Thou Shalt Have No Other Gods before Me

This book is among the most thorough and comprehensive analyses of the causes of religious discrimination to date, complete with detailed illustrations and anecdotes. Jonathan Fox examines the causes of government-based religious discrimination (GRD) against 771 minorities in 183 countries over the course of twenty-five years, while offering possible reasons for why some minorities are discriminated against more than others.

Fox illustrates the complexities inherent in the causes of GRD, which can emerge from secular ideologies, religious monopolies, anticult policies, security concerns, and more. Western democracies tend to discriminate more than Christian-majority countries in the developing world, whether they are democratic or not.

While the causes of GRD are ubiquitous, they play out in vastly different ways across world regions and religious traditions. This book serves as a method for better understanding of this particular form of discrimination, so that we may have the tools to better combat it and foster compassion across people of different religions and cultures.

JONATHAN FOX is the Yehuda Avner Professor of Religion and Politics at Bar Ilan University in Ramat Gan, Israel, and director of the Religion and State Project. He writes about government religion policy, religious freedom, and religious conflict.

Thou Shalt Have No Other Gods before Me

Why Governments Discriminate against Religious Minorities

JONATHAN FOX

Bar Ilan University

CAMBRIDGE
UNIVERSITY PRESS

CAMBRIDGE
UNIVERSITY PRESS

University Printing House, Cambridge CB2 8BS, United Kingdom

One Liberty Plaza, 20th Floor, New York, NY 10006, USA

477 Williamstown Road, Port Melbourne, VIC 3207, Australia

314-321, 3rd Floor, Plot 3, Splendor Forum, Jasola District Centre, New Delhi - 110025, India

103 Penang Road, #05-06/07, Visioncrest Commercial, Singapore 238467

Cambridge University Press is part of the University of Cambridge.

It furthers the University's mission by disseminating knowledge in the pursuit of education, learning and research at the highest international levels of excellence.

www.cambridge.org
Information on this title: www.cambridge.org/9781108715676
DOI: 10.1017/9781108773171

© Jonathan Fox 2020

This publication is in copyright. Subject to statutory exception and to the provisions of relevant collective licensing agreements, no reproduction of any part may take place without the written permission of Cambridge University Press.

First published 2020
First paperback edition 2022

A catalogue record for this publication is available from the British Library

ISBN 978-1-108-48891-4 Hardback
ISBN 978-1-108-71567-6 Paperback

Cambridge University Press has no responsibility for the persistence or accuracy of URLs for external or third-party internet websites referred to in this publication, and does not guarantee that any content on such websites is, or will remain, accurate or appropriate.

Contents

Figures

Tables

Acknowledgments

I would like to thank Roger Finke, who helped me conceive of this project, especially the societal religious discrimination variables, and for his support and comments throughout the project. I'd also like to thank Matthias Basedau, Daniel Philpott, Jocelyne Cesari, Lene Kuhle, Yasemin Akbabba, Chris Bader, Jeff Haynes, Patrick James, Shmuel Sandler, Ariel Zellman, Torkel Brekke, Tom Konzack, Dane Mataic, and Baruch Susser, as well as the anonymous reviewers for their advice and comments at various points in the project. Thanks to the research assistants for round 3 of the project, including Sherrie Feigelson, Mora Deitch, Tanya Haykin, and Eytan Meir. As always, my heartfelt thanks to Ted R. Gurr for teaching me the skills I needed to attempt a project like this one.

Finally, I thank the Israel Science Foundation (Grant 23/14), The German-Israel Foundation (Grant 1291-119.4/2015), and the John Templeton Foundation for funding this project, as well as the Association of Religion Data Archives for their help with the data. The opinions expressed in this study are solely my own and do not necessarily reflect those of any of the funders.

1

Introduction

If there is one aspiration shared by all religious people worldwide, it is the desire to practice their religions freely and without hindrance or restriction. While many of these people may not feel that members of other religions should have this same right, this desire for the free exercise of religion is universal among the religious. Yet, as I discuss in more detail in Chapter 2, religious discrimination is ubiquitous against religious minorities. Thus, this yearning for religious freedom is far more often a dream than it is a reality for religious minorities.

Government-based restrictions on religious minorities are common even in Western democracies. In fact, this study will show that the relationship between democracy and discrimination is not as straightforward as many assume, this assumption being that democracies, especially liberal Western democracies, discriminate less. More specifically, this relationship does exist in statistical models but myriad other factors that influence levels of discrimination can overshadow this relationship to the extent that absolute levels of religious discrimination are higher in Western democracies than in many other parts of the world. Thus, for example, non-Western Christian-majority democracies as well as non-Western Christian-majority nondemocracies have lower average levels of religious discrimination than do Western democracies. I discuss this finding in more detail in Chapters 5, 7, and 8.

Norway provides a good illustration of this phenomenon. Norway, which is by no means the most restrictive among Western democracies, engages in substantial restrictions on religious minorities. Laws requiring the stunning of animals before slaughter effectively ban the ritual slaughter of meat by both Jews and Muslims. This means Kosher and Halal slaughter in Norway are illegal, though Kosher and Halal meat may be imported. While Norway has many Mosques, there are reports of local councils delaying or denying permits to build more. Similarly, while there are cemeteries set aside for Muslims, not all Muslim religious requirements for burial are always accommodated, so some Muslims are buried in their country of origin. In 2013 the Norwegian Parliamentary Intelligence Monitoring Committee reported that the Security Police were illegally keeping members of Muslim communities under surveillance. Some Norwegian uniformed services such as the police restrict the wearing of the hijab by Muslim women in those services, but this is primarily determined by the uniform regulations of the particular institution. In addition, until 2018 municipalities were allowed to set their own rules for religious head coverings that also cover the face in schools. In 2018 Norway passed a law banning all clothing that partially or fully covers the face in all public schools and universities. This applies to both teachers and students ("Must provide," 2010; "Norway bans," 2018; Ryland, 2012, 2013a, 2013b; Solholm, 2009). All of these types of restrictions are common in Western democracies.

The Norwegian government's efforts to control religion are not limited to overt restrictions on religious minorities. Rather, the government's system of financially supporting religion can be an explicit means of control over both the majority religion and minority religions. In the past, the government has used its control over the (as of 2017) former national church to alter its stance on issues like female clergy (Kuhle, 2011).

Interestingly the extent and nature of this control was discussed openly at a public conference in response to Norway's decision to disestablish the Evangelical Lutheran Church (ELC) as of January 1, 2017. The discussion at this conference, which was held the following October, focused on the issue of the nature and extent of the government's future involvement in religion. While opinions on this issue differed, the opposing sides of the debate illustrated the power of Norway's government to control religion and its influence on religious freedoms. Some conservatives felt that all funding for religion, including to the ELC, should be terminated. This is because the seduction of "free" money is difficult to refuse and is not really free. It comes with significant government control and oversight. Others wanted to continue the existing system of government funding for religion. One advocate for this stance explicitly stated that this should include funding for Muslim religious institutions in order to "keep the Muslim radicals under control."[1]

---

[1] I attended this conference, and this description is based on my recollections.

While, like every country in the world, Norway's religion policy is unique, its components are not. More specifically, restrictions on burials, ritual slaughter, building places of worship, and female religious headwear are each present in multiple Western democracies, though the exact manifestation and application of each of these restrictions is different across countries. Yet the basic types of restrictions are comparable across countries. On a more general level, most governments restrict religious minorities. In addition, most governments support religion in some manner, and this support almost inevitably leads to some control over the supported religions. In many cases this support is part of an intentional strategy to control religion. Also, this support can in complex ways be connected to restricting religious minorities.

The motivations for and influences on Norway's policy toward its religious minorities and religion in general are complex and crosscutting. This book's objective is to delve into these motivations and causes across the 183 countries and 771 religious minorities included in this study.

THE TOPIC OF STUDY

This book seeks to explain the nature, causes, and dynamics of government-based religious discrimination. Given this, it is important to define religious discrimination at the outset of this study. This is because religious discrimination is a deceptively simple term, but it can have different meanings to different people. For example, in the West, religious discrimination is at the center of recent intensive debates. In these debates religious freedom is often defined broadly to include the freedom of personal expression and even the freedom to discriminate against those who somehow violate one's religious beliefs.

In this study, the definition of discrimination is far narrower. Specifically, I examine the causes of a subset of all religious discrimination, government-based religion discrimination (GRD). In brief, for the purposes of the study contained in this book, I define GRD as restrictions placed by governments or their agents on the religious practices or institutions of religious minorities that are not placed on the majority religion. I discuss this definition in more detail and how it compares to other definitions and the general concept of religious freedom in Chapter 2.

The central goal of this study is to explore the causes of GRD. These causes are complex in two respects. First, there are multiple and often crosscutting factors that influence GRD. Second, these crosscutting influences manifest differently in different groupings of states. That is, the same universe of causes of GRD are present in most groupings of states, but which causes are more important and the specific manner in which each of these causes influences GRD differs across groupings of states based on majority religion and world region. In addition, many of the findings of this study run counter to the prevailing wisdom.

An example of both the complexity of GRD's causes and how my findings contradict common wisdom is the link between democracy and GRD. Many assume that the liberal democracies of the West are the strongest bastions of religious freedom in the world and that, in general, democracies discriminate less than nondemocracies. My findings contradict both of these assumptions. For example, Western democracies engage in more GRD than the Christian-majority democracies of Asia, Africa, and Latin America. Furthermore, among all Christian-majority countries in Asia, Africa, and Latin America, the average levels of GRD are similar between democracies and nondemocracies. Thus, Western democracies are not the grouping of states with the highest level of religious freedom for minorities in the Christian world, and there is even a large grouping of nondemocracies that engage in less GRD than the West. However, among non-Christian-majority states as well as Christian Orthodox-majority states, democratic states engage in less GRD. This indicates that there is a complex relationship between democracy and GRD, which I address in more detail, particularly in Chapters 5, 7, and 8.

In this study, I examine GRD using round 3 of the Religion and State-Minorities dataset (RASM3), which includes 771 religious minorities in 183 countries and independent territories. RASM3 covers the 1990–2014 period. GRD is very common: 162 (88.5%) of these countries engage in GRD against 574 (74.4 percent) of minorities at some point during the study period. I also examine other forms of religious discrimination, primarily societal religious discrimination (SRD), which I define as societal actions taken against religious minorities by members of a country's religious majority who do not represent the government. I use SRD in this study primarily as a means to explain levels of GRD, though I do address the issue of the causes of SRD. Interestingly, I find that SRD only causes GRD in a limited number of circumstances. I argue here that a trigger is required for SRD to influence levels of GRD. That is, some other factor, usually the presence of an existential threat, is required to activate the latent potential of SRD to cause GRD. I discuss this in more detail in later chapters.

Both GRD and SRD increased between 1990 and 2014. GRD in 2014 was 23.6 percent higher than it was in 1990, and SRD was 29.6

percent higher. As I discuss in more detail throughout this study, this finding is consistent across countries in different world regions and belonging to different majority religious traditions. Thus, discerning the causes of religious discrimination is becoming increasingly important.

This focus on discrimination that is specifically against religious minorities is not to deny that many governments also restrict the religious freedom of their majority religion and that religion can motivate discrimination against other types of minorities such as the LGBTQ community. These issues, as well as many others related to government religion policy, are important and worthy of study. For example, based on the general Religion and State round 3 (RAS3) data, 88.5 percent of the 183 countries in this study restrict or regulate the majority religion to its institutions in some manner. This is certainly related to the concept of religious freedom, which I discuss in more detail in Chapter 2, but the focus of the book is narrower.

Put differently, this focus on GRD against religious minorities in some ways limits the discussion and excludes many aspects that would be included in a discussion of religious freedom, more broadly defined. I make this choice because while related, the causes and dynamics of GRD are different from those of repression or limiting religion in general, for example. As I argue in another context, the distinction between GRD and repressing religion in general "is critical because actions that can be quite similar can have different implications" and causes "depending on the object of those policies" (Fox, 2015: 106). None of this is to deny the importance of the wider range of issues that may be included in a broader definition of religious freedom. Rather, despite the narrower focus of this book, explaining GRD is a complex task, and expanding the purview of the study would, in my assessment, limit my ability to explain GRD. In addition, as I discuss in more detail in Chapter 2, a ban on GRD is the one thing that many diverse and sometimes contradictory conceptions of religious freedom all agree is an essential element of the concept. So in that sense it is the minimum common denominator of all conceptions of religious freedom.

As will be seen in this study, the causes of GRD are complex and crosscutting. I find uncovering these causes a sufficiently complex task and choose to focus on it exclusively in this study. I believe that to do otherwise would further complicate an already complex task. All other elements of government religion policy addressed in this study are included for the purpose of explaining the causes of GRD. In addition the RASM3 data used in this study provides an unprecedented wealth of information designed specifically to discover the causes of GRD against religious minorities. I therefore refer the reader to other studies that take a broader look at the influences on the religious freedom of both religious majorities and minorities, as well as the impacts of government-religion connections and polices on a wide range of other important issues and populations (e.g., Fox, 2015; Grim & Finke, 2011; Philpott, 2019).

THE CORRELATES OF GRD

In Chapter 2, I discuss the causes of GRD in theory. There are multiple potential causes. This makes the theoretical causes of GRD potentially complex. However, this study's findings paint an even more complex picture of the causes of GRD in practice. One aspect of this complexity is that when addressing the causes of GRD, one must explain both what types of states are more likely to engage in GRD and which minorities in these states are more likely to be subject to GRD. This is because most states that discriminate do so unequally. That is, in most countries, some minorities are subject to more GRD than others.

Perhaps the least surprising finding is that ideology plays a strong role in causing GRD. However, it is not just religious ideology that causes GRD. Both secular and religious ideologies, even in democratic states, result in more GRD. Thus, the second commandment, "Thou shalt have no other Gods before me," or its equivalent in non-Abrahamic religions, is still observed in practice by many governments. To be clear, the "God" that will tolerate no competition is often a secular one or the state itself.

In theory, secular ideologies should treat all religion equally. This means that if there are restrictions, they ought to apply equally to all religions in a country, including the majority religion. As Philpott (2009) points out, all uses of the term *secular* are either not religion, the negation of religion, or antireligion. While Philpott (2019) argues that some secular states will restrict and regulate religion more than others, the extent of this restriction and regulation should be uniform against religion. Positive-secular states tend to be neutral but tolerant toward religion and will restrict it less. Negative-secular states are those states that are explicitly antireligious and, accordingly, restrict it more. I discuss these distinctions in more detail in Chapter 4.

Philpott (2019) is correct in that the negative-secular states restrict religion more than do the positive-secular states. However, few of these states treat all minorities equally. This is true of both types of secular states. A number of positive-secular states engage in little or no GRD, but many do engage in at least some GRD, and this GRD is usually applied differently to different religious minorities.

The antireligious negative-secular states tend to engage in restrictions that apply to all religions, including the majority religion, which is not GRD by the definition used here. Yet, even countries with the most antireligious secular ideologies restrict religious minorities in a manner that they do not restrict the majority religion, which is precisely this study's definition of GRD. On average, the more antireligious a state's ideology, the higher the level of GRD. I argue that this is because the antireligious elements of secular ideologies can be a force that magnifies other motives for GRD. That is, secularism, by itself, will likely motivate equal restrictions on all religions, but when combined with other motivations and causes of GRD that are minority-specific, it will amplify GRD against those minorities. As such potential motives are almost always present, there is ample opportunity for secular ideologies to interact with these motives to enhance levels of GRD.

In addition, in some cases, secular ideologies can cause a focus on restricting religious practices that are counter to the secular ideology in question. For example, many secularists consider Muslim women covering their hair an affront to woman's rights, the ritual slaughter of animals for food by Jews and Muslims a violation of animal's rights, and male infant circumcision, a ritual present in Islam and Judaism, a barbaric violation of the child's right to bodily integrity. All of these religious practices are limited in at least some Western liberal democracies. Thus, the secular Gods are also, in a way, jealous of those who follow ideologies, including religious ideologies that contradict their secular ideals. Thus, the liberal ideal of religious freedom is often trumped by secular ideology and beliefs.

All of this is linked to government religion policy, that is, how a government chooses by policy to address the issue of religion, including its majority religion, in general. Both states that support religion and those that are hostile to religion are more likely to engage in GRD, though for different reasons. Those that support religion are more likely to engage in GRD for reasons linked to religious ideology and intolerance of competing religions. Those hostile to religion, as I noted earlier, engage in GRD at least in part due to their distaste of all religion. In addition, both states that strongly support religion and states that are hostile to religion are more likely to regulate the majority religion. States that do this, on average, engage in more GRD. This means that an absence of GRD against religious minorities is most likely to be found in states that are neutral on the issue of religion and are not strongly linked to secular ideologies. Thus, this combination of ideology and government religion policy is likely the most important state-level cause of GRD, but there are others.

Regime also has an influence on GRD. However, as noted earlier, democracy's influence on GRD is less straightforward than many assume. In part, this is because many democratic states support a single religion over all others, often through declaring it the state's official religion. Other democratic states espouse secular ideologies that can have antireligious elements. Also, many democratic states that have technically neutral religion policies and maintain high levels of separation of religion and states are still influenced by secular ideologies that can be intolerant of religious practices that contradict these ideologies. Also, not all democracies are fully liberal democracies. "Rule by the people" does not imply tolerance of religious minorities in any necessary way. Without sufficient protections for minority rights and civil liberties, the will of the majority can be to discriminate against minorities.

Thus, there are two kinds of neutrality in government religion policy. The first is ideological neutrality. This neutrality is based on secular ideologies that demand that in some manner the state separate itself from religion, but it can also include other ideological imperatives for regulating government and society that can potentially clash with religious views on the same issues. The second form of neutrality is more of a laissez-faire neutrality where the state simply chooses to leave religion alone. This may be for pragmatic reasons or simply a lack of desire to regulate and influence religion. As I argue in Chapters 7 and 8, it also may be due to a scarcity of the resources necessary to regulate it.

This perhaps explains one of this study's more interesting findings – that among Christian-majority democracies, those found in the developing world engage in significantly less GRD than do Western democracies. In fact, even Christian-majority nondemocracies in the developing world engage in less GRD than do Western democracies. Thus, this difference between ideological neutrality and nonideological laissez-faire neutrality can, under some circumstances, have a stronger impact on GRD than regime.

Other state-level factors also influence GRD. States with some religious traditions engage in higher levels of GRD. For example, Muslim-majority states engage in the highest levels of GRD, on average. However, as I discuss in more detail in Chapter 4, this general finding conceals a wide diversity among Muslim-majority states that includes both countries that are among the most tolerant of religious minorities as well as countries that are among the most intolerant. World region matters. For example, many of the Muslim-majority states that are tolerant of religious minorities are found in West Africa. In addition, more populous and wealthier countries engage in more GRD.

That being said, state-level factors are not sufficient to understand the causes of GRD. Most countries that engage in GRD do so unequally. By this, I mean that some minorities are subject to different levels and types of GRD than others within the same country. Thus, there must be minority-level factors that cause these differential levels of GRD.

Ideology can also play a role in differential GRD. Some minorities or their practices may be in some way more objectionable to the majority ideology. As I alluded earlier, secular ideologies often do identify such objectionable practices, and the advocates of these ideologies often seek to limit these objectionable practices. For example, in France wearing "ostentatious" religious symbols in public such as a Muslim woman's head covering or modest "burkini" garb at a beach violates its secular *laicite* ideology. Other minorities that do not engage in this behavior will not attract this type of attention.

Nationalism and the desire to protect the local culture can play a role. This motivation directs GRD primarily at minorities that the majority or the government considers nonindigenous. North American Protestant denominations that actively proselytize around the world are common targets for GRD inspired by this motivation. Minorities considered to pose a security or political threat to the majority may be subject to more GRD. For example, in many Christian countries Muslims are seen as a security threat (Saiya, 2018). This stimulates GRD against them.

Minorities seen as cults are also often subject to higher GRD. While this phenomenon has some overlap with nationalism and protection of culture as well as threat perception, the nature of this perceived threat is different. These cults are seen as both poaching members of the majority religion as well as causing their members to engage in dangerous behavior. For example, both France and Belgium passed anticult laws after incidents of mass suicides by cults in their countries.

Some types of motivation are minority-specific. This study finds anti-Semitism to be present and increasing in the Christian-majority states of the West and former-Soviet bloc. However, this mostly manifests as SRD rather than GRD. In fact, between 1990 and 2014, SRD against Jews in these states has increased dramatically. I discuss this in more detail in Chapters 5 and 6.

SRD is also a common but complex motivation for GRD. In a major study of the topic Grim and Finke (2011) found that societal prejudices lead to government-based restrictions on religious freedom. Their study uses state-level variables. This study's use of the minority level of analysis reveals that SRD causes GRD only for some minorities but not others. I argue that this is because this dynamic requires a trigger. That is, SRD only causes GRD when some other factor activates this latent potential cause of GRD. These triggers are usually linked to a perceived existential threat.

All of these causes of GRD interact in a complex manner. I discuss all of them in more detail in the body and conclusions of this study.

WHY IS GRD IMPORTANT?

Why study the causes of GRD? I argue that GRD is important because it has multiple and overlapping influences on important political, social, and economic factors. First, and perhaps most important, GRD is in and of itself consequential. The majority of the world's population is religious, and there exist no countries lacking religious minorities (Norris & Inglehart, 2004). Thus, GRD can potentially influence the daily lives of many people across the world.

Second, GRD has implications for citizenship and justice. In theory, all citizens should be treated justly and equally. The presence of GRD not only undermines this equality, but also it is likely a sign that the government may be willing to disregard other rights normally granted to citizens. Third, GRD has similar implications for the nature of a regime. What does it say about a democracy when it singles out some religious minorities for restrictions that it does not place on the majority religion? As the majority of liberal democracies engage in GRD, this raises the question of whether religious freedom is truly a necessary trait of a liberal democracy or, perhaps, whether those countries that many consider to be liberal democracies actually are (Perez & Fox, 2018; Perez et al., 2017). This question is even more pertinent because the liberal democracies of the West engage in far more GRD that Christian-majority states in the developing world, including those that are nondemocracies.

Fourth, Gill (2008) argues that religious freedom is good for the economy. His argument is based on the free market. If a country restricts certain religions, members of that religion will be less likely to be interested in trading with that country. Thus, religiously free countries will have more potential trading partners, which is good for the economy.

Fifth, significant levels of GRD can result in migration and population shifts. For example, the Christian population of the Middle East is shrinking dramatically due to the persecution of Christians in the region (Cantilero, 2015; Griswold, 2015). According to the RASM3 data, during the study period forty-seven religious minorities experienced GRD sufficiently severe that a significant portion emigrated from their country. This includes ten Middle Eastern minorities, including Christians from Egypt, Gaza, Iraq, Lebanon, Libya, and the Palestinian Authority. Subsequent to 2014 many Christians fled Syria. This phenomenon is not limited to the Middle East. For example, a significant number of Jews left Belgium, Germany, France, and Sweden, though this was mostly due the inability of these governments to protect Jews from rising anti-Semitic violence. Migration and refugees can be an important political issue in both the countries they leave and the countries in which they seek to settle.

Sixth, about 90 percent of the world's constitutions promise some form of religious freedom (Fox, 2008, 2015), and many international treaties guarantee religious freedom. This demonstrates that most of the world's countries support religious freedom in theory. Yet this contrasts sharply with the finding that most of these same countries that promise religious freedom in their constitutions and signed these international treaties engage in GRD. This demonstrates that the value of religious freedom is sufficiently prominent in world politics that most states see it as necessary to, at a minimum, pay lip service to this value. This makes the question of why most states fall short of fully observing this value a significant one.

Seventh, a growing number of NGOs actively promote religious freedom worldwide. These include general human rights groups that include religious freedom on their agenda like Amnesty International, Human Rights without Frontiers, and Forum 18, among others. There are also NGOs that focus specifically on religious freedom such as the Religious Freedom Institute.

Eighth, several Western countries include promoting religious freedom as an explicit part of their foreign policies. For example, both the United States and Canada have passed laws specifically setting up an office for religious freedom as part of their foreign policy apparatus, though Canada eliminated this office in 2016. The United States has an ambassador at large for religious freedom heading this office. In addition, many European governments and the European Union have incorporated religious freedom into their foreign policies (Joustra, 2018; Philpott, 2019). While there is some debate over how much religion truly influences foreign policy (Sandal & Fox, 2013), religious freedom is formally on the agenda.

Ninth, GRD is often a predictor of religiously motivated violence, both by and against the religious minority (Finke & Harris, 2012; Grim & Finke, 2007, 2011). Finally, there are a number of theoretical and practical advantages to focusing a study on GRD, which I discuss in more detail in Chapter 2.

ROUND 3 OF THE RELIGION AND STATE-MINORITIES (RASM3) AND RELIGION AND STATE (RAS3) DATASETS

This study uses round 3 of the Religion and State-Minorities (RASM3) dataset as its source for information on GRD and SRD. The RASM3 dataset is a module of the larger Religion and State (RAS3) dataset. RAS3 collects a wide variety of information on government religion policy using the state as the unit of analysis. It covers 183 states and territories with independent governments for the 1990–2014 period. RASM3 focuses on GRD and SRD. Rather than using the state as the level of analysis, RASM3 uses a religious minority within a state as the unit of analysis and includes 771 religious minorities. This is an increase from round 2 of the dataset, which includes 587 religious minorities in 177 countries.

RASM3 includes every religious minority that is at least 0.2 percent of the country's population (RASM2 used a 0.25 percent cutoff). In addition, it includes some minorities where population estimates varied, and while they are likely under the 0.2 percent cutoff, there is at least one source that puts them at 0.2 percent or above of the country's population. RASM3 also includes a selection of smaller minorities. For example, it includes all Christian minorities in Muslim-majority states and all Muslim minorities in Christian-majority states. In addition, it includes all Jewish minorities in both Muslim-majority and Christian-majority states. This additional focus on Muslim, Christian, and Jewish minorities is due to the international political significance of discrimination against these minorities.

While identifying most religious minorities is generally noncontroversial, this is not always the case. For example, some mainstream Sunni Muslims would say that Bahais, like Ahmadis and Yazidis, are apostate Muslims – and thus a sect of Islam and should not be considered minorities in Muslim-majority countries. I address this in two ways, one theoretical and one practical. First, theoretically I rely on Gurr (1993), who argues that a minority's identity is about how that minority is perceived by itself and others. In the cases of the Bahai, Ahmadis, and Yazidiz, whether they are truly a sect of Islam or not, they are perceived by many Muslims to be the "other." In addition, these groups perceive themselves as separate. One of the most basic of religious freedoms is the ability to define for oneself to which religion one belongs. On a practical level, this study includes not only minorities that belong to a different religion as the majority, it also includes minorities that are members of different denominations or sects of the same religion as the majority religion.

RASM3 is unique in that it both uses the religious minority as the unit of analysis and includes all relevant religious minorities. Most other data collections that address religious discrimination or religious freedom in general use the country as the unit of analysis. As such, they have a single score for each country and cannot assess whether governments or society treat some minorities differently from others (e.g., Grim & Finke, 2011). The other datasets that use the minority as the unit of analysis focus on ethnic minorities (Cederman & Girardin, 2007; Cederman et al., 2010; Gurr, 1993, 2000). Some of these datasets include modules for religious discrimination (Akbaba & Tydas, 2011; Fox, 2002, 2004). However, these datasets focus on ethnic minorities. Thus, while Gurr's *Minorities at Risk* dataset includes 119 ethnoreligious minorities, this is only a subset of religious minorities whose ethnic and religious identities overlap.

There are also datasets that have a different focus but include variables on religious discrimination. They also use the state as the unit of analysis and often have additional limiting factors. For example, the *World Christian Encyclopedia* includes a state-level religious discrimination variable, but it measures only discrimination against Christians (Barret et al., 2001). Human rights datasets such as Abouharb and Cingranelli (2006) often include country-level variables for restrictions on religious rights, but these variables provide far less detail than the RASM3 variables.

In contrast, RASM3 includes thirty-five types of GRD, each coded yearly for 1990–2014. This is six more types than the twenty-nine included in RASM2. They are listed in detail in Chapter 2.[2] RASM3 also added a battery of variables on SRD that includes twenty-seven distinct types of SRD that are listed in detail in Chapter 3. Each of them is coded yearly for 1990–2014. This total of sixty-two religious discrimination

---

[2] The Main RAS3 dataset contains thirty-six types of religious discrimination. They are identical to the thirty-five included in RASM3 but include an extra variable for restrictions on foreign missionaries. This variable was not included in the RASM3 version of the dataset because RASM3 is intended to measure the treatment of indigenous minorities.

variables is far more than are included in any other relevant dataset. RASM3's twenty-five-year time span is also longer than all of the preceding datasets other than Gurr's (1993, 2000) *Minorities at Risk* dataset.

This makes RASM3 the most detailed and comprehensive dataset on the topic of religious discrimination. It also includes considerably more information and variables than its previous iteration, RASM2. This allows analyses previously not feasible. In particular, the SRD variables allow an analysis of how societal factors influence GRD at the minority level. That is, it can examine, for example, whether SRD against Jews is related to GRD against Jews. In contrast, Grim and Finke (2011) can measure whether societal restrictions in general are related to whether the government restricts religious freedom in general. However, Grim and Finke (2011) cannot determine whether the societal restrictions are placed on the same minority that experiences governmental restrictions. Furthermore, Grim and Finke's (2011) governmental restrictions also includes restrictions on the majority religion in their government restrictions variable.[3] Thus, RASM3's ability to use the minority as the level of analysis allows a type of analysis of religious discrimination not previously possible.

In addition, the 771 religious minorities included in RASM3 arguably constitute the entire universe of cases that meet the project's 0.2 percent minimum population cutoff and not just a representative sample. The ethnic minority datasets that are at the minority level of analysis (Cederman & Girardin, 2007; Cederman et al., 2010; Gurr, 1993, 2000) all only include politically active ethnic minorities, which means they do not include all ethnic minorities. This has two implications. First, RASM3 is the only dataset at the minority level of analysis that includes the entire universe of cases. Second, this means that technically statistical significance – which is intended to measure the likelihood that a finding from a sample is representative of the entire universe of cases – is not necessary for a finding to be valid. However, in this study I nevertheless use statistical significance as a measure of the strength of a relationship.

As noted earlier, RASM3 follows Gurr's (1993) conception of defining ethnic minorities to arrive at this list of 771 religious minorities. Gurr argues that while many traits can contribute to making a minority a minority, the key traits are whether the group perceives itself as a minority

---

[3] This is also true of the PEW data collection on religious freedom, which is a continuation of Grim and Finke's (2011) data collection and uses essentially the same variable structure (www.pewforum.org/topics/restrictions-on-religion/).

and whether others perceive it as a minority. All other traits are important only to the extent that they contribute to these perceptions. Thus, identity is key. In most cases the minority group in question perceives itself to have a separate identity. However, in some cases the identity can be imposed from the outside. Also, it is important to note that many religious minorities in this study are different sects of the same religious tradition as the majority such as Protestants in Catholic-majority countries and Shi'i Muslims in Sunni-majority countries.

The RAS3 dataset includes state-level variables that are important in predicting and understanding GRD. In particular, it includes three types of variables on government religion policy: (1) The state's official religion policy – this is a thirteen-category classification system on the "big-picture" aspects of a government's religion policy. It includes whether the government declares an official religion, supports one or some religions without declaring an official religion, are neutral toward all religions, or are hostile to religion. (2) Religious support measures fifty-one ways a government might support the majority religion. (3) Religious regulation measures the extent to which the government restricts and regulates all religions in the country including the majority religion. It is appropriate that these variables be measured at the state level because they measure aspects of government policy that are uniform, no matter the religious minority. As I discuss in more detail, particularly in Chapter 4, all of these factors influence GRD.

As was the case with previous rounds of RASM and RAS, the data for RASM3 and RAS3 is based on a wide variety of sources. The project's researchers investigated each country separately and produced a country report based on all available sources. These sources include (1) government and intergovernment reports on human rights or religious freedom, including reports and other information from sources such as the UN, the EU, and the US State Department; (2) reports by nongovernmental human rights organizations such as Amnesty International, Human Rights without Frontiers, and Forum 18; (3) news articles primarily taken from the Lexis/Nexis database, but also from other sources; (4) relevant academic articles and books; (5) primary sources such as laws and constitutions; and (6) an internet search for relevant sources. These reports were the basis for coding all of the RASM3 and RAS3 variables.[4] This range of

---

[4] For a full discussion of how the data was collected see Fox (2008, 2011, 2015, 2018) and Fox et al. (2018). This discussion includes a more detailed listing of sources and an analysis of the data's reliability.

sources is wider than all competing datasets noted earlier other than the *Minorities at Risk* dataset, which uses a similar range of sources.[5] The project produced a report of this nature for each of the three rounds of the RAS. They cover, respectively, 1990–2002, 2003–2008, and 2009–2014. All of these reports were used for the coding of RAS3 and RASM3.

As I noted earlier, this study covers the 1990–2014 period with each variable coded separately for each year during this twenty-five-year period. There are exceptions to this general rule. First, if the country did not exist in the year in question, it was not coded. Most, but not all, of these cases are former–Soviet bloc states that were not independent until after 1990. Armenia, Azerbaijan, Belarus, Croatia, Estonia, Georgia, Kazakhstan, Kyrgyzstan, Latvia, Macedonia, Moldova, Slovenia, Tajikistan, Turkmenistan, Ukraine, and Uzbekistan, all became independent in 1991. Eritrea and Slovakia became independent in 1993. Timor became independent in 2002, and Montenegro did so in 2006. Gaza and the Palestinian Authority are coded from the election of their governments in 2006. Second, countries are not coded in years in which there was no functioning government. It is not possible to code government policy in cases where there is no government. These cases include Afghanistan until 1992, Bosnia until 1995, Iraq in 2002, and Syria after 2011.[6]

Finally, both RAS3 and RASM3, other than the societal variables, focus on government religion policy. The definition of government policy used to collect the data is broad. It includes policies created not just by constitutions and formal legislation. It can also include bureaucratic regulations, actions taken by public officials, and decisions by courts. For example, in several countries, there is no law against proselytizing, but the police or other government security officials consistently harass and arrest minorities who proselytize. This is effectively a government policy even in the absence of a written law or regulation.

---

[5] In fact, the RAS project's data collection methodology was modeled after the *Minorities at Risk* project.

[6] I used a very broad definition for the presence of a government, so even in war-torn states such as Somalia for much of this period, the presence of even a nominal government that had control over some territory was deemed sufficient to code that government's policy. This allows researchers who wish to use these cases to do so and allows those who feel that using them is unwarranted to drop them from the study. The analyses presented here use all coded cases.

RESEARCH STRATEGY AND STRUCTURE

The research based on RASM2 (Fox, 2016; Fox & Akbaba 2014, 2015) revealed three dynamics and findings that inform this study. First, GRD is unequal. By this, I mean that most states that discriminate and have multiple religious minorities usually treat at least some of them differently. Some minorities are subject to more GRD, and the types of GRD can vary across minorities within the same country. In Chapter 2, I begin to address this issue. I provide a full discussion of GRD in both theory and practice. This discussion includes the theoretical foundation for how I define GRD, a discussion of all thirty-five components of the GRD variable, and how common each one of these components is. I confirm the previous findings that GRD is common and unequal in Chapter 2 and later chapters.

Second, in previous studies of religious discrimination and religious freedom, most of the independent variables used to predict these phenomena were at the state level. However, this type of variable cannot differentiate between minorities. As GRD is unequal, we need minority-level variables to explain its causes. That is, we need variables that can tell us why a certain minority is subject to more GRD than another in the same country. State-level variables, which are effectively coded identically for all minorities within a given state, cannot accomplish this. As I discussed earlier and in Chapter 3, most previous studies used country-level data including the dependent variable. In the analysis of RASM2, the previous round of the dataset used here, the only minority-specific variables were demographic. Specifically, it measures the religious identity of the minority. This type of variable proved significant. For example, when looking at all minorities, Christians experienced higher levels of GRD (Fox, 2016: 187). However, this cannot tell us why Christians experienced more GRD.

Given this, we require better minority-level variables. RASM3 added two such variables in round 3. The first is SRD, which measures actions taken by societal actors who are not representatives of the government against the minority religion. The second is violent and semiviolent societal actions taken by the minority against the majority. Both are posited to increase levels of GRD. I discuss both of these variables in detail in Chapter 3. I find in this study that both influence GRD, but their influence is complex. In addition, I added another demographic variable, the population size of the minority. This I took from "The Religious Characteristics of States" dataset (Brown & James, 2017). While there is some theory that predicts this will influence GRD, the variable did not prove significant in predicting GRD. I discuss all the potential causes of GRD in Chapter 2. In Chapter 4 I discuss how all variables not described in Chapters 2 and 3 are measured.

The final finding from Fox (2016) that informed this study is that patterns of GRD are different across groupings of states. Accordingly, this study divides the world into seven groups of relatively homogeneous states and analyzes them separately. By relatively homogeneous, I mean that they are more similar to each other based on majority religion, world region, and regime than they are to states from other groupings. These include (1) Muslim-majority states (Chapter 4), (2) non-Orthodox European and Western democracies (Chapter 5), (3) Orthodox-majority states (Chapter 6), (4) Communist states (Chapter 6), (5) noncommunist Buddhist-majority states (Chapter 6), (6) all other democracies (Chapter 7), and (7) all other nondemocracies (Chapter 8). The results from this study confirm that the dynamics of GRD are different in each of these groupings, which helps to justify this particular manner of breaking the world into parts.

Breaking up a dataset into distinct sections and analyzing each separately rather than performing an analysis of the entire dataset as a single unit is unusual in quantitative analyses. This would not be a matter of concern if this was a classical comparative analysis that, by its nature, examines each state or group of states separately and can easily account for nuances and differences across these units of analysis. In fact, classical comparative methodology is designed to do exactly this.

However, breaking the data up into smaller parts complicates things considerably in a quantitative study. Rather than performing a single meta-analysis of the entire RASM3 dataset, this study finds its answers by breaking the data up into chunks, based on the majority religion, ideology, world region, and regime of the countries and analyzing each separately. While this provides a much better explanation for GRD, it is considerably messier than analyzing the entire dataset as a single cluster.

One may ask, based on this, why use quantitative as opposed to qualitative methodology? The answer is twofold. First, qualitative methodology can handle only a limited number of cases. While I am uncertain what the upper limit is for this methodology, 771 minorities in 183 countries is simply unworkable. Second, even with its complications, results emerge from this methodology that would be unlikely to emerge from comparative methodology. This includes, but is by no means limited to, the findings that societal religious discrimination (SRD) causes GRD only for some minorities and that not only are democracies often intolerant of religious minorities, but also they are less tolerant than many types of nondemocracies.

In addition, doing a meta-analysis of all the data in a single test would also obfuscate these findings on SRD and democracy. Thus, this study's strategy of breaking the dataset into parts and analyzing each part separately, I argue, is the optimum strategy to discover the causes of GRD.

As I discussed in more detail earlier in this chapter, the findings of this study show that the causes of GRD across these groupings are similar on a general level, but the specifics of how these causes manifest and influence GRD can be very different across groupings. This is because GRD is influenced by the majority religion, regional culture, and regime. For example, among Muslim-majority states there are commonalities, but those that are more democratic discriminate less, and there are pockets of regional culture that have a heavy influence. GRD is particularly high in the Middle East, especially the Persian Gulf region. However, there is a cluster of Muslim-majority states in West Africa that engages in less GRD than Western democracies. Of course, other factors such as nationalism and the extent to which a government supports religion also influence GRD among Muslim-majority states,

Also, while the causes of SRD is not the focus of this study, Chapters 4 through 8 nevertheless address the issue and compare the causes of SRD to the causes of GRD

Chapter 9 summarizes the findings of this study, taking the findings on each individual grouping of states and placing them together to understand the bigger picture. The result is a complex but comprehensible model for the causes of GRD that has important policy implications for those whose agenda is to promote religious freedom.

CONCLUSIONS

Overall GRD is influenced by a complex and crosscutting mixture of causes. This multifaceted concoction of causes includes both religious and secular ideologies, regime, religious identity, world region, economic development, threat perceptions, nationalism, culture, anti-Semitism, and GRD, among other more context-specific causes. In the following chapters, this study delves deeper into how discrimination is defined and understood in the context of this study, how it manifests differently in different contexts, and how these multiple and complex influences interact to cause GRD.

2

Government-Based Religious Discrimination

Religious discrimination is one of a series of contested terms including religious freedom, religious tolerance or intolerance, religious repression, and religious human rights. There is no agreement in the literature on what these terms, and other related terms, mean. Accordingly, it is critical to define one's terms when addressing any of these issues in order to achieve transparency on what is being discussed.

In this chapter, I address government-based religious discrimination (GRD). My goal is to define and thoroughly discuss the dependent variable for this study. In brief, I define GRD as restrictions placed by governments or their agents on the religious practices or institutions of religious minorities that are not placed on the majority religion. This definition is intentionally narrow and specific in order to isolate a specific type of government discriminatory behavior that is unambiguously related to religion. In order to explain why I focus in this definition, I briefly discuss the contested nature of the terms I listed earlier. I then discuss in detail what I mean in practice by GRD. I measure it using 35 specific types of discriminatory actions a government might take against a religious minority as well as the extent of this discrimination against 771 religious minorities in 183 countries. Finally, I briefly discuss the general causes of religious discrimination in theory. I analyze these causes in practice in subsequent chapters.

The analysis in this chapter shows that GRD increased substantially between 1990 and 2014. During this period 172 of the 183 countries in the study engaged in GRD against at least 1 minority, and 150 of these countries discriminated unequally, that is some minorities were singled out for more GRD than others. This means that in explaining GRD it is not only important to explain which states are more likely to engage in GRD but also why they might single out certain minorities for more GRD than others.

CONTESTING RELIGIOUS DISCRIMINATION, FREEDOM, INTOLERANCE, REPRESSION, AND HUMAN RIGHTS

In Genesis 11:1–9 the Bible tells the story of why men speak many different languages. In order to prevent men from building a tower intended to reach to the Heavens, God made the men speak different languages to confound their efforts. In many ways the discussion of religious freedom, discrimination, intolerance repression, human rights, and so on is similarly confounded by different understandings of similar terms. In order to understand the specific definition of GRD used in this study, I explore briefly this larger dissonance regarding how to understand this term and related terms.

First, it is important to understand that I distinguish between GRD and societal-based religious discrimination (SRD). For discrimination to be government-based its origin must be a government, whether through laws, policies, the judiciary, or other actions taken by government officials or agents. SRD, which I discuss in more detail in Chapter 3, is discrimination against religious minorities by actors other than government actors. Accordingly, the discussion in the rest of this chapter focuses on the former. As most of the literature on religious freedom, discrimination, and related terms focuses on GRD, this does not unduly complicate the discussion.

While this study focuses on discrimination, the debate in the literature focuses on other terms and revolves around the term *religious freedom* more than any other term. Religious freedom and its related terms have many possible interpretations. I focus here on eight of the more common usages in order to demonstrate the complexity of the debate and that how one defines these terms can have important practical implications. Each definition of religious freedom must answer five questions:

1. May the government restrict public religious practices or institutions?
2. May the government restrict private religious practices?
3. May the government support religions unequally?
4. May the government support all religions equally?
5. May the government treat religious minorities unequally in matters other than religion?

The eight terms and their answers to each of these questions are summarized in Table 2.1 and do not include the term *religious freedom.* This is because the debate is essentially over what religious freedom means. For many, religious freedom means the right to *free exercise.* This term is taken from the first amendment of the US Constitution. Setting the specific legal meaning of this term in the US context aside, "the concept of free exercise of religion can be defined as the ability to freely practice one's religion" (Fox, 2016: 14). Many consider this interpretation of religious freedom essential to democracy. For example, Casanova (2009: 1062) argues, "One could advance the proposition that it is the free exercise of religion ... that appears to be a necessary condition for democracy. One cannot have democracy without freedom of religion." Saiya (2015: 377) similarly argues that "the free exercise of religion works against tendencies towards authoritarianism and tyranny." As I discuss in more detail later, restrictions on free exercise can be placed on individuals or religious institutions. These include limitations on religious practices, religious institutions, clergy, proselytizing, conversion, and other religious activities.

In the terms of our five questions, this means that the government may not restrict religious institutions or practices in public or in private (questions 1 and 2). However, there are no limitations on government support for religion (questions 3 and 4). Also, restricting religious minorities in areas other than religion (question 5), such as economic and political restrictions, are forms of discrimination but do not violate the right to free exercise.

Religious persecution and repression are closely related to the concept of free exercise with one distinction. These concepts also ban non-free-exercise-related forms of discrimination against religious minorities (question 5). Jenkins (2007: 3) defines religious persecution as "an effort by a government to repress major activities by a given religious group, commonly with the goal of eliminating that group in the long or short term." Bowen (2010: 1750) more explicitly argues that the freedom of religion includes both free exercise, which he defines as including two elements. The first is "equal rights and capacities to practice religion." The second is freedom from other forms of persecution targeted at religious minorities that occurs when "certain individuals or groups do not enjoy the same rights or privileges as do members of other religious groups (or nonreligious people) in the society."

Discrimination on the basis of religion, the third conception of religious freedom, centers on any restriction placed on a religious group that

TABLE 2.1 *What the government is allowed to do under competing conceptions of religious freedom*

Religious freedom standard	Types of government policy allowed				
	Restrict public practices & institutions	Restrict private practices	Unequal support for religion	Equal support for religion	Restrict religious minorities
Free exercise	No	No	Yes	Yes	Yes
Persecution or repression	No	No	Yes	Yes	No
Discrimination on the basis of religion	Yes, if applied equally	Yes, if applied equally	Yes	Yes	No
Tolerance/intolerance	No	No	Yes	Yes	No
Neutrality	Yes, if applied equally	Yes, if applied equally	No	Yes	No
Separationism	No	No	No	No	No?
Laicism/secularism	Yes (even mandated), if applied equally	Yes, if applied equally	No	No	No
Religious discrimination	Yes, if applied equally	Yes, if applied equally	Yes	Yes	Yes

is not placed on the majority group. It does not matter whether these restrictions involve limitations on free exercise or not. Farr (2008) uses this conception when he defines religious persecution as "egregious abuse – torture, rape, unjust imprisonment – on the basis of religion." Other than that the restrictions in question are placed on a religious minority, these restrictions are similar to those that may be placed on other types of minority groups based on race, ethnicity, political affiliation, or sexual preference, among others. For example, studies of ethnic conflict examine precisely these types of repression and persecution (e.g., Gurr, 1993, 2000; Horowitz, 1985). Thus, this conception allows restrictions on the right to free exercise as long as these restrictions are placed on everyone, including members of the majority religion (questions 1 and 2), and it does not address support for religion (questions 3 and 4).

The fourth conception of religious freedom, *religious tolerance,* means to put up with those you dislike or with whom you disagree (Eisenstein, 2008: 15). *Religious intolerance* is the absence of this tolerance. Put differently, this means that a government does not have to like a religious minority but it must grant them the same rights and privileges as everyone else. This is inherent in all definitions of religious tolerance. For example, Little (1996: 81) defines religious tolerance as responding "to a set of beliefs and practices regarded as deviant or objectionable without forcible interference." Similarly, Stepan's (2000) concept of "twin tolerations" include "the minimal boundaries of freedom of action that must somehow be crafted for political institutions vis-à-vis religious authorities, and for religious individuals and groups vis-à-vis political institutions." That is, to be tolerant of religious minorities is to refrain from persecuting or repressing then. Thus, while based on a different set of reasoning, this conception of religious freedom is, in practice, the same as the one developed by the literature on religious persecution and repression.[1]

The fifth conception of religious freedom is *neutrality.* The government is expected to be neutral with regard to religion, treating all religions equally. Essentially this means that the government may restrict religion or support it as long as it does so in the same manner for all religions (Stepan, 2012). Roger Finke (1990, 2012; Grim & Finke, 2011; Stark & Finke, 2000), among others (e.g., Farha, 2012; Flere et al., 2016; Toft et al., 2011), argues that restrictions on unequal support are essential to religious freedom. Religion is not free. Places of worship, clergy, and

---

[1] For a discussion of how religion is related to tolerance and intolerance, see Djupe and Calfino (2013) and Eisenstein (2008).

other religious materials and services cost money. This gives religions funded by the state, the most common form of government support for religion (Fox, 2015), a competitive advantage over other religions when they compete for congregants. The supported religions will be less expensive, and those belonging to nonsupported congregations will have to pay twice for their religion, once through taxes and once in contributions to their chosen congregation. Thus, the end result is the same as discrimination, disadvantaging the nonsupported religions.

Providing religious education in public schools, another common form of support, has a similar result both because it makes religious education less expensive for the religion that is taught, and it can stigmatize students who do not wish to attend the religion classes (Fox, 2015). Some other forms of support such as enforcing religious laws are essentially a form of discrimination for those who do not believe in these religious laws. Bader (1999) and Gill (2004) argue that such neutrality is impossible because by favoring no religion, the government essentially favors secularism, which disadvantages all religions.

The *separationist* conception of religious freedom holds that any government involvement in religion is a threat to religious freedom. This conception, of which the US model is a prime example, requires that the state neither support nor hinder any religion. While it does not address the issue of how religious minorities may be treated on matters other than religion, this doctrine is usually combined with a liberal view of minority equality and rights. There is some debate over to what extent government and religion should be separated within this conception. In the United States, conservatives and many liberals agree that despite this separation, religion has a place in public life but argue over exactly what this role should be. Most consider the use of religious language by politicians acceptable, and some even believe that religious organizations can receive government funds to engage in nonreligious activities such as welfare, as long as this is in a context where religious and secular institutions compete equally for such funds. On the other side of the debate, some believe that there should be a Jeffersonian wall of separation between religion and state that bans religious motivations for policy decisions and even the use of religious language in political discourse (Esbeck, 1988; Kuru, 2009).

The *laicist* conception of religious freedom, which takes its name from France's national policy concerning religion, is, perhaps, the strictest because it both bans state support for religion *and* restricts religion's presence in the public sphere by all members of society, including both religious majorities and minorities. This restriction clearly also applies to public religious expression by members of the majority religion. Yet most such countries, in practice, further restrict minority religions. This is certainly true of France and pre-Erdogan Turkey, classic examples laicist policies. This can include restrictions on religious institutions, public religious activities, and wearing religious clothing or symbols in public places. While in democracies these bans are generally limited to the public sphere, in nondemocratic states this can extend to the private sphere (Durham, 1996: 21–22; Esbeck, 1988; Haynes, 1997; Hurd, 2004a, 2004b; Keane, 2000; Kuru, 2009; Stepan, 2000). For example, in 2004 France passed a law banning overt religious symbols in public schools, including the traditional head coverings worn by Muslim women. From the laicist perspective, these head coverings are an aggressive religious encroachment into the public domain. Thus, bans on free exercise in the public sphere are not only acceptable, they are mandated but must be applied equally to all religions. As equality is an essential element of this doctrine, it implicitly bans unequal treatment of religious minorities in matters other than religion.

As demonstrated in this discussion and in Table 2.1, each of these conceptions of religious freedom, as well as the final one that I discuss next and use as the basis for this study, places different requirements on what the government must, may, or may not do. Determining which standard is the correct one is a normative issue that is beyond the purview of this study. However, it is important to define exactly what is being measured in this study for purposes of clarity and transparency. In addition, a prohibition against GRD – unequal limitations on religious practices or institutions – is the one thing that all of these conceptions of religious freedom have in common. Thus, as I discuss in more detail later, while this study focuses on what is perhaps the narrowest of these definitions of religious freedom, any act of GRD violates all of these conceptions of religious freedom. This makes it a particularly relevant topic of study.

DEFINING GOVERNMENT-BASED RELIGIOUS DISCRIMINATION IN THEORY

The final conception of religious freedom I discuss is based on an absence of religious discrimination. I define government-based religious discrimination (GRD) as restrictions placed by the government or its agents on the religious practices or institutions of a religious minority that are not placed on the majority religion (Fox, 2008, 2015, 2016). In this section I discuss how this conception of religious freedom relates to the other conceptions.

This is the most lenient of all the conceptions of religious freedom, but it is also a basic element of all of them. It allows many actions the other conceptions of religious freedom ban. This includes support for religion and discrimination against members of minority religions in matters other than religion. It even allows restrictions on religious institutions and practices if they are applied equally to all religions, including the majority religion. The only disallowed government policy is one that restricts minority religious practices or institutions in a manner that the majority religion is not restricted. This is because to discriminate, by definition, means to treat differently or unequally.

Focusing on GRD in this study has a number of advantages. The first is that it is the one element of the concept of religious freedom that all agree upon. That is, a violation of this conception of religious freedom is a violation of all of the conceptions I discussed earlier. GRD is the one state action that no conception of religious freedom allows. Throughout this study I show that GRD is very common. Consequently, few countries have full religious freedom, however the contested term is defined.

A second advantage is simplicity. While the elements included in other conceptions of religious freedom are worthy of study, focusing on 35 types of GRD against 771 religious minorities in 183 countries and independent territories is sufficiently complicated. Adding in elements such as nonreligious discrimination and comparative levels of support would add a further level of complexity to an already complex study.

Third, GRD is a core aspect of religious freedom. This is not only because it is the one element of religious freedom agreed upon by all definitions. It is also the canary in the coal mine. Religious minorities are the most vulnerable populations when it comes to religious freedom. If a state violates religious freedom on any substantial level, religious minorities are most likely among those affected.

A fourth advantage of focusing on GRD is that there is a difference between unequal government support for religious minorities and restricting religious practices and institutions. Supporting one religion, or a few religions, more than others or even to the exclusion of others does not necessarily entail any actual restrictions on the practices or institutions of other religions. For example, funding the Catholic Church exclusively does not in any way limit the right to free exercise for Protestants, or for that matter for any non-Christian religion. It is entirely possible to construct a policy that favors one or a few religions, but no other religion is restricted in any way. However, certain types of support such as enforcing the majority religion on the entire population are effectively GRD, and the codings I discuss later reflect this.

Many theorists make precisely this argument. Mazie (2004, 2006), argues that while restrictions on minority religions are not compatible with liberal democracy, some forms of support can be compatible. For example, a state's use of religious symbols on its national flag may alienate minorities, and declaring religious holidays such as Christmas to be national holidays may inconvenience religious minorities. However, many democratic states have religious symbols on their flags, and nearly all of them declare religious holidays national holidays. Also, blocking this type of policy, Mazie (2004: 6) argues, "would transform liberalism into a doctrine denying independent states the moral right to even the most rudimentary form of political culture."

More substantial support for religion, such as unequal financing of religious institutions, are not, according to Mazie (2004, 2006), incompatible with liberal democracy as long as they do not restrict a minority's right to free exercise. While many might not be happy with this unequal support, it is not unusual for democratic governments to enact policies that are unpopular with some segments of society. Thus, for Mazie (2004, 2006), only government actions that violate the right to free exercise are incompatible with his conception of religious freedom.

Casanova (2009: 1063) similarly argues that an established religion only undermines religious freedom when it "claims monopoly over a state territory, impedes the free exercise of religion, and undermines equal rights or equal access of all citizens." Driessen (2010) takes this a step further and argues that support for religion can be healthy for a democracy.

> Heavy handed ruling against religion in democracies, by contrast, not only runs the risk of provoking the counter-productive, anti-democratic forces which lie within religious fundamentalism but also obscures the full breadth of options open for healthy relationships between religion and state and, by doing so, weakens the potential religion possesses to help legitimize and strengthen new democratic regimes.
>
> (Driessen, 2010: 57)

However these governments must protect religious freedom, and there must be no religious veto of government policies.

A fifth advantage of focusing on GRD is that if one looks solely at limitations on religion in general, all governments restrict religion to some extent. For example, no country would allow a sect to perform human sacrifice. Or consider the less extreme but not uncommon case where a religion's worship practices include the use of an illegal drug. To allow any action, even illegal ones, because they are a religious practice would be to invite anarchy. In the 1879 case *Reynolds vs. United States*, US Supreme Court Chief Justice Morrison Waite made exactly this argument: "Can a man excuse his practices to the contrary because of his religious belief? To permit this would be to make the professed doctrines of religious belief superior to the law of the land, and in effect to permit every citizen to become a law unto himself. Government could exist only in name under such circumstances." All societies need to decide what is and is not acceptable behavior. While there is a line between legitimate government regulation and violations of religious freedom, where that line is drawn is subjective. However, to limit some religions but not others undermines this argument of the government's prerogative to maintain social order.

That being said, general restrictions on religion can be substantial and violate the right to the free exercise of all citizens of a state, including the majority religion. The RAS dataset includes a variable that measures this, and this variable is used in this study as an independent variable that predicts GRD. Nevertheless, the focus of this study is specifically on GRD. As I noted earlier, this endeavor is sufficiently complicated in and of itself. Attempting to add additional factors such as regulation of the majority religion to the factors I attempt to explain would likely to be to bite off more than I can properly chew in this endeavor. The dynamics causing the regulation of the majority religion are related to those casing GRD but different and deserve separate consideration. Put differently, attempting to explain too much would likely undermine my ability to explain anything at all.

DEFINING GOVERNMENT-BASED RELIGIOUS DISCRIMINATION IN PRACTICE

The Religion and State-Minorities round 3 (RASM3) dataset measures thirty-five distinct government policies that restrict the institutions or practices of minority religions. In this section, I present each of these thirty-five types of restrictions and how common they were in 1990 and 2014, or the first and most recent years available. In the discussion I will refer to them as 1990 and 2014. I also present the 2014 results on (1) how common they were based on the majority religion in the country, that is, for example, do Catholics discriminate more than Muslims? (2) how common they were against six types of religious minority, that is, for example, are Jews discriminated against more than Bahai? and (3) what proportion of states discriminate against at least one minority. In this latter category, I include discrimination against any minority, even if it is not among the 771 included in this study because the main Religion and State round 3 (RAS3) dataset includes this information.

Thus, the tables in this section focus on demographic identity traits. I chose this focus rather than some other means of dividing the minorities and countries into groups such as world region or regime because, as I show in later chapters, religious identity plays a major role in explaining GRD. In fact, arguably, this is the most important factor in predicting GRD other than government religion policy, which I analyze in detail in subsequent chapters. In addition, this demonstrates that GRD is something that is found across all religions.

The purpose of this exercise is threefold. First, this represents a practical discussion of all of the ways governments engage in GRD, as defined by this study. As the RAS project has, in each of its three rounds, researched each country's government religion policy, I am confident that this list is inclusive of all types of GRD currently present in government policy across the world. Second, it provides a basic analysis of the commonality of each type of GRD. As discussing all thirty-five types of GRD in detail would be too lengthy, in this discussion I focus on those that are particularly common or that I consider to be of particular import, but all of them are listed in the tables. The purpose of the discussion and examples in this chapter is to give the reader a more qualitative understanding of the events and policies that underlie the data. Third, I demonstrate that levels of GRD vary considerably across different types of states and within these states against different types of minorities. This will prove to be important in explaining levels of GRD.

Each of the thirty-five types of GRD is coded on the following scale:

2 = The activity is significantly restricted or the government engages in a severe form of this practice.

1 = The activity is slightly restricted or the government engages in a mild form of this practice.

0 = Not significantly restricted or the government does not engage in this practice for any.

The composite variable combines all 35 of these variables into a single index, which in theory ranges from 0–70, though no minority's score reaches 70. However, the analysis in this chapter focuses primarily on the presence or absence of GRD.

Restrictions on Religious Practices

I divide these thirty-five types of GRD into four categories I developed in Fox (2015, 2016). These categories place each of the types of GRD into groupings with a similar theme. The first category, presented in Table 2.2, is restrictions on religious practices. While individually few of these restrictions are particularly common, in 2014, 38.9 percent of minorities experienced at last one type, and 60.1 percent of states engaged in at least one type against at least one minority. These types of restrictions are overall most common against minorities in Muslim-majority countries and least common in Catholic-majority countries.

The right to practice one's religion freely is at the core of the concept of the free exercise of religion. Even the smallest and seemingly inconsequential restriction on the right to free exercise is unlikely to be seen as trivial by the religious community that is restricted. While it is difficult to compare across forms of GRD and determine which most obstructs religious freedom, it is certainly true that religious freedom is not possible without the right to freely practice all aspects of a religion. When this category of GRD is placed only on minority religions, it is a sign that the government considers the religious minority or the specific practice undesirable.

The most common form of restriction in this category are restrictions on the public observance of religion, which, in 2014, was present in one out of three countries against 18.7 percent of minorities. While this type of restriction is most common in religiously exclusive states such as Saudi Arabia, which bans all public religious observance by any religion other than the state-approved version of Wahhabi Sunni Islam, it is also present in other types of countries. For example, Russia's 1997 law on religion required all religious organizations to register or be dissolved. As many were not allowed to register, this left them vulnerable to severe limitations, especially by local and regional governments. This denial of registration as a basis for restricting minority religions is common in nondemocratic governments (Finke, Mataic, & Fox, 2017; Sarkissian, 2015).

In June 2012 Russia's government significantly increased administrative penalties for individuals and for organizers violating the law against unsanctioned demonstrations. While the law is intended to restrict political dissent and does not apply specifically to religious rites, some local authorities broadly interpret the law to cover the activities of some minority religions. Also, Russian courts apply this type of creative

TABLE 2.2 *Restrictions on religious practices against religious minorities*

	All cases		Controlling for majority religion in 2014					At least one minority in the country in 2014 (%)
	1990 (%)	2014 (%)	Catholic (%)	Orthodox (%)	Other Christian (%)	Muslim (%)	Other (%)	
Public observance of religion	14.1	18.7	3.1	25.0	5.5	39.2	29.7	33.3
Private observance of religion	5.2	8.8	0.0	11.9	3.1	21.1	12.9	18.0
Forced observance: religious laws of another group	11.9	14.4	8.8	4.7	7.0	34.0	9.3	19.7
Make/obtain materials necessary for religious rites/customs/ceremonies	2.7	3.0	0.0	6.2	0.0	7.7	4.4	7.1
Circumcisions or other rite of passage ceremonies	0.0	0.3	0.0	0.0	1.0	0.0	0.0	0.5
Religious dietary laws	1.6	1.8	0.0	0.0	6.5	0.5	0.0	4.9
Write/publish/disseminate religious publications	14.5	17.5	0.0	20.3	3.6	48.5	19.5	26.2
Import religious publications	11.9	14.0	0.0	17.2	1.0	36.1	21.2	21.3
Religious publications for personal use	4.3	6.2	0.0	8.8	1.0	21.1	1.7	13.7
Religious laws concerning marriage and divorce	6.7	7.3	0.0	11.9	0.5	19.6	8.5	12.0
Religious laws concerning burial	6.4	9.1	3.1	17.2	6.5	14.9	9.3	20.8
Religious symbols or clothing	3.0	4.5	3.6	6.2	3.5	6.7	3.4	16.9
At least one type	32.9	38.9	16.0	54.7	22.9	70.1	44.1	60.1

Controlling for minority religion in 2014

	Christian (%)	Muslim (%)	Hindu (%)	Buddhist (%)	Jewish (%)	Animist (%)	Bahai (%)	Other (%)
Public observance of religion	24.1	15.3	27.9	16.7	6.6	18.7	14.1	22.2
Private observance of religion	14.7	6.1	7.0	6.2	2.6	7.7	4.7	11.1
Forced observance: religious laws of another group	13.8	11.7	25.6	22.9	3.9	12.1	21.9	17.5
Make/obtain materials necessary for religious rites/customs/ceremonies	5.2	1.8	7.0	6.2	0.0	0.0	0.0	3.7
Circumcisions or other rite of passage ceremonies	0.0	0.6	0.0	0.0	1.3	0.0	0.0	0.0
Religious dietary laws	0.0	4.3	0.0	2.1	7.9	0.0	0.0	0.0
Write/publish/disseminate religious publications	22.4	14.1	31.2	22.9	6.6	8.8	15.6	24.1
Import religious publications	20.3	9.2	27.9	16.7	6.6	5.5	12.5	14.8
Religious publications for personal use	10.3	3.7	14.0	6.2	2.6	0.0	7.8	3.7
Religious laws concerning marriage and divorce	7.3	6.7	18.6	12.5	1.3	1.1	9.4	11.1
Religious laws concerning burial	11.1	9.2	11.6	14.6	10.5	1.1	9.4	3.7
Religious symbols or clothing	1.3	15.3	4.7	6.2	1.3	0.0	0.0	1.9
At least one type	40.9	41.7	46.5	43.7	30.3	30.8	31.2	46.3

All scores in this table use a minority within a country as the unit of analysis except the "at least one minority in the country" column, which uses the country as the unit of analysis.

interpretation of the law on public demonstration to keep evangelical Protestants from gathering for worship (Forum 18 News Service, 2012). In 2014, there were twenty-three known cases of fines for holding public religious activities without prior state permission, mostly against Jehovah's Witnesses and Protestants (UNHCR, The UN Refugee Agency, 2015).

The second-most-common form of GRD in this category is restrictions on religious publications. An inability to obtain basic religious publications such as the Bible or Koran are a serious burden on the ability to practice a religion. Between the three types of discrimination in this category listed in Table 2.1, this type of restriction was present in 30.5 percent of countries and against 19.5 percent of religious minorities. For example, in Kuwait the government allows no religious publishers for any religion other than Islam, although registered churches can produce materials for use by their own congregations. One private company may import religious materials for use by registered churches, as long as they do not contain any material insulting to Islam. Private individuals may not import any religious materials contrary to Islam (Importing personal property into Kuwait, 2010).

Finally, while only 9.1 percent of religious minorities experience restrictions on burying their dead, this type of restriction exists in 20.8 percent of countries. In several Western countries, this type of restriction is in place for a variety of reasons. In Sweden, despite being disestablished in 2000, the Lutheran Church of Sweden still controls most cemeteries and burials, though it is expected allow burial for all religions and make available premises without any religious symbols for the holding of funeral ceremonies (Ministry of Culture Sweden, 2000). In Switzerland, many municipalities and cantons refuse zoning approval to build Muslim cemeteries. In Greece, there are few Muslim cemeteries outside Thrace. Greek law requires exhumation of bodies after three years, which violates Islamic religious law. Most Greek Muslims are buried in Thrace or in their country of origin. Also, until 2006 cremation, which is part of the burial rites of several religions, was illegal in Greece. While a cremation facility is planned, it has been delayed for over a decade due to objections by the Greek Orthodox Church (The National Herald, 2017). German law requires burial in a coffin, which is in opposition to Muslim religious rites. In recent years, some states (Berlin, Bremen, Hamburg, and Hesse) have made agreements with Muslim communities permitting burial in a shroud, but in other states the restriction remains.

In later chapters I will discuss restrictions on the Kosher and Halal slaughter of meat (coded here under restrictions on dietary laws) and on male infant circumcision. These types of restrictions are not overly common worldwide but are emerging issues in Western democracies and raise an interesting issue. They are generally applicable laws that, at least technically, do not target minority religions. Rather, they ban practices that are considered objectionable by some interpretations of liberal secular ideology. It is certainly true that if religious law trumps state law, any form of government other than a theocracy would be difficult to maintain. However, the RAS project codes these types of restrictions in cases where they restrict long-standing religious practices that are considered central and nonoptional to a religion. Circumcision and ritual slaughter both meet these criteria for Muslims and Jews. In addition, passing laws that technically are general but in practice restrict only certain minority religions or can otherwise be applied selectively is a common means governments use to restrict minority religions.

Restrictions on Religious Institutions and Clergy

The second category of GRD, presented in Table 2.3, is restrictions placed on religious institutions and clergy. Organized religion relies upon clergy and institutions. While there are examples of organized religions that lack either clergy, such as the Quakers, or formal institutions, such as many tribal religions, there are few that lack both. Clergy and institutions are usually responsible for maintaining a religion's theology and doctrines as well as transmitting them from generation to generation. They are central to most religious ceremonies and rites of passage. Without them, practicing a religion and even maintaining its presence in a location becomes more difficult. Thus, restrictions upon them have serious consequences.

In 2014, 55.3 percent of minorities experienced at least one of these eight types of restriction, and they were present in 74.9 percent of countries. Restrictions on building, repairing, and maintaining places of worship is the most common form as measured by the proportion of countries that restrict minorities in this manner (51.9 percent). In Western democracies, this type of restriction is common. In most cases, it is a result of local governments denying permits or using zoning rules to limit minority places of worship. Much of this focuses on Muslims. Muslims experienced this type of restriction in Australia, Belgium, Denmark, and Italy for the entire 1990–2014 period, and local governments in Andorra, Austria, Iceland, Malta, and the United States began restricting Mosques

TABLE 2.3 *Restrictions on religious institutions and clergy against religious minorities*

	All cases		Controlling for majority religion in 2014					At least one minority in the country in 2014 (%)
	1990 (%)	2014 (%)	Catholic (%)	Orthodox (%)	Other Christian (%)	Muslim (%)	Other (%)	
Building/leasing/repairing/maintaining places of worship	24.4	30.6	9.3	73.3	9.5	59.3	32.4	51.9
Access to existing places of worship	10.6	14.4	6.2	40.6	3.5	20.6	22.0	32.8
Formal religious organizations	8.4	12.8	5.2	23.4	4.0	23.7	16.9	27.9
Ordination of and/or access to clergy	8.6	8.7	1.5	10.9	3.0	18.6	12.7	18.6
Minority religions (as opposed to all religions) must register	29.3	33.1	44.3	67.2	19.4	35.1	16.1	44.8
Minority clergy access to jails	14.4	14.3	17.5	48.4	8.0	8.8	10.2	21.3
Minority clergy access to military bases	18.9	19.6	26.8	64.1	8.0	16.0	9.3	24.9
Minority clergy access to hospitals & other public facilities	10.6	12.5	13.4	43.7	7.5	5.2	8.5	15.3
At least one type	50.2	55.3	59.8	92.2	40.3	71.6	43.2	74.9

Controlling for minority religion in 2014

	Christian (%)	Muslim (%)	Hindu (%)	Buddhist (%)	Jewish (%)	Animist (%)	Bahai (%)	Other (%)
Building/leasing/repairing/maintaining places of worship	42.2	35.6	39.5	27.1	18.4	22.1	21.9	20.4
Access to existing places of worship	24.6	17.8	9.3	4.2	11.8	4.4	3.1	7.4
Formal religious organizations	15.5	14.7	9.3	12.5	9.2	8.8	14.1	10.3
Ordination of and/or access to clergy	10.3	10.4	14.0	12.5	3.9	2.2	4.7	11.1
Minority religions (as opposed to all religions) must register	44.0	28.2	18.6	27.1	36.8	26.4	31.2	25.9
Minority clergy access to jails	19.8	14.7	11.6	12.5	17.1	6.6	6.2	9.3
Minority clergy access to military bases	23.7	17.2	14.0	22.9	30.3	11.0	17.7	11.6
Minority clergy access to hospitals & other public facilities	17.2	12.9	4.7	10.4	4.5	4.4	3.1	7.4
At least one type	66.4	59.5	44.2	54.2	56.6	38.5	45.3	42.6

All scores in this table use a minority within a country as the unit of analysis except the "at least one minority in the country" column, which uses the country as the unit of analysis.

in this manner at some point after 1990. In Switzerland, in addition to restrictions by local governments, a 2009 national referendum restricts the building of Minarets on Mosques.

However, these types of restrictions also exist in some Western democracies against minorities other than Muslims. Some municipalities in Spain use legal hurdles to make it difficult for all minority places of worship to be built and operated, including but not limited to Mosques. In Cyprus, as of 2014, only 8 of about 110 mosques still operate, and some of those are not open for public use (Fox News, 2014; Islam Today, 2011). Also, in 2010, Cyprus's Jewish community complained that the government did not respond to requests for land to build a synagogue. In Greece, municipalities limit the building of places of worship by Muslims as well as nonregistered religions, including many non-Orthodox Christian denominations. France is the only Western country where restrictions apply only to a non-Muslim group. The Jehovah's Witnesses are limited in a variety of manners as part of France's anticult program. In contrast, in Latin America, other than in Cuba's highly restrictive Communist regime, no minority included in RASM experiences this type of restriction.

The most common form of restriction in this category, based on the number of minorities restricted, are restrictions on registration. In some cases, this merely means that minorities must register in a manner that the majority religion does not, but this registration is rarely if ever denied. This form of restriction only becomes substantial when governments deny registration, and failure to register has consequences. For example, Bulgaria's *Religious Denominations Act of 2002* recognizes the Bulgarian Orthodox Church and requires all other religions to register. Nonregistered groups are open to significant limitations. While registered organizations for Jews and Muslims exist, Muslim and Jewish groups not affiliated with these organizations have been restricted. For example, a Chabad-Jewish community had its registration application rejected in 2009 on the grounds that the group violated the *Religious Denominations Act* by operating a synagogue and kindergarten without the consent of the registered Jewish organization. Similarly, in 2011, thirteen Muslim leaders were arrested and charged with undermining rule of law by running an unregistered religious association affiliated with Salafi Islam and funded by Saudi Arabia. As discussed earlier, many of Russia's local governments have used the inability of some groups to register to limit their religious practices.

Restrictive registrations laws are a common method used by autocracies to restrict religious organizations they consider undesirable. This allows them to claim they provide religious freedom for legal religious organizations while in practice denying that freedom by refusing to let religious organizations become legal (Sarkissian, 2015).[2]

Restrictions on Conversion and Proselytizing

The third category of GRD, presented in Table 2.4, is restrictions placed on conversion and proselytizing. While not all religions seek converts, most do. Many regimes and nearly all religions see proselytizing and conversion away from the majority religion as threatening. In fact, as I argue in more detail in later chapters, this threat can be seen as an existential threat. Why this is true for religious ideological reasons is obvious. But it is also true for demographic and political reasons. Conversion can alter the demography of a country. As religion and identity are both potentially important elements of politics including perceptions of national identity and culture, this type of demographic shift can have significant political implications. Voting and other forms of support for political parties is influenced by religious identity in many countries. Conversion can also have social implications, as leaving one's religion can also mean leaving one's social group and family. This can result in resentment of the proselytizing minority religions. This, in turn, can have political implications (Grim & Finke, 2011).

Overall restrictions in this category are most common in Muslim-majority countries. Afghanistan represents one of the extreme cases. Converts away from Islam legally have three days to recant. The official punishment for this crime of apostasy is deprivation of all property and possessions, the invalidation of the person's marriage, and beheading. Beheading is generally not enforced against women, who are sent to prison until they recant. Lawyers often refuse to represent these "apostates" (Ahmed, 2014; Bingham, 2014). In addition, Afghanistan's government considers the Bahai faith a form of blasphemy. All Muslims who convert to the religion are considered apostates, and Bahai practitioners are labeled as infidels. While proselytizing is not technically illegal in Afghanistan, the 2000 NGO law bans organizations from engaging in proselytizing activities, and foreigners who proselytize are deported. Also, according to a government official, the government searches the websites of those organizations requesting visas and denies visas if they detect any

---

[2] For a more detailed discussion on restrictions on religious registration, see Finke, Mataic, and Fox (2017).

TABLE 2.4 *Restrictions on conversion and proselytizing against religious minorities*

	All cases		Controlling for majority religion in 2014					At least one minority in the country in 2014 (%)
	1990 (%)	2014 (%)	Catholic (%)	Orthodox (%)	Other Christian (%)	Muslim (%)	Other (%)	
Conversion to minority religions	9.6	9.6	0.0	0.0	0.5	34.0	5.9	15.3
Forced renunciation of faith by recent converts to minority religions	4.0	4.4	0.0	0.0	0.5	13.4	5.9	8.2
Forced conversions	1.9	3.2	0.5	0.0	0.0	7.7	7.6	6.6
Efforts/campaigns to convert members of minority religion (no force)	7.7	9.6	2.6	7.2	0.0	23.2	16.9	13.7
Proselytizing by permanent residents to members of the majority religion	16.9	21.1	1.5	40.6	2.0	52.6	23.7	33.9
Proselytizing by permanent residents to members of minority religions	10.1	13.2	2.6	38.5	2.0	24.2	18.6	21.3
At least one type	22.8	26.3	5.7	45.3	2.0	60.8	34.7	56.3

Controlling for minority religion in 2014

	Christian (%)	Muslim (%)	Hindu (%)	Buddhist (%)	Jewish (%)	Animist (%)	Bahai (%)	Other (%)
Conversion to minority religions	10.3	4.3	23.3	16.7	2.6	3.3	17.2	16.7
Forced renunciation of faith by recent converts to minority religions	7.3	1.8	7.0	6.2	0.0	2.2	4.7	5.6
Forced conversions	4.3	3.1	2.3	0.0	0.0	2.2	3.1	9.3
Efforts/campaigns to convert members of minority religion (no force)	10.8	5.5	18.6	12.5	3.9	7.7	14.1	13.0
Proselytizing by permanent residents to members of the majority religion	30.2	14.7	30.2	25.0	14.5	9.9	20.3	20.4
Proselytizing by permanent residents to members of minority religions	18.5	11.7	11.6	18.7	9.2	5.5	7.8	16.7
At least one type	33.2	17.8	37.2	35.4	19.7	15.4	23.4	37.0

All scores in this table use a minority within a country as the unit of analysis except the "at least one minority in the country" column, which uses the country as the unit of analysis.

hint of proselytizing. Non-Muslims in prisons are often pressured and beaten in order to induce them to convert to Islam (Ireland, 2008).

While this type of restriction is most common in Muslim-majority countries, many of them do not engage in this type of restriction at all, including Burkina Faso, Djibouti, Gambia, Guinea, Mali, Niger, Senegal, and Sierra Leone. Also, while restrictions on conversion are uncommon in non-Muslim-majority countries, restrictions on proselytizing are more common. For example, Belarus bans public proselytizing in the context of more general restrictions on all public religious activities. In Laos, a Buddhist-majority country with a Communist government, all religious groups including proselytizers must have government permission to preach or disseminate religious materials outside their house of worship. Some local authorities arrest Christians for proselytizing. There are also cases of local authorities pressuring Christians to recant their faith. This can include confiscating their homes, exiling them from their villages, and sometimes imprisonment.

Other Types of Restriction

The final category, presented in Table 2.5, looks at the nine types of GRD that do not fit into the other three categories. The Bahai minority in Iran is the only minority that experiences all nine types of GRD in this category. In fact, the Bahai in Iran experience more GRD than any other minority included in RASM3 and are subject to twenty-eight of the thirty-five types of GRD included in RASM3.

The Bahai, are the largest non-Muslim religious community in Iran. The government considers them heretics, apostates, and a "deviant sect." The Bahai faith is illegal. This explicitly includes teaching and practicing the Bahai faith. The Bahai community may not assemble officially nor may it maintain administrative institutions. This results in systematic harassment, arrest, and persecution. The government regularly arrests and detains Bahai, either on trumped-up charges such as espionage or without reason. In most cases, a condition for their release is recanting their faith. Bahai are even sometimes subject to summary executions and extrajudicial killings. In addition, the government regularly confiscates Bahai private and commercial property, as well as religious materials. The government holds many Bahai properties that were seized following the 1979 revolution, including cemeteries, holy places, and historical sites. The government prevents Bahais from burying their dead in accordance with their faith and sometimes destroys their cemeteries. The Iranian

TABLE 2.5 *Other restrictions against religious minorities*

	All cases		Controlling for majority religion in 2014					At least one minority in the country in 2014 (%)
	1990 (%)	2014 (%)	Catholic (%)	Orthodox (%)	Other Christian (%)	Muslim (%)	Other (%)	
Religious schools/ education	12.5	16.9	5.2	34.4	6.0	30.9	22.0	23.0
Mandatory education in the majority religion	15.4	18.7	8.8	23.1	10.9	39.2	11.9	24.6
Arrest/detention/ harassment other than for proselytizing	7.0	12.8	3.6	20.3	7.5	22.2	17.8	35.0
Failure to protect religious minorities against violence or punish perpetrators	5.6	7.5	1.5	26.6	0.5	13.9	8.5	20.2
State surveillance of religious activities	7.5	11.3	3.1	14.1	7.0	18.6	18.6	29.0
Child custody granted on basis of religion	9.2	9.7	0.5	1.6	0.0	37.6	0.0	15.3
Declaration of some minority religions dangerous or extremist sects	2.2	4.2	2.6	7.8	4.0	4.6	4.2	21.3

(continued)

TABLE 2.5 (continued)

	All cases		Controlling for majority religion in 2014					At least one minority in the country in 2014 (%)
	1990 (%)	2014 (%)	Catholic (%)	Orthodox (%)	Other Christian (%)	Muslim (%)	Other (%)	
Antireligious propaganda in official/semiofficial government publications	8.0	8.7	1.0	29.1	1.0	16.5	11.0	27.3
Other forms of governmental religious discrimination	10.6	14.1	11.9	20.3	9.0	21.6	11.0	33.3
At least one type of other restrictions	37.4	45.9	27.8	76.6	33.7	69.6	42.0	68.3
At least one type for all religious discrimination	64.2	71.6	75.3	95.3	51.2	86.1	63.6	88.5
Mean for all religious discrimination	7.66	8.72	2.37	11.11	2.02	12.27	6.42	–

	Controlling for minority religion in 2014							
	Christian (%)	Muslim (%)	Hindu (%)	Buddhist (%)	Jewish (%)	Animist (%)	Bahai (%)	Other (%)
Religious schools/education	23.7	14.7	18.6	18.7	15.8	8.8	10.9	13.0
Mandatory education in the majority religion	17.6	19.6	30.2	16.7	15.8	16.5	20.3	18.5
Arrest/detention/harassment other than for proselytizing	19.0	20.2	4.7	2.1	1.3	8.8	4.7	13.0
	13.4	8.6	7.0	2.1	6.6	1.1	3.1	1.9

Failure to protect religious minorities against violence or punish perpetrators								
State surveillance of religious activities	13.4	19.6	9.3	8.3	1.3	6.6	4.7	11.1
Child custody granted on basis of religion	12.5	4.3	20.9	12.5	6.6	2.2	4.1	14.8
Declaration of some minority religions dangerous or extremist sects	6.9	2.5	0.0	2.1	0.0	6.6	4.7	4.7
Antireligious propaganda in official/semiofficial government publications	13.4	8.6	7.0	4.2	9.2	3.3	3.1	10.3
Other forms of governmental religious discrimination	18.5	19.0	9.3	4.2	11.8	9.9	10.9	10.4
At least one type of other restrictions	51.3	44.6	48.8	35.4	42.1	34.1	31.2	46.3
At least one type for all religious discrimination	74.6	78.5	62.8	68.7	76.3	60.4	62.5	70.4
Mean for all religious discrimination	8.09	5.85	7.65	6.54	4.20	3.15	5.11	5.75

All scores in this table use a minority within a country as the unit of analysis except the "at least one minority in the country" column, which uses the country as the unit of analysis.

state-run media and even school textbooks denigrate the Bahai faith. The government bans Bahai schools, and Bahais may enroll in schools and university only if they hide their faith. In public schools, teachers and administrators pressure Bahai children to convert to Islam, and universities expel students discovered to be Bahai. Economic discrimination is rampant. The government denies licenses and leases to Bahai businesses or forces them to close in another manner. The government also pressures private businesses to fire Bahai employees. Bahais may not serve in leadership positions in the government and military. They are denied access to the social pension system as well as compensation for injury or criminal victimization. They may not inherit property. The government does not recognize Bahai marriages and divorces, but it does allows a civil attestation of marriage to serve as a marriage certificate (Erdbrink, 2016; Iran Press Watch, 2016; MacEoin, 2014; Oweis, 2016; Shaheed, 2015; UK Home Office, 2013; USCIRF Press Briefing, 2012; Zaimov, 2016).

GENERAL PATTERNS OF GOVERNMENT-BASED RELIGIOUS DISCRIMINATION

There are two important general patterns in the data. First, overall GRD is increasing. Thirty-three of the thirty-five types of GRD included in RASM3 were present against more minorities in 2014 than they were in 1990. Of the 771 minorities in the dataset, GRD decreased against 59 (7.7 percent), remained stable against 415 (53.8 percent), and increased against 305 (39.6 percent). As shown in Figure 2.1, this increase is mostly consistent over time and across categories of GRD.

The second pattern is that GRD is most often unequal. That is, in countries that discriminate, some minorities are singled out for more GRD or different types of GRD than others. Looking at the entire 1990–2014 period, of the 183 countries included in RASM3, 15 engage in no GRD, and 5 have only 1 minority. Of the remaining 163, 144 (88.3 percent) treat at least 1 minority in RASM3 different from the others. An additional six countries treat all coded minorities the same but discriminate differently against an uncoded minority. For example, in Suriname in several school administrators banned Rastafarians, a group too small to be included in RASM3, on the grounds that they may not wear dreadlocks, a basic element of their faith. Similarly, Botswana denied Scientologists registration. Thirteen countries discriminate but discriminate equally against all coded minorities. Thus, overall, 150 (81.9 percent) countries in RASM3 discriminate unequally.

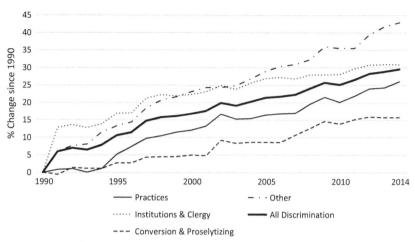

FIGURE 2.1 Change over time in government-based religious discrimination against religious minorities
Significance of change between practices for 1990 and marked year: <.05 in 1994, <.01 in 1995–1996, <.001 from 1997 onward
Significance of change between institutions and clergy for 1990 and marked year: <.05 in 1995–1996, <.001 from 1991 and 1997 onward
Significance of change between conversion and proselytizing for 1990 and marked year: <.05 in 1991–1994, <.01 in 1995–1996, <.001 from 1997 onward
Significance of change between other for 1990 and marked year: <.05 in 1991, <.01 in 1991, <.001 from 1993 onward
Significance of change between all cases for 1990 and marked year: <.05 in 1992, <.001 from 1994 onward

This unequal discrimination is an important finding. Most data on discrimination or human rights violations has a single score for the entire country. For example Freedom House has a widely used human rights score (Puddington & Roylance, 2017), but this score is for entire countries. The same is true of many other studies (e.g., Abouharb & Cingranelli, 2006; Grim & Finke, 2011). While some studies have minority-level data, these studies focus on ethnic minorities and do not include all relevant minorities (e.g., Cederman et al., 2007, 2010; Gurr, 1993, 2000). This finding shows that using a religious minority as the unit of analysis matters. That is, we must ask not only why does a government discriminate against minorities in general, but also why does it discriminate against a particular minority.

Put differently, clearly certain types of governments are more likely to discriminate in general, regardless of the target of this GRD. However, this finding shows that there must be factors that make a government more likely to discriminate against some minorities more than others. A major focus of this book is to examine exactly what factors in what contexts make governments more likely to discriminate unequally and what motivates them to target certain minorities for more GRD.

WHY DO GOVERNMENTS DISCRIMINATE?

While I discuss this issue in more detail in the following chapters using specific contexts and examples, it is useful at this point to list the various reasons the literature posits governments may discriminate. As noted in the previous chapter the question of why governments discriminate has two elements. First, what makes a government more likely to discriminate in general? Second, why would a government single out a particular minority for discrimination?

In this section, I discuss a number of potential causes of GRD. I make no claim that this list is all-inclusive, nor do I claim that any one of these factors is likely to be driving levels of GRD in isolation. Also, many of these factors are complex and can cause GRD in general as well as focus it on a specific group in particular. While the discussion here focuses on the causes of GRD, most of these causes also apply to other forms of discrimination including SRD. For this reason, I refer to them as causes of discrimination in general rather than GRD specifically. I present a summary of these potential causes in Table 2.6.

Primarily Influences All Minorities

Religious ideologies are among the most often cited cause of religious discrimination. Religious ideologies identify an exclusive truth and are usually intolerant of incompatible beliefs. This is particularly true of the Abrahamic faiths (Jelen & Wilcox, 1990; Stark, 2001, 2003; Wald, 1987). One way to reduce competition from other religions is to repress their believers. Thus, states connected to a religious ideology will be more likely to discriminate against religious minorities in general and in particular against minorities considered especially objectionable to the majority religion.

The rational choice literature focuses not on ideologies but on *religious monopolies*. This literature focuses on the rational motivations of politicians and religious institutions to maintain a religious monopoly. While the ultimate motivation for religious institutions to desire a monopoly is

TABLE 2.6 *Predictors of religious discrimination*

Cause of religious discrimination	Higher in states that ...	Higher levels of discrimination against minorities that ...
Primarily a general influence		
Religious ideology	Are more strongly associated with a religious ideology	Are particularly objectionable to the majority religion
Antireligious secular ideologies	Have antireligious secular ideologies	Are discriminated against for other reasons, and the antireligious ideology amplifies this discrimination
Religious monopolies	Are more strongly associated with a religious ideology	Pose a demographic challenge to the majority religion
Religious tradition	Have majorities belonging to more intolerant traditions	Are particularly objectionable to the religious tradition
Regime	Are less democratic	–
Regime stability	Unclear	–
World region	Varies on regional culture and religious tradition of majority	–
Primarily causes unequal discrimination		
Nationalism and protection of culture	Seek to protect their national culture and identity	Are nonindigenous and considered threats to national culture
Anticult policies	None	Are perceived as cults
Objectionable practices	None	Engage in "objectionable" practices
History of conflict	Have a history of civil war	Have a history of conflict with the government
Past discrimination	Discriminated in the past	Experienced discrimination in the past
Perceived security threats	Perceive a security threat	Are perceived to be a security threat
Perceived political threat	Perceive a political threat	Are perceived to be a political threat
Minority size	–	Unclear
Societal discrimination	Have high levels of societal discrimination	Experience high levels of societal discrimination

theological, this perspective focuses on the mechanics and power politics. Politicians are willing to support this monopoly because it can lend them legitimacy and enforce morals, which makes ruling less expensive. That is, when people accept a government's rule and behave morally, the government needs to invest less into police, courts, jails, and security (Gill, 2008). From this perspective, those groups that demographically pose the greatest threat to the religious monopoly are the most likely to be targeted.

Given this, states that are associated with a particular religion are more likely to engage in GRD just as individuals who are more religious are more likely to hold negative attitudes toward other religions. I discuss the dynamics of how this works in practice in more detail in subsequent chapters, particularly Chapter 4.

Antireligious secular ideologies can also be a source of religious discrimination. While in theory this should apply to all religions equally, in practice most antireligious regimes single out some minorities for an extra dose of repression (Fox, 2016). While this is usually the result of other motivations listed in this section such as political or security challenges, the hostility of these regimes toward religion likely amplifies these other motivations for GRD. I address this topic in more detail in Chapter 6.

Religious Tradition. Huntington (1993, 1996) argues that some religious traditions, particularly Islam, are more intolerant and conflict prone. While this theory is highly controversial,[3] many studies have examined this topic with some finding a basis for it (e.g., Grim & Finke, 2011; Toft, 2007) while others find less support for the theory, especially when controlling for other factors (e.g., Basedau et al., 2011; Cesari & Fox, 2016; Fox, 2004). In this study I find that religious tradition can have an impact on patterns of GRD, but not in the specific manner that Huntington predicted.

Regime. Most who address the topic argue that democratic regimes discriminate, on average, less than nondemocratic regimes (Brathwaite & Bramsen, 2011; Rebe, 2012). However many democracies still discriminate (Fox, 2016; Gurr, 1988). The findings of this study show that this relationship is in practice complicated. I address this issue in more detail in Chapters 5, 7, and 8.

Regime Stability. The influence of this factor is unclear. On the one hand conflict, and by analogy discrimination, is more common in new

---

[3] For a discussion of this theory and its critics, see Fox (2004).

and unstable regimes. On the other hand, discrimination is a policy, and this policy can take time to develop so it might be common in more stable regimes (Fox, 2016; Gurr, 1988). In addition, strong and stable regimes are in a better position to engage in discrimination due to their increased resources (Gill, 2008).

World Region. In Fox (2016), I demonstrate that the culture and patterns of GRD are different across world regions. For example, among Christian countries, those in the developing world engage in the least GRD, and former-Soviet states engage in the most. I address this issue in more detail in Chapters 7 and 8. Mataic (2018), using a previous version of the RAS data, finds that GRD is spatially clustered. He argues that while coercion from other states and international normative pressure are factors in this, the primary explanation is mimicry.

All of the preceding factors primarily should influence GRD against all minorities in a state in a similar manner. However, they can also cause GRD against some minorities more than others. For example, it is possible for certain minorities to more easily run afoul of both religious and secular ideologies.

Primarily Causes Unequal Discrimination

In contrast, the causes of GRD that I discuss in this section are more likely to focus on some minorities within a state more than others. Thus, these are factors that are likely to help explain unequal discrimination.

Nationalism and Protection of Culture. Many states seek to preserve and defend their national cultures, which are often linked to religion. As a result, religious minorities that are considered new to the country, and therefore not part of the national culture, can be seen as threats (Fox, 2015, 2016).

Anticult policies can result in substantial levels of GRD against religions considered cults. There is no agreed-upon definition of the term *cult*, but most academic definitions focus on a cult's small size, dangerous or violent practices, and the presence of a charismatic leader (Almond et al., 2003: 91, 103; Appleby, 2000: 204; Grim & Finke, 2011: 47–48). However, in practice most countries that persecute cults focus on religions that are small and new to the countries, even though these religions may be mainstream elsewhere. As Thomas (2001: 529) puts it, "there is ... [an] informally defined universe of acceptable religions and spiritualties. Those which fall outside this universe are stigmatized as cults."

Objectionable Practices. While other categories earlier address this issue indirectly, I find it important to emphasize this cause of GRD with its own category. Religious minorities that engage in practices considered objectionable by the majority religion or the majority's secular ideology can be targets of discrimination. For example, in the West many consider the requirement that Muslim women cover their hair or, for some Muslim women, their entire body a violation of liberal values. Many in these countries consider the ritual slaughter of meat by Jews and Muslims cruel to animals and the rite of male circumcision, also present in both of these religions, barbaric and a violation of the rights of the child. Yet banning these practices is a form of GRD as defined in this study. In other cases the objectionable practices, whatever they may be, can lead to a more general campaign of restrictions on the minority religion in question.

Perhaps the most common type of objectionable practice is proselytizing. As I discussed in more detail earlier in this chapter, this practice agitates religious majorities for ideological reasons because few religions welcome other religions "poaching" their members. Conversion results in a shift of identity that can have both nationalist and cultural implications. Shifting identities can also result in politically relevant demographic changes that are unwelcome to governments.

History of Conflict. Most basic theories on conflict between the state and minorities link discrimination and conflict. While most of these theories focus on ethnic conflict (e.g., Gurr, 1993, 2000; Horowitz, 1985), they are also applicable to religious minorities (Akbabba & Tydas, 2011; Fox, 2004; Fox et al., 2017). It is a dynamic relationship where discrimination against a minority can be a cause of conflict, but it can also be a government's response to conflict. Henne and Klocek (2017) argue that past conflict increases repression of minorities because it increases the threat perception of political elites as well as lowering their perception of the costs of repression. Religious conflict also constrains which strategies political elites consider as a response to such violence" (Henne & Klocek, 2017: 9). They find that "countries in which rebel groups mobilized followers along religious lines or made religious demands tended to have higher levels of religious repression than those in which combatants were leftist or solely ethnonationalist in nature" (Henne & Klocek, 2017: 17–18). However, all of their data is at the country level so they are unable to test whether this relationship holds for specific minority groups. That being said, when focusing on specific religious minorities, most religious minorities are not in active conflict with the state, so this potential cause of GRD can explain only a small proportion of cases.

Past Discrimination. One of the best predictors of current discrimination is past discrimination. States that have successfully used repression in the past are more likely to do so in the present and future, and their most likely targets are those that have been repressed in the past (Gurr, 1988).

Perceived Security Threats. A minority does not have to be in a state of active conflict with the majority for it to be perceived as a potential security threat. That being said, if a minority is seen as a security threat, this can lead to discrimination whether this threat is real or imagined. Securitization theory posits that if a group is "securitized," this lifts policy toward the group from ordinary politics and can justify policies that would otherwise be considered beyond the pale (Buzan & Segal, 1998; Mabee, 2007; Wæver, 1995). This can be especially true of religious minorities who are often seen as more threatening (Laustesen & Wæver, 2000). While this process can easily explain security-related restrictions such as arrests of suspects and immigrations restrictions, Cesari (2013) and Chebel d'Appolonia (2015) argue that the hysteria surrounding security can also result in restrictions on religious activities and institutions, even if there is no obvious or perhaps only a tenuous connection between the minority and increased security.

This body of theory was developed primarily to explain how democracies justify acts that on their face violate liberal democratic norms. However, the argument that security concerns can lead to GRD is certainly also applicable to nondemocracies (Sarkissian, 2015). I discuss this cause of discrimination in more detail in Chapter 5.

Perceived Political Threats. Sometimes the perceived threat posed by a religious minority is a political rather than a security threat. For example, demographic shifts can give a religious minority increased clout, which challenges the political status quo (Grim & Finke, 2011: 46). In other cases, the presence of the minority in the country can pose an ideological challenge to the majority (Finke, 2013) or it can be competing with the majority for resources (Bohman & Hjerm, 2013: 4). In any case, if a religious minority is seen as threatening to the political survival of leaders, it is likely to attract discrimination (Gill, 2008).

Minority Size. The influence of this factor is unclear. On the one hand, smaller minorities are weaker and more vulnerable to discrimination. On the other hand, larger minorities are more likely to be perceived as a security or political threat.

A final cause of GRD that is found in the literature is *societal religious discrimination* (SRD). Grim and Finke (2011), in their book, *The Price of Freedom Denied*, argue that SRD is a significant cause of GRD. That is, GRD is more common when societal prejudices against a religious minority exist. More specifically, Grim and Finke (2011: 9) argue that

legal restrictions on religion as well as the easing of legal restrictions arise from social origins. Popular religious movements, religious plurality, immigration patterns, political stability, and economic interests have all driven changes in the legal regulations placed on religion around the globe.

This regulation is often mobilized by a dominant religion that either lacks the authority of the state or wants to go beyond the state's actions ... Religions, social movements, cultural context, and institutions beyond the state can all foster regulatory actions that lead to persecution.

(Grim & Finke, 2007: 637)

In addition, the enforcement of GRD relies upon social cooperation.

While Grim and Finke (2007, 2011) focus on societal explanations for this dynamic, there is also clearly a political component. If a minority is unpopular, this unpopularity can be a signal to political leaders that repressing this group may enhance their political careers or that they are free to follow their own prejudices. This is especially likely when a significant proportion of the majority group is prejudiced against the minority and some members of the majority are willing to engage in concrete actions against the minority. It is also more likely that the prejudices of the leader will reflect those of the population they lead. Grim and Finke (2011: 211) imply this type of logic when they argue that "heightening the tension between groups and socially isolating them from other groups also serves to stimulate the growth of religious, social, and political movements that drive conflict." They also argue that when there is societal violence against a minority, the government may choose to "restrict religious freedoms in an effort to maintain order, protect the citizenry, and reduce potential violence" (Grim & Finke, 2011: 211).

Grim and Finke (2007, 2011) test this theory with a panel of country-level data for 143 countries and find strong support for the SRD-GRD link. However, their study has some significant limitations. First, these measures look only at countries as a whole and cannot distinguish whether some minorities experience different levels of GRD or SRD. This is important because, as shown in this study, levels of both SRD and GRD usually vary across different minorities in the same country. Second, their GRD measure also includes restrictions on the religious freedoms of the majority. Thus, their government-societal link found in their study included elements that are not even specific to religious minorities.[4]

Accordingly, the tests presented in this study will, if nothing else, examine this theory with a greater level of specificity. In addition, the findings of this study show that the SRD-GRD relationship is a complex one that does not apply in all cases, and when it applies, it can have different dynamics across different groupings of states and minorities. I examine these complexities in subsequent chapters.

CONCLUSIONS

GRD is very common to the extent that it is the norm rather than the exception. Most countries engage in GRD, and a majority of the world's religious minorities experience GRD. GRD has also been increasing over time. Yet there is a wide variety of types of GRD, and there is considerable diversity in the levels and types of GRD applied to the world's religious minorities. This diversity is also present within states, as most countries that discriminate do so at different levels and in different manners to different minorities.

This chapter is intended to provide some insight into the definition of GRD and the specific government actions that underlie this definition. This chapter also provides a basic theoretical understanding of what may cause GRD in theory. In practice, these causes are multiple, crosscutting, and complex. The exact mix of causes and how they manifest varies from country to country as well as from minority to minority within a single country. Subsequent chapters in this book focus on using this theoretical foundation to explain GRD in practice as well as to test and improve these theories using real-world examples.

---

[4] Grim and Finke's (2011) data is the precursor to the Pew data on religious freedom (www .pewforum.org/topics/restrictions-on-religion/). Accordingly, the Pew data have similar limitations.

3

Societal Discrimination

Much of the literature on human rights in general and religious freedom in particular focuses on how governments restrict religious freedom and human rights. Yet nonstate actors are often responsible for frequent and severe discrimination. Rodney Stark and Katie Corcoran (2014: 2) recently proposed that in "earlier times, religious wars were fought by armies. Today they are mainly fought by civilian volunteers." This study's findings bear this out partially. On the one hand, societal religious discrimination (SRD) – which I define as societal actions taken against religious minorities by members of a country's religious majority who do not represent the government – is common to the extent that it can be considered the norm rather than an exception. It increased over time between 1990 and 2014. Of the 771 religious minorities included in this study, 442 (54.7 percent) experienced some form of SRD between 1990 and 2014. This includes at least 1 minority in 172 (94 percent) of the 183 countries in this study. On the other hand, as I demonstrated in Chapter 2, government-based religious discrimination (GRD) is also very common. So it is perhaps more accurate to say that these "civilian warriors" are working in parallel to or in some cases in conjunction with their governments. This complex relationship between SRD and GRD is a recurring theme throughout this book.

In this chapter, I focus in on the more straightforward task of defining SRD as it is measured in this study and providing a basic description and analysis of the variables that measure SRD in order to provide a baseline for the rest of the study. Specifically, the SRD data used in this study takes a different approach to measuring societal relations between religious majorities and minorities than have most studies in the past. In order to place this in the proper context I also discuss previous measures of phenomena similar to the SRD index used in this study, the findings of the studies based on these measures, and several related issues.

The findings in this chapter show SRD to be significant across the world. As I noted earlier, it is common and increasing over time. Jews are the minority most likely to experience SRD. In fact, Jews are almost twice as likely to experience SRD as Christians, who are the second most likely to experience SRD. Muslim minorities are the third most likely to experience SRD. Given the relatively small number of Jews worldwide compared to religions like Islam, Christianity, Buddhism, and Hinduism, this finding demonstrates that unique forces may be at work with regard to SRD against Jews. This is a topic I explore in more detail in later chapters.

SRD is most likely to occur in Orthodox Christian-majority states and second most likely to occur in Muslim-majority states. Thus, both as targets and perpetrators, the three Abrahamic religions are the most involved in SRD. Interestingly, violence is the most common form of SRD, even more common than simple public speech acts.

Finally, while in Chapter 2 I discussed *why* many believe SRD is a cause of GRD, in this chapter and in subsequent chapters I discuss *how* it causes GRD. That is, in later chapters this study demonstrates that the dynamics of the SRD-GRD relationship are complicated. Specifically, the relationship applies to some types of religious minorities in some groupings of states but not others. For example, as I show in Chapter 5, in Western democracies, SRD predicts GRD against Muslim minorities but not against other religious minorities. I argue that this is because the SRD-GRD relationship needs a trigger of some kind to activate it. Most often this trigger is some form of perceived existential threat.

PAST STUDIES OF SOCIETAL RELIGIOUS DISCRIMINATION

There are few previous variables that measure societal actions taken against religious minorities. Rather, most previous variables focus on societal attitudes toward religious minorities rather than actions. This is important for at least two reasons. First, attitudes, unless they lead to actions, are not discrimination. One can dislike a religious minority, but this does not mean that, for example, one will vandalize their place of worship. Second, on a methodological level, many argue that actions can be a more precise measure of how people feel than reported attitudes. For example, a long line of research in social psychology has established that past behavior, rather than reported attitudes, is a better predictor of future behavior.[1]

In addition, reported attitudes, especially when based on surveys, have standard disadvantages. First, there is always some question as to whether the people surveyed are truly representative of the population. Second, surveys assume people report their attitudes truthfully. Attitudes about prejudices are particularly problematic in this respect. Finally, cross-country data on attitudes assumes that the questions are understood similarly across cultures and languages.

It is also possible to criticize the type of action-based measure used here by questioning whether these actions represent society as a whole or just a racist or prejudiced segment within the majority group. For instance, violent attacks on a religious minority do not necessarily mean that the assailants' attitudes represent society as a whole. They may represent a subgroup within the majority. Often the precise identity the perpetrators of SRD is unknown.

Another issue is that such a measure can include only incidents reported in the sources examined, and it is likely that some incidents go unreported. However, the more common the occurrence of SRD and the higher the intensity of these incidents, the more likely they will be reported. Thus, while a measure based on actions will likely underreport incidents, I posit that this is mitigated by two factors. First, this under-reporting likely happens in most countries for most minorities, so it has a relatively uniform influence across cases. Second, the cases where SRD is more common and more intense will likely have more reported incidents, so such a measure will effectively differentiate between cases with low and high levels of SRD. This also means that the cases that are underreported will be those at the low end of the scale, so its impact on the overall measures will likely not heavily influence the results.

Taking all of this into account, I posit that action-based variables are useful measures of discrimination for at least six reasons. First, though the specific problems differ, both attitude and action-based measures are imperfect. The problems with action-based measures are no greater than those found in attitude-based measures. Despite their imperfections, attitude-based measures are regularly used in research. Thus, action-based variables are arguably no less suitable for research. Second, action-based variables measure concrete actions that occurred in public.

---

[1] For a brief overview on the relationship between attitudes and behavior, see Myers (1990: 34–40).

This leaves little doubt that at least an element of society has chosen to engage in SRD. Third, these actions directly influence the targets of the SRD and arguably society as a whole. This makes them both socially and politically relevant. Fourth, the scale used here for SRD is a detailed and comprehensive one that includes a broad range of action types. Each type of SRD is measured on a scale creating a composite measure differentiates between countries where a few low-level types of SRD occurred and countries where multiple and more severe types of SRD occurred. Fifth, it is possible to collect these variables for all relevant countries in a manner that is unambiguously consistent across countries. Finally, SRD is in and of itself a form of discrimination. This makes it directly relevant to any study of religious discrimination.

Furthermore, attitudes and actions, while not the same, are highly correlated. The Religion and State project collected an attitudes variable that replicates the Grim and Finke (2011) attitudes variable. It measures, separately, attitudes regarding nontraditional religions, conversion to other religions, and proselytizing by religious minorities.[2] This variable was only collected with the state as the unit of analysis, but it has a strong correlation with the SRD variable of .615 (significance = .000).[3]

Many studies use survey data to examine the causes and consequences of attitudes toward other religions. While this is by no means a complete survey of this literature, some typical findings include the following. Participation in the Haj increases tolerance by Muslims (Alexeev & Zhemukkov, 2016). Several studies show that increased religious commitment or belief results in less tolerance (Eisenstein, 2008; Karpov, 2002; Laythe, Finkel, Bringle, & Kirkpatrick, 2002; Laythe, Finkel, & Kirkpatrick, 2002; Milligan et al., 2014). Studies on the Muslim minorities in Europe find mixed effects. Europeans who are more religious show more tolerance of Muslim religious practices such as the wearing of head coverings by Muslim women, but those who are educated and more politically liberal are more tolerant of Muslims in general (Fetzer & Soper, 2003; Helbling, 2014). State support for religion is associated with lower tolerance of Muslims (Helbling & Traunmuller, 2015). Anti-Israel opinions predict anti-Semitism in Europe (Kaplan & Small, 2006).[4] The

---

[2] Each of these variables is measured on a scale of 0–3, resulting in an index that ranges from 0–9.

[3] For a more detailed discussion of the reliability of the SRD variable see Fox et al. (2018).

[4] For a review of the literature on the link between religion and political tolerance, see Eisenstein (2008: 23–28).

measures used in these studies rarely cover more than a few countries. Even the World Values Survey, which is multinational, includes less than half of the world's countries, so it is not useful for anything more than a limited cross-country analysis.

Grim and Finke (2006, 2007, 2011) collected the only truly cross-national measure of "social regulation of religion."[5] This measure includes five components, as opposed to the twenty-seven used in the SRD measure in the Religion and State-Minorities round 3 dataset (RASM3). Three examine attitudes toward nontraditional religions, conversion to other religions, and proselytizing. The others measure actions: "existing religions try to shut our newcomers" and "social movements against certain religious brands." While it would be feasible to construct a measure using only those components that measure societal actions, no study to my knowledge has done so. In addition, the measure was collected at the state level, which means it is not possible to determine from the data at which minority these attitudes and actions are directed.

Despite these limitations, this index has held strong associations with many variables of interest. Past research has reported that this "Social Regulation Index" is a significant predictor of reduced women's rights (Ben-Nun Bloom, 2015) and reduced economic growth (Alson et al., 2017). It also has a significant influence on variables related to religion in general and GRD in particular. It is associated with reduced religious freedoms (Finke & Martin, 2014), increased religion related violence (Finke & Harris, 2012), increased religious persecution by governments (Grim and Finke, 2011) and increased GRD against the membership of religious minorities (Finke, Mataic, & Fox, 2017).

That being said, the form of discrimination most often used in studies of religious discrimination, whether as the dependent or independent variable, is one based on government actions. Studies based on societal discrimination are less common. Accordingly, we can learn much from a more accurate and refined measure of SRD. As I discuss in more detail later, the SRD variable used here has considerably more detail than the Grim and Finke (2011) variable. It has twenty-seven components and is collected separately for each of 771 minorities in 183 countries.

The Grim and Finke (2011) measures differ from the RASM measures in two additional respects. First, their measure of government restrictions

---

[5] Grim and Finke's (2011) data is the precursor to the PEW data on religious freedom, which use essentially the same variable structure. Thus these comments also apply to the PEW data (www.pewforum.org/topics/restrictions-on-religion/).

on religious freedom is a single measure of restrictions on both the majority and minorities. Second, their study assigns a single score to a state, so societal restrictions on Jews, for example, might, in practice, be used to explain government restrictions on another minority such as Muslims or on the country as a whole, including the majority religion.

SOCIETAL RELIGIOUS DISCRIMINATION IN PRACTICE

The Religion and State-Minorities round 3 (RASM3) dataset measures twenty-seven distinct types of societal actions taken by individuals and groups from the majority religion who are not government officials nor are their actions against religious minorities acting explicitly on behalf of the government. In this section, I present each of these twenty-seven types of SRD and how common they were in 1990 and 2014, or the first and most recent years available, though in the discussion we will refer to them as 1990 and 2014.

One of the most important issues with patterns of SRD is that unlike GRD, which I discussed in more detail in Chapter 2, it is often sporadic. That is, while in some cases any given type of SRD may occur consistently from year to year, in many cases it occurs in some years but not others. In contrast, GRD, is usually present consistently from year to year, and when there is a change in GRD, the new equilibrium tends to persist over time. For this reason, much of the analysis in this chapter looks at whether a given form of SRD occurred against a minority at any point between 1990 and 2014. In order to demonstrate that SRD is common across groupings of states and minorities, the tables in this chapter also present the results using the same majority and minority religion categories as I used in Chapter 2 for GRD.

The purpose of this exercise is threefold. First, this represents a practical discussion of all types of SRD present in the world, as defined by this study. As the Religion and State round 3 (RAS3) project has collected extensive information on SRD on a country-by-country basis and found few societal actions taken against minorities that do not fit into these categories, I am confident that this list is comprehensive. Second, this discussion, in practice, provides a detailed definition and discussion of what I mean by SRD. That being said, the devil can be in the details, and this discussion provides the relevant details. These details also include a more concrete set of examples of the types of actions and events that underlie the data. Third, it provides a basic analysis of the commonality of each type of SRD. As discussing all twenty-seven types of SRD in detail would be too lengthy, in this discussion, I focus on those that are particularly common or that I consider to be of particular import, but all of them are listed in the tables.

Each of the twenty-seven types of SRD is coded on the following scale:

2 = This action occurs on a substantial level,

1 = This action occurs on a minor level.

0 = There are no reported incidents of this type of action against the specified minority.

Thus, the composite variable includes all types of SRD and ranges in theory from 0–54, though no minority's score reaches 54. However, the analysis in this chapter focuses primarily on the presence or absence of SRD.

Also, it is important to note that many reports on SRD are nonspecific. That is they tend to mention the general situation in a country and provide approximate numbers of incidents, but often contain few details. Nevertheless, details are available on a sufficient number of incidents to form a good impression of the details of the types of SRD that occur. The examples presented in this chapter are intended to give the reader a sense of the typical and interesting incidents of SRD occurring throughout the world.

Economic SRD

I divide the twenty-seven types of SRD into six categories, which I consider separately. The first category is economic discrimination, which is presented in Table 3.1. During the study period, 16.2 percent of minorities experienced some form of societal-based economic discrimination. This includes at least one minority in 47 percent of countries, nearly half, of all countries in the study. Discrimination in the workplace was by far the most common type. The targeting of minority businesses and other types of economic discrimination was far less common. All three categories of economic discrimination were more common in 2014 than in 1990.

Workplace discrimination is particularly common against Muslims in Western countries, including in Austria, Canada, Cyprus, Denmark, Finland, France, Germany, Ireland, Liechtenstein, the Netherlands, Norway, Portugal, Spain, Sweden, Switzerland, the UK, and the United States. The businesses of eighteen minority groups worldwide are targeted for boycotts or other societal nonviolent harassment. This includes Jews in Belgium, South Africa, Iran, Turkey, and the UK as well as Muslims in Denmark, Israel, Myanmar, the UK, and the United States.

The "other" economic discrimination included many instances of discrimination in housing. For example, in 2006, a judge in Argentina decided that a landlord is allowed to refuse to rent his apartment to a Jewish couple because of the landlord's fear of a possible terrorist attack. Other groups that experienced discrimination in housing included the Muslim minorities in Cyprus, Denmark, Ecuador, and France and Orthodox Christians (mostly Serbs) in Croatia. Scientologists in Germany suffered all three types of economic discrimination. In Germany, being a scientologist can often get one fired, and many employers refuse to hire them. Their businesses are often boycotted, and some find it difficult to purchase land.

Speech Acts

The second type of SRD is speech acts, also presented in Table 3.1. Speech acts are defined here as antiminority speech, propaganda, rhetoric, or statements by (1) the nongovernment media, (2) clergy of the majority religion, and (3) political parties (in some manner that is not directly connected to government office holders such as occurring in election campaigns), as well as (4) the dissemination of antiminority publications. All these acts are public acts, as opposed to private ones. That is, they do not represent individuals expressing their opinions in private. Rather, these statements or publications are consciously intended to be public. Thus, they represent not only the presence of antiminority sentiment in the public sphere but demonstrate the fact that people, often public figures, feel that it is safe and appropriate to engage in antiminority rhetoric in public.

All of these types of acts are common. The study shows 28.8 percent of minorities had such speech acts directed against them at some point between 1990 and 2014, and this occurred to at least one minority in 67.2 percent of the countries in the study. They are particularly common against Jewish minorities worldwide, 73.6 percent of which experience this form of anti-Semitism. Orthodox-majority states stand out as the environment in which this type of SRD is most likely to occur. The study found speech acts against 64.1 percent of minorities in Orthodox-majority states. All four categories of speech act were more common in 2014 than 1990.

TABLE 3.1 *Economic discrimination and speech acts against religious minorities*

	All cases			Discrimination any time between 1990 and 2014 Controlling for majority religion				
	1990 (%)	2014 (%)	Any time 1990–2014 (%)	Catholic (%)	Orthodox (%)	Other Christian (%)	Muslim (%)	Other (%)
Economic discrimination (at least one type)	11.0	12.8	16.2	13.4	17.2	15.4	18.6	17.8
In the workplace	10.0	11.2	13.6	11.3	12.5	12.9	16.5	13.6
Boycott of business/denial of access to businesses, stores, etc.	0.5	1.6	2.3	0.5	4.7	3.0	2.6	2.3
Other economic discrimination	1.4	2.2	3.0	3.6	4.7	3.0	1.0	4.2
Speech acts (at least one type)	16.3	21.4	28.8	23.7	64.1	23.4	35.6	16.1
Antiminority propaganda/ statements/articles in the media	10.4	14.9	18.5	14.9	42.2	18.9	21.6	5.9
Antiminority rhetoric by majority religion's clergy	6.9	8.0	11.5	5.7	32.2	4.5	19.6	9.3
Antiminority rhetoric in political campaigns or by political parties	6.1	8.2	10.6	9.3	32.8	8.5	10.3	5.1
Dissemination of antiminority publications	3.8	4.8	9.6	10.8	31.2	9.0	3.6	6.8

Discrimination any time between 1990 and 2014
Controlling for minority religion

	Christian (%)	Muslim (%)	Hindu (%)	Buddhist (%)	Jewish (%)	Animist (%)	Babai (%)	Other (%)	At least one minority in country (%)
Economic discrimination (at least one type)	15.9	31.9	14.0	6.2	17.1	4.4	6.2	11.1	47.0
In the workplace	13.8	28.8	14.0	4.2	7.9	2.2	6.2	12.1	38.8
Boycott of business/denial of access to businesses, stores, etc.	2.6	3.1	0.0	0.0	6.6	0.0	1.6	1.7	8.2
Other economic discrimination	2.2	6.1	0.0	2.1	3.9	2.2	0.0	3.7	12.0
Speech acts (at least one type)	31.51	41.1	9.3	6.2	73.6	7.7	6.2	9.3	67.2
Antiminority propaganda/statements/articles in the media	15.1	23.9	7.0	2.1	72.4	4.4	6.2	3.7	53.0
Antiminority rhetoric by majority religion's clergy	21.1	11.1	4.7	2.1	15.8	4.4	1.6	3.7	39.9
Antiminority rhetoric in political campaigns or by political parties	9.9	16.0	0.0	0.0	40.8	1.1	0.0	1.9	31.7
Dissemination of antiminority publications	7.3	11.0	0.0	2.1	47.4	0.0	0.0	3.7	29.0

All scores in this table use a minority within a country as the unit of analysis except the "at least one minority in the country" column, which uses the country as the unit of analysis.

All these types of speech acts occur in Russia against multiple minorities. This includes public speech acts against Jews, "sects," and Protestants, by Russian Orthodox Church clergy and activists. They also disseminate negative publications and occasionally stage demonstrations throughout the country against Catholics, Protestants, Jehovah's Witnesses, and other minority religious groups. Local politicians, as well, use antiminority campaigns to strengthen their Russian Orthodox constituency. For example, in a debate Oleg Bolychev, a member of the ruling United Russia party who was at the time a representative in a regional parliament in Kaliningrad called his detractors "Jews, mired in opposition ... You destroyed our country in 1917 and you destroyed our country in 1991" (JTA, 2014).

Nonviolent Attacks on Property

The third type of SRD, which is presented in Table 3.2, is nonviolent attacks on property. These include vandalism of religious property and graveyards, vandalism of other property owned by a religious minority, and antiminority graffiti. I differentiate nonviolent vandalism from arson and bombings. Bombings and arson are included in acts of violence, which I discuss later, because they have the potential to harm and kill.

While nonviolent attacks on property are public acts, they are different from speech acts in at least three ways. First, it is possible for the perpetrators to remain anonymous, in fact that is usually their preference. Because of this limitation, in this study I assume all property attacks were perpetrated by the majority group unless there is evidence to the contrary. While this likely places some minority on minority acts in the category of SRD by the majority, these acts represent treatment of a minority by society as a whole, and it is likely that most such cases were, in fact, perpetrated by members of the majority. Second, while it is possible that these acts include words, as is often the case with graffiti, these constitute tangible physical acts that cause physical damage and are usually intended to cause fear. While explicit threats of violence are a separate category, in this study, these acts are a short step from escalating to violence and can be perceived as a threat to engage in violence. Third, while antireligious hate speech is banned in many countries (ninety-seven, or 53 percent of countries in 2014 according to the RAS3 project), these laws often go unenforced. In contrast, vandalism and graffiti are criminal acts in most countries. In most countries, authorities tend to attempt to find and prosecute offenders. These laws are usually only unenforced in countries that themselves engage in severe GRD against minorities or in weak states that are unable to enforce these laws. That being said, levels of effort and success at catching and prosecuting perpetrators of these types of acts vary.

This type of SRD is common, with 27.2 percent of minorities being the targets for such attacks at some point between 1990 and 2014, and at least one minority was targeted for these property crimes in 62.3 percent of countries. Like speech acts, Jews were by far the most likely to be targeted. In 76.3 percent of countries in which Jewish minorities are included in RASM, they were targeted for property attacks. This is nearly twice the level of the next most targeted group, Christians, 33.6 percent of which experienced nonviolent property crimes. Orthodox-majority states were the most likely place for such acts to occur, with 62.5 percent of religious minorities living in these states being the targets of vandalism or graffiti. In contrast, in Muslim-majority states, which had the second-highest score, 29.6 percent of minorities experienced this type of SRD.

Most vandalism and graffiti were similar across countries – consisting of property damage and the painting of hate speech or symbols such as swastikas on religious property or property owned by religious minorities. However, some types of vandalism were more creative. A particularly disturbing trend is the leaving of pig heads, carcasses, other body parts, feces, or blood to deface Mosques or sites where Mosques are to be built. This occurred in Australia, Bulgaria, Canada, the Czech Republic, France, Germany, Georgia, Iceland, Israel, Italy, Montenegro, Northern Ireland, Norway, South Africa, Sweden, the UK, and the United States. For example, in Iceland in 2012 and 2013, the site for a proposed Mosque was strewn with pig heads, blood, and desecrated pages of a Koran ("Protest against Mosque," 2013). In some cases, people bring live pigs to Mosques. In 2007 Roberto Calderoli, who was at the time vice president of the Italian Senate, bragged of previously taking his pig for a walk on a proposed Mosque site and offered to do the same on the site of another planned Mosque ("Un maiale-day contro," 2007). Similarly, in 2014 the head of the Czech Republic's Dawn of Direct Democracy party and member of Parliament led a Facebook campaign urging people bring pigs and dogs to Mosques as a protest against Islamization ("MP Urges Czechs," 2015). There was also a case of an apparent minority on majority application of this form of vandalism in Malaysia, where, during the controversy over use of the word *Allah* by non-Muslims, a Mosque was vandalized and pig heads were placed at two others, in apparent

TABLE 3.2 *Nonviolent attacks on property and other SRD against religious minorities*

	All cases			Discrimination any time between 1990 and 2014 By majority religion				
	1990 (%)	2014 (%)	Any time 1990–2014 (%)	Catholic (%)	Orthodox (%)	Other Christian (%)	Muslim (%)	Other (%)
Nonviolent attacks on property (at least one type)	11.7	16.6	27.2	21.6	62.5	21.4	29.9	22.9
Vandalism of religious property (places of worship, community centers, schools, cemeteries)	9.7	15.3	24.5	19.6	60.9	18.9	27.3	17.8
Vandalism of other minority property	4.2	4.8	9.9	9.3	12.5	7.5	11.9	10.2
Antireligious graffiti	6.7	8.7	11.9	15.5	28.1	13.4	4.1	7.6
Other types of acts (at least one type)	8.7	13.1	20.6	17.5	39.1	13.9	23.7	22.0
Efforts to deny access to or close existing religious sites	1.4	2.2	5.2	2.1	8.8	1.0	11.9	5.1
Efforts to prevent religious sites from being built/opened/rented	2.5	5.7	9.7	6.7	29.7	7.5	10.8	5.9
Other types of discrimination	6.2	7.8	11.7	12.4	17.2	9.0	9.8	15.3

Discrimination any time between 1990 and 2014
Controlling for minority religion

	Christian (%)	Muslim (%)	Hindu (%)	Buddhist (%)	Jewish (%)	Animist (%)	Bahai (%)	Other (%)	At least one minority in country (%)
Nonviolent attacks on property (at least one type)	33.6	32.5	20.9	4.2	76.3	5.5	3.1	6.6	62.3
Vandalism of religious property (places of worship, community centers, schools, cemeteries)	29.7	29.4	20.9	4.2	72.4	5.5	1.6	1.6	54.6
Vandalism of other minority property	9.6	13.5	4.7	2.1	28.9	2.2	3.1	5.4	27.3
Antireligious graffiti	8.6	14.7	2.3	0.0	60.5	0.0	1.6	0.0	34.4
Other types of acts (at least one type)	25.4	31.3	25.6	6.2	18.4	12.1	4.7	13.0	57.1
Efforts to deny access to or close existing religious sites	10.8	4.9	4.7	2.1	2.6	1.1	0.0	1.9	18.0
Efforts to prevent religious sites from being built/opened/rented	12.9	20.9	7.0	0.0	5.3	0.0	3.1	3.7	31.1
Other types of discrimination	14.2	14.7	14.0	4.2	11.8	12.1	1.6	8.4	39.3

All scores in this table use a minority within a country as the unit of analysis except the "at least one minority in the country" column, which uses the country as the unit of analysis.

revenge attacks following the vandalism of numerous churches (Ahmad, 2010; Hookway, 2010).

To a lesser extent, Jews have also been the target of this particular type of vandalism. In January 2014 in Italy, boxes containing pig heads were mailed to the synagogue in Rome, the Jewish museum, and the Israeli Embassy (Anti-Defamation League, 2014). In November 2013, pig heads were placed overnight near a synagogue under construction in the Ukraine. In 1990 pig heads were placed outside a synagogue in South Africa (Carlin, 1990). In 2011, in California, the house of a Jewish college student was covered in pig guts and feet and pieces of pork jerky, and a fountain in the front yard wrapped in Christmas paper. In 1998, vandals painted a swastika and left a pig head outside a synagogue in Philadelphia (Burling, 1998). In 1991 a Jewish memorial in Berlin was vandalized with Swastikas and pig heads (Bridge, 1991). In Belgium in 2013 British rock musician Roger Waters used a pig-shaped balloon painted with a Star of David as a prop (Bond, 2013). However, this particular pig-themed incident is technically classified as a speech act. Speech acts calling Jews "Jewish pigs" are more common (Anti-Defamation League, 2011). For example, during the 2012 presidential election campaign in Venezuela, President Chavez called his opponent, Capriles Radonski, a practicing Catholic of Jewish ancestry, a pig.

Nonviolent Harassment

Table 3.3 presents nonviolent harassment, the fourth type of SRD. I define nonviolent harassment as acts of harassment and persecution taken against individuals and groups that fall short of violence and do not constitute an overt threat of violence. RASM3 measures separately harassment of (1) clergy, (2) proselytizers, missionaries, (3) converts away from the majority religion, and (4) other members of the minority religion. It also has measures for (5) expulsion or harassment so severe that it leads to minority members leaving the area (though not necessarily the country) and (6) mass nonviolent demonstrations and protests against religious minorities.

Unlike property crimes, this type of SRD involves actions taken directly against people. While, by definition, no one is physically harmed, otherwise it would be considered violence, this type of SRD can involve an implied threat of violence and can certainly cause its targets to fear that it will escalate to violence. This willingness to engage in up close and personal harassment and intimidation may, from the perspective of the perpetrators, be an act of expression or it may be intended to terrorize.

Nonviolent acts of harassment are slightly more common than vandalism and graffiti. Between 1990 and 2014, members of 29.2 percent of minorities were harassed in this manner, and at least one minority in 72.7 percent of the countries in the study experienced this type of harassment. Jews are the most likely targets of nonviolent harassment, with 63.2 percent of Jewish minorities being nonviolently harassed, which is almost twice the level for Muslim (33.1 percent) and Christian (37.5 percent) minorities, who themselves are harassed far more often than other religious minorities. Societal actors in Orthodox-majority countries (100 percent) and Muslim-majority countries (82.4 percent) were the most likely to engage in this type of SRD. Interestingly the most common targets for harassment are not clergy, proselytizers, missionaries, and converts, but rather the general population of religious minorities. Perhaps this is because the general membership is more likely to be a target of opportunity, while harassment of clergy, proselytizers, missionaries, and converts is more likely to be a premeditated act. All six types of nonviolent harassment were more common in 2014 than they were in 1990.

In most cases of significant amounts of nonviolent harassment, violent harassment (which I discuss later) is also present. One of the rare exceptions is the case of Christians in Israel. There are several types of Christians in Israel. These include Israel's indigenous Christian population, clergy from a number of major religions who are present at holy sites, various religious monasteries and institutions, tourists, converts, and missionaries. There are numerous incidents of Ultra-Orthodox Jews in Israel insulting and spitting on priests and nuns. Attitudes and behavior in Israeli society against converts and missionaries is more widespread. Open missionary activity in Israel sometimes attracts significant harassment of missionaries, usually intended to deter them from their missionary activity, but it rarely turns violent. However Ultra-Orthodox organizations whose self-described mission is to protect Jews from missionary activity instigate protests against missionary organizations and messianic Jews – Jews who consider themselves Jewish but believe in Jesus. These protests occasionally involve low-level violence such as the throwing of vegetables and stones. These organizations also distribute flyers with rhetoric such as "damned evil people are here to murder people and souls in Israel, like in the days of the inquisition, when Jews were slaughtered cold bloodedly" and "these are the corrupt missionaries who are hunting Jewish souls for money. Different elements calling

TABLE 3.3 *Nonviolent harassment against religious minorities*

	All cases			Discrimination any time between 1990 and 2014 Controlling for majority religion				
	1990 (%)	2014 (%)	Any time 1990–2014 (%)	Catholic (%)	Orthodox (%)	Other Christian (%)	Muslim (%)	Other (%)
Nonviolent harassment of clergy	2.3	2.7	3.9	3.1	4.7	1.5	5.7	5.9
Nonviolent harassment of proselytizers or missionaries	3.2	3.4	3.6	2.6	7.8	0.0	7.7	2.5
Nonviolent harassment of converts away from the majority religion	8.2	8.2	8.6	2.6	1.4	1.0	26.3	5.9
Nonviolent harassment of other members of religious minorities	13.7	16.9	20.9	16.0	39.1	17.3	26.3	16.1
Expulsion or harassment so severe that it leads to a significant number of minority members leaving a town or region	2.7	3.9	6.1	3.1	1.6	2.5	12.9	8.5
Organized demonstrations and public protests against religious minorities	1.3	2.3	7.4	5.2	21.9	5.0	7.2	7.6
At least one type	20.8	24.1	29.2	19.6	48.4	18.9	48.9	22.9

Discrimination any time between 1990 and 2014
Controlling for minority religion

	Christian (%)	Muslim (%)	Hindu (%)	Buddhist (%)	Jewish (%)	Animist (%)	Babai (%)	Other (%)	At least one minority in country (%)
Nonviolent harassment of clergy	6.9	4.3	2.3	0.0	6.6	0.0	0.0	1.9	13.1
Nonviolent harassment of proselytizers or missionaries	9.9	1.2	0.0	2.1	1.3	0.0	2.6	0.0	13.1
Nonviolent harassment of converts away from the majority religion	18.5	4.9	7.0	6.2	3.9	1.1	6.2	1.9	25.1
Nonviolent harassment of other members of religious minorities	22.0	25.2	16.3	8.3	57.1	6.6	4.7	9.3	47.5
Expulsion or harassment so severe that it leads to a significant number of minority members leaving a town or region.	9.1	5.5	4.7	2.1	7.9	4.4	1.6	5.6	19.1
Organized demonstrations and public protests against religious minorities	8.6	8.6	2.3	0.0	25.0	1.1	3.1	0.0	23.5
At least one type	37.5	33.1	18.6	15.6	63.2	7.7	12.5	11.1	72.7

All scores in this table use a minority within a country as the unit of analysis except the "at least one minority in the country" column, which uses the country as the unit of analysis.

themselves 'Jews' are helping these criminals carry out their scheme in public, for a bribe, and have allowed them to come to our city ... and preach their impure and poisonous beliefs" (Posner, 2012; Zitun, 2010).

Violence against Minority Religions

The fifth and most extreme form of SRD is violence, which is presented in Table 3.4. RASM3 examines eight categories of violence. This includes (1) overt threats of violence; (2) violence targeted against clergy; (3) violence targeted against proselytizers, missionaries, or converts away from the majority religion; and (4) violence targeted against other members of the minority religion. It also includes (5) large-scale violence; (6) lethal violence; (7) arson, bombing, or concerted attacks against religious property; and (8) arson, bombing, or concerted attacks against other property owned or associated with the minority. While the latter two categories do not necessarily target people and could be included in the attacks on property category, they still have the potential to harm or kill so I include them in the violence category.

I consider it self-evident that violence targeted against religious minorities is a significant form of SRD. It is the most extreme form of SRD measured in this study. Yet it is no less common than the other types. In fact 34.0 percent of minorities experienced some form of societal violence, which is higher than for any of the other categories examined here. Similarly, 72.7 percent of countries had at least one minority that experienced violent SRD, which ties nonviolent harassment for the highest score among the six categories examined here. All eight types of violent SRD were more common in 2014 than in 1990. As is the case for speech acts, nonviolent property attacks, and nonviolent harassment, Jews are by far the most likely to experience violent attacks. In the study, 69.7 percent of Jewish minorities were attacked violently at some point between 1990 and 2014 as compared to 46.0 percent of Muslim minorities and 41.8 percent of Christian minorities, whose scores are, respectively, the second and third highest in this category. Orthodox-majority states have majorities that are the most likely to engage in violent SRD.

Overt *threats of violence* were common; 17.4 percent of minorities in 47.5 percent of countries received such threats. Threats of killings and bombings against Jews across the world were common. In countries like Argentina, Australia, Brazil, France, the UK, and the United States, all of which have large Jewish communities, there are dozens or even hundreds of such threats reported each year. For example, in Australia in 2000 one typical call threatened to kill fifteen Jewish schoolgirls for every Palestinian killed by Israel. Brazil's Rio de Janeiro Jewish Federation reports receiving an average of six threats per week via telephone.

Attacks on clergy happened to approximately one in ten minorities (10.1 percent) at some point between 1990 and 2014. This often takes place in the context of larger violent campaigns against religious minorities. In Pakistan, for example, violent campaigns exist against many religious minorities, including Christians, Ahmadis, Hindus and Shi'i Muslims. This campaign often targets clergy and religious leaders. For example in 2010 unidentified assailants in Faisalabad shot dead two Ahmadi religious leaders as well as one of their sons. In 2014, unidentified gunmen killed the president of a local Hindu association.

Attacks on proselytizers, missionaries, or converts were less common and occurred to 5.1 percent of minorities, perhaps because members of several religions such as Jews and Hindus usually do not actively seek converts. As some Christian groups send missionaries all over the world, it is not surprising that Christian missionaries, proselytizers, and converts are targeted for violence most often. These attacks are particularly common in former-Soviet-bloc Orthodox-majority states such as Armenia, Bulgaria, Moldova, Romania, and Russia, particularly against Mormons and Jehovah's Witnesses engaged in missionary activities. In Bulgaria, for example, there are multiple reports of youth gangs associated with nationalist movements attacking Mormon missionaries as well as others. In one incident in 2000, volunteer workers for the Christian Unity Foundation were severely beaten by several "youths" under the apparent direction of a local Bulgarian Orthodox priest at a scheduled screening of a documentary-style film on the life of Jesus Christ. In February of 2008, an Armenian Apostolic priest physically assaulted a Jehovah's Witness. The priest had several prior incidents of attacking Jehovah's Witnesses.

Other violence against a minority due to its religious affiliation is the most common form of violent attack focused on people rather than property. Statistics show that 18.8 percent of minorities experienced such attacks, which interestingly is slightly more common than threats of violence. Lethal violence and large-scale violence as well as arson bombings or concerted attacks on religious property or property owned by members of minority religions were present against 8.8 percent, 14.8 percent, 20.2 percent, and 10.2 percent of minorities, respectively.

All of these types of attacks occurred in India, particularly against its Christian and Muslim minorities. For example, all of the following

TABLE 3.4 *Violence against religious minorities*

	All cases			Discrimination any time between 1990 and 2014 Controlling for majority religion				
	1990 (%)	2014 (%)	Any time 1990–2014 (%)	Catholic (%)	Orthodox (%)	Other Christian (%)	Muslim (%)	Other (%)
Overt threats of violence	7.5	10.8	17.4	14.9	34.4	12.9	21.6	12.7
Violence targeted against clergy	2.1	3.5	10.1	6.2	23.4	7.5	14.4	6.8
Violence targeted against proselytizers or converts	2.5	2.9	4.9	1.0	11.9	0.0	12.7	3.4
Other violence against minority due to their religious affiliation	9.6	12.1	18.8	12.4	42.2	14.9	23.2	16.1
Large-scale violence against minority due to their religious affiliation	2.5	3.0	8.8	5.7	15.6	3.0	14.4	11.0
Lethal violence against minority due to their religious affiliation	3.6	6.4	14.8	8.8	12.5	7.0	30.4	13.6
Arson, bombing, or concerted attacks against religious property	4.5	7.4	20.2	14.9	37.5	17.42	26.3	15.4
Arson, bombing, or concerted attacks against other property	3.9	4.3	10.2	5.7	10.9	7.0	17.5	11.0
At least one type	14.0	19.2	34.0	27.3	62.5	24.4	46.4	27.1
At least one type of SRD	37.0	42.7	54.7	45.4	81.2	42.3	72.7	44.7
Mean for all SRD	4.86	5.28	–	1.64	5.00	1.77	4.13	1.87

Discrimination any time between 1990 and 2014
Controlling for minority religion

	Christian (%)	Muslim (%)	Hindu (%)	Buddhist (%)	Jewish (%)	Animist (%)	Bahai (%)	Other (%)	At least one minority in country (%)
Overt threats of violence	21.1	21.5	2.3	2.1	50.0	6.6	1.6	5.6	47.5
Violence targeted against clergy	15.9	12.7	2.3	2.1	23.7	2.2	0.0	0.0	29.5
Violence targeted against proselytizers or converts	14.7	1.2	0.0	0.0	1.3	0.0	1.6	0.0	21.3
Other violence against minority due to their religious affiliation	20.3	27.6	7.0	6.2	47.4	6.6	1.6	8.4	46.4
Large-scale violence against minority due to their religious affiliation	10.8	20.2	4.7	2.1	3.9	4.3	0.0	1.9	23.5
Lethal violence against minority due to their religious affiliation	19.8	22.7	7.0	4.2	19.7	8.8	1.6	3.7	36.6
Arson, bombing, or concerted attacks against religious property	27.2	31.9	7.0	4.2	38.2	5.5	0.0	3.7	50.3
Arson, bombing, or concerted attacks against other property	11.6	7.8	2.3	2.1	19.7	2.2	1.6	5.6	29.0
At least one type	41.8	46.0	14.0	8.3	69.7	19.8	3.1	13.0	72.7
At least one type of SRD	60.3	71.4	55.8	22.9	90.8	29.7	23.4	33.3	94.0
Mean for all SRD	3.36	3.38	1.45	0.40	6/07	0.46	0.56	1.17	–

All scores in this table use a minority within a country as the unit of analysis except the "at least one minority in the country" column, which uses the country as the unit of analysis.

occurred in 2013. Hindu nationalists attacked Christians across the country including clergy, individuals, schools, and churches. In November, the seven-year-old son of a Christian missionary was found dead in a pond with signs of torture in Sadar Thana, Dungarpur, Rajasthan. The boy's father had previously received death threats demanding he stop his missionary activities ("Police in India Slow," 2013). Sixty-five people were killed in riots between Hindus and Muslims in Muzaffarnaga. In addition, dozens more were injured and tens of thousands of people fled their homes (Bhalla, 2013; Jain, 2013). Hindu-Muslim riots in Chandan Negar led to multiple injuries but no reported deaths ("Curfew Imposed," 2014).

The year 2014 was similarly violent. Members of Hindu Vahini, a youth organization, assaulted and murdered Orucanti Sanjeevi, a Christian pastor. In the village of Bajrang Dal, Hindu activists disrupted the screening of a film about Jesus, alleging Christians were forcibly converting viewers ("Hindu Extremists Accused," 2014). A Christian prayer hall was attacked in Kandhamal, Odisha district. Christian houses in the state of Odisha were set on fire. New Delhi's St. Sebastian Church was destroyed by arson. Another New Delhi church, Our Lady of Fatima Forane, was attacked by unknown persons, who threw stones at the church window while 200 parishioners were inside praying (US State Department, 2014). Hindu groups in Mumbai used protests and threats to force the closing of a play based on the life of Mohammed Ali Jinnah, the first political leader of Pakistan (Kumar, 2014). At the urging of Pravin Togadia, leader of the Vishva Hindu Parishad (VHP) a Hindu nationalist party, protestors forcibly occupied a house purchased by Muslims in order to prevent them from moving in. Communal riots in Pune against Muslims included the arson of Muslim-owned shops and Mosques, multiple assaults including of a Muslim cleric, and at least one death (Parmar, 2014). Communal clashes between Muslims and Hindus in Vadodara included multiple incidents of arson and stabbing. They were instigated by an image circulated via text message of a Hindu deity atop a picture of the Kaaba in Mecca (Express News Service, 2014; Nair, 2014).

Other Types of SRD

This category, which is presented in Table 3.2, covers those three types of SRD that do not fit into the other five categories. Two of them focus on societal efforts to block access to or prevent the opening of minority religious sites. Efforts to block access to or close existing sites affected

5.2 percent of minorities, and 9.7 percent experienced efforts to prevent religious sites from being opened or built. As noted earlier in Italy, efforts to prevent Mosques from opening included walking pigs on the sites of proposed Mosques. In 2014 in Algeria, dozens of Salafists demonstrated against the reopening of synagogues that had previously been closed for security reasons during Algeria's civil war in the 1990s ("Anti-Semitic Protests Rage," 2014). In Georgia, societal attempts to restrict minority places of worship are common. Often led by leaders of the Georgian Orthodox Church, protesters have sought to prevent the building of Mosques on several occasions, and there have been incidents of protesters preventing Muslims from worshiping together in private homes. In one typical incident in 2013, Georgian Orthodox Church congregants protested the building of a Mosque in Samtatskaro and prevented Muslims from holding prayer services once it was built. A group surrounded the imam's house, assaulted his wife, and threatened to burn down the house and drive them from the village (Corley, 2014; Tolerance and Diversity Institute, 2014; United Nations Association of Georgia, 2015). While less common, there have been similar protests against Catholic, Baptist, and Pentecostal churches.

The "other" category is intended to cover all acts of SRD that do not fit onto the other twenty-six categories. In some cases the SRD was too general to classify. For example in Bhutan there is general societal pressure to uphold Buddhist traditions (The Institute of Religion and Public Policy, n.d.). There are also general reports of discrimination against minorities in schools in various countries, including Djibouti, Jamaica, Kenya, Madagascar, Mexico, and Timor. Others were for more specific reports. For example, in Ethiopia members of the Orthodox majority accused Protestants of heresy. In Iraq minorities were forced to wear Islamic clothing and adhere to Islamic law. In Mexico, in a number of rural villages Protestants are forced to participate in local Catholic Syncretic festivals. Until 2001 in Lima, Peru, prestigious private social clubs refused to accept Jewish members.[6] In Pakistan there are multiple incidents of non-Muslim girls being kidnapped and forced to convert to Islam and marry a Muslim. Muslims in South Korea complained of lack of appropriate dietary options, and denial of prayer breaks by employers during work hours. In the Ukraine, Jehovah's Witnesses and the Roman

---

[6] RASM did not code cases where specifically religious organizations hired or accepted only members of their own religion. Only cases where secular organizations explicitly excluded members of certain minority religions were coded.

Catholic Church were victims of "property raiders." These raiders unlaw-
fully sell land without the knowledge of the owner. This starts lengthy and
costly legal proceedings in which the owner can lose rights to the land (US
Department of State, 2011).

PATTERNS AND TRENDS

Overall the trends in SRD between 1990 and 2014 show four trends of
note. First, it is increasing over time. Of the twenty-seven types of SRD
included in RASM3, all but one was more common in 2014 than in 1990.
Nonviolent harassment of converts away from the majority religion
remained at the same level in 2014. The analysis presented in this chapter
primarily looks at levels of SRD as a proportion of religious minorities
that experience this SRD but does not take into account the extent of this
SRD. As shown in Figure 3.1, an examination of mean levels of SRD
confirms a statistically significant increase over time between 1990 and
2014. This is similar to previous findings as well as findings presented in
Chapter 2 that GRD has been rising since 1990 (Fox, 2015, 2016). This is
consistent with the finding by Grim and Finke (2011) that there is a
relationship between SRD and GRD. However, as I demonstrate in later
chapters, this relationship is a complex one that is present only under
some circumstances.

Second, overall, Jews are the most likely to experience SRD. This is
also true of fifteen of the twenty-seven specific types of SRD and when
looking at the speech acts, attacks on property, nonviolent harassment,
and violence categories but not the economic and "other" categories. This
is confirmed by a comparison of mean levels of SRD presented in
Figure 3.2. Overall levels are slightly under double the level of Christians
who experience the second-highest levels of overall SRD. Muslims experience mean levels just under those of Christians. This means that the three
Abrahamic religions are subject to higher mean levels of SRD than all
non-Abrahamic religions. Also, as I show in subsequent chapters, Jews
experience the most SRD in all groupings of states that have Jewish
minorities other than Muslim-majority states where SRD is highest
against Christian minorities.

Third, despite impressions that religion is most salient in the Muslim
world (e.g., Huntington, 1993, 1996), this study finds that overall
Orthodox-majority states engage in the highest levels of SRD. However,
Muslim-majority states have the highest levels of economic discrimination, nonviolent harassment, and violence against minorities, while

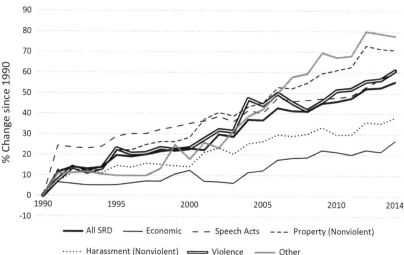

FIGURE 3.1 Percent change in SRD since 1990
All scores in this figure use a minority within a country as the unit of analysis
Significance of change between all SRD for 1990 and marked year <.05 in 1992,
1993, 1998–2000 <.01 in 1994, 2002, 2003
Significance of change between Economic for 1990 and marked year <.05 in
2000, 2006–2008, 2011, <.01 in 2009, 2010,
Significance of change between Speech Acts for 1990 and marked year <.05 in
2002, 2005 <.01 in 2004, <.001 in 2006–2014
Significance of change between Property 1990 and marked year <.05 in
1997–1999, <.02 in 2000, <.001 in 2001–2014
Significance of change between Harassment for 1990 and marked year <.05 in
2001, 2002 <.01 in 2004–2008, <.001 in 2009–2014
Significance of change between Violence for 1990 and marked year <.05 in 1992,
1995, 2007–2009, <.01 in 2004–2006, 2919–2013, <.001 in 2014
Significance of change between Other for 1990 and marked year <.05 in 1998
<.01 in 2000, 2002 <.001 in 1999, 2001, 2003–2014

Orthodox-majority states have the highest levels of speech acts, attacks on
property, and SRD in the "other" category, which is primarily restrictions
on places of worship. I explore the reasons for these differences across
majority religions in subsequent chapters.

Finally, counterintuitively, violence is the most common form of SRD.
Intuitively, one would expect that the more extreme and violent forms
of SRD would be less common than the nonviolent ones. For example,
based on this result speech acts, simply publically saying something
negative about religious minorities, are less common than physically
attacking them, bombings, and arson. Perhaps this is an artifact of the

Societal Discrimination

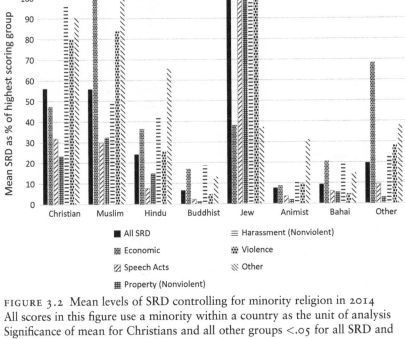

FIGURE 3.2 Mean levels of SRD controlling for minority religion in 2014
All scores in this figure use a minority within a country as the unit of analysis
Significance of mean for Christians and all other groups <.05 for all SRD and
violence, and other <.001 for harassment
Significance of mean for Muslims and all other groups <.05 for all SRD and
violence, and other <.001 economic
Significance of mean for Muslims and all other groups <.001 for speech
Significance of mean for Buddhists and all other groups <.01 for economic, <.001
for all SRD, speech property, harassment, violence, and other
Significance of mean for Jews and all other groups <.05 for violence, <.01 for
harassment, <.001 for all SRD, speech, property,
Significance of mean for Animists and all other groups <.01 for other, <.001 for
all SRD, speech, economics, property, harassment, and violence
Significance of mean for Bahai and all other groups <.01 for econ, <.001 for all
SRD, speech, property, harassment, violence, and other
Significance of mean for Other and all other groups <.01 for speech <.001 for all
SRD, property, and harassment

fact that speech acts in this study are limited to those by political parties,
clergy, and the media. Research methodology also requires that they are
made in public and reported in a manner that enables the RASM3 project
to discover and document these speech acts. Violence, by its very nature,
is more likely to be reported, both by human rights organizations and the
press. It is likely that if we had perfect information we would find speech

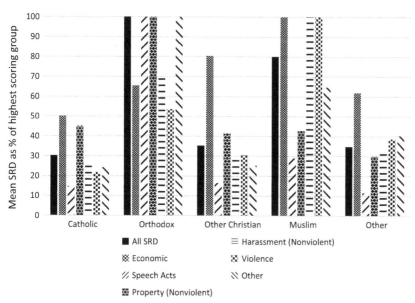

FIGURE 3.3 Mean levels of SRD controlling for majority religion in 2014
All scores in this figure use a minority within a country as the unit of analysis
All scores in this table use a minority within a country as the unit of analysis
except the "at least one minority in the country" column, which uses the country
as the unit of analysis
Significance of mean for Catholics and all other groups <.05 for economic, <.001
for all SRD, speech, harassment, violence, and other
Significance of mean for Orthodox and all other groups <.05 for other, <.001 for
all SRD, speech, and property
Significance of mean for other Christians and all other groups <.01 for all SRD,
speech, violence, and other, <.001 for harassment
Significance of mean for Muslims and all other groups <.001 for all SRD,
harassment, and violence
Significance of mean for "other" and all other groups <.05 for all SRD and
property, <.01 for harassment, <.001 for speech

against all minorities by at least some members of the general population
of the majority.[7]

---

[7] While it is not possible to rule out the possibility that this result that violent SRD is more
common than other forms of SRD due to differential reporting in the sources, I do not
believe this to be the case. The sources used widely reported nonviolent forms of SRD, and
these sources were often the same sources that reported the violent forms of SRD. In most
cases where nonviolent harassment, for example, was reported, it was reported in multiple
sources.

TABLE 3.5 *Correlation matrix for SRD in 2014*

	Economic	Speech acts	Property	Harassment	Violence
Speech acts	.308				
Property	.327	.606			
Harassment	.300	.490	.525		
Violence	.295	.395	.536	.689	
Other	.255	.326	.241	.466	.440

All correlations in this table are significant at <.001 level.

That being said, this raises the question of whether the different types of SRD are interconnected. In particular, one would expect that speech acts are signals by leaders to engage in SRD, or at least might be interpreted as such by potential assailants. This is a form of political mobilization that has in particular been linked to mobilization using religion (Calfino & Djupe, 2009; Isani & Silverman, 2016). As shown in Table 3.5, not surprisingly all of the types of SRD are strongly and significantly correlated. However, speaking in relative terms, speech acts are more weakly correlated with violence and harassment than violence and harassment are correlated with each other. This indicates that while mobilization by elites is likely a factor in causing violent SRD, societal attitudes and factors likely play an independent role. In addition, even when societal attitudes are present, many elites may be reluctant to openly engage in speech acts because "politicians who use overt religious cues run the risk of alienating a large portion of potential voters" (McLaughlin & Wise, 2014: 366).

TRIGGERS AND THE COMPLEX LINK BETWEEN SRD AND GRD

As I discussed in more detail in Chapter 2, theorists predict SRD is a cause of GRD, and studies that use the state as the level of analysis find that there is a link between the two (Grim & Finke, 2007, 2011). Overall, the findings in subsequent chapters replicate this finding when using a universal SRD variable. However, when using SRD variables specific to each minority present in a grouping of states, it emerges that the SRD-GRD link is present for some minorities but not others.

I posit that the reason for this is that the SRD-GRD relationship requires a trigger to activate it. That is, SRD on its own does not cause GRD. Rather, there must be some factor that catalyzes this relationship. Only when this trigger or catalyst is present will societal attitudes toward a minority religion, as measured by SRD, influence GRD. Essentially, it is not sufficient that society or elements of a society dislike a minority; the government must also perceive the minority to be in some manner a threat, likely an existential threat.

I posit that the dynamic of this relationship works as follows. Under normal circumstances, SRD does not greatly influence GRD. In democratic states, this may be due to liberal norms of tolerance. Also, both democratic and nondemocratic governments often have an interest in maintaining social order as well as accommodating and even working with religious minorities because it makes their rule less expensive and more efficient (Gill, 2008; Mantilla, 2016). Koesel (2014: 5) explains this motivation to accommodate as follows:

even in repressive political settings, religious and regime actors have needs that converge and develop mutually reinforcing and supportive relations. Although religious and political authority differ, each side has a set of resources at its disposal that can be offered to the other to minimize uncertainly and meet strategic needs. For instance, government officials may attempt to establish cooperative relations with religious communities as a means of preserving political power, governing more efficiently, and diffusing local conflicts. At the same time religious leaders may seek vertical alliances to safeguard their survival, gain access to resources and promote their spiritual agenda.

Sarkissian (2015: 21) begins with a similar premise but notes that when a religious group is seen by the state as a threat, it may be targeted:

Because of the costs of enforcement, politicians are unlikely to seek to regulate religion in the absence of political motivations. Aside from suppressing the potential oppositional capabilities of religious groups, governments may target specific religious groups because they threaten the identity or unity of a society.

Once such a trigger is present, SRD can influence GRD. This trigger or perceived threat becomes more important than any government motivation for cooperation and tolerance. SRD then can influence GRD because it is related to the extent to which society considers the religious minority in question to be a threat. This can influence governments through at least three avenues. First, politicians are likely to have similar attitudes and threat perceptions toward religious minorities as the population from which they come. Second, SRD is likely related to societal pressure on governments to deal with the perceived threat and may in and of itself constitute such societal pressure (Grim & Finke, 2011). Finally, the SRD is related to the level of the perceived threat. The higher the threat, the higher the SRD and GRD, but in this case it is not SRD causing GRD but, rather, the perceived threat is causing both simultaneously.

The nature of this threat that triggers the SRD-GRD relationship can vary across minorities and groupings of states. In subsequent chapters the types of threats, as perceived by the relevant governments, include security threats, proselytizing, perceived associations with external enemies, heresy, cultural threats, and protection of national culture from foreign influences. In most cases, the threat rises to the level that it can be perceived by political actors as an existential threat of some form. I discuss all of these triggers in more detail in the context of the relevant governments and minorities in subsequent chapters.

SOCIETAL ACTIONS BY MINORITIES

Not all societal actions are taken by the majority group. There are instances of minority on majority and minority on minority SRD. RASM3 collects five types of SRD by minority groups against both the majority group and other minority groups. As shown in Table 3.6, SRD by minority groups is far less common than by majority groups but it does occur. Muslim minorities are by far the most likely to engage in these types of actions, and violent actions are more common than nonviolent ones. While this study focuses on the interaction between SRD by members of the majority group and GRD, this minority SRD is important because it is a factor that can potentially influence levels of both SRD and GRD by the majority.

In some cases these actions are taken by organized terror or separatist movements. For example, in the Philippines the Moro Islamic Liberation Front as well as other Muslim militant groups were active throughout the study period. This conflict included clashes with government troops, attacks, often lethal, on Christian civilians, and kidnappings. In some cases the violence is less organized and in reaction to inflammatory local events. For example, in 2012 in Ghana, in response to a ruling by a traditional chief banning Muslim burials in his area, and the subsequent exhumation of the corpse of an imam, Muslims rioted, burning cars and destroying property. However, in some cases these actions are primarily nonviolent. For example, in Norway, some Muslim men harass women who they consider to be dressed immodestly.

TABLE 3.6 *Societal actions by minorities*

	Societal actions taken by minorities any time between 1990 and 2014								
	All Minorities (%)	Christian (%)	Muslim (%)	Hindu (%)	Buddhist (%)	Jewish (%)	Animist (%)	Bahai (%)	Other (%)
Against the majority religion (at least one type)	9.2	8.8	25.8	4.7	2.1	0.0	4.4	0.0	3.4
Violence	5.4	3.9	16.0	2.3	2.1	0.0	3.3	0.0	3.4
Acts of terror	3.0	0.0	13.5	0.0	0.0	0.0	1.1	0.0	0.0
Nonviolent harassment	1.3	1.8	3.1	0.0	0.0	0.0	1.1	0.0	0.0
Vandalism, graffiti, or other attacks on property	3.5	3.9	8.0	2.3	2.1	0.0	3.3	0.0	0.0
Other relevant acts	2.2	2.2	6.7	0.0	0.0	0.0	1.1	0.0	0.0
Against the minority religion (at least one type)	7.5	7.0	20.2	4.7	0.0	0.0	6.6	0.0	1.7
Violence	4.2	3.5	12.3	2.3	0.0	0.0	2.2	0.0	1.7
Acts of terror	1.0	0.0	4.3	2.3	0.0	0.0	0.0	0.0	0.0
Nonviolent harassment	2.9	2.2	9.2	0.0	0.0	0.0	2.2	0.0	0.0
Vandalism, graffiti, or other attacks on property	2.9	1.8	8.6	2.3	0.0	0.0	2.2	0.0	1.7
Other relevant acts	2.1	2.6	4.5	0.0	0.0	0.0	1.1	0.0	0.0

All scores in this table use a minority within a country as the unit of analysis.

CONCLUSIONS

This chapter is intended to provide a thorough discussion of the extent and nature of SRD. SRD is common, widespread, and increasing. Like GRD, it is the norm rather than the exception. During the study period for this book, overt public actions of discrimination by non-government-affiliated individuals and groups against religious minorities was present in 94 percent of countries. There is a wide variety of types of SRD, but interestingly the most common are violent acts. While it is most common against some minorities, particularly Jews, Christians, and Muslims, in that order, it is present against a large proportion of all types of religious minorities included in this study.

Understanding the nature of SRD is important because, as I show in subsequent chapters, SRD is a significant predictor of GRD. This relationship is present mostly when some form of perceived threat or challenge triggers the SRD-GRD relationship. Usually, this threat can be classified as an existential threat. For this reason, SRD influences levels of GRD against certain minorities in certain places but not all religious minorities. This is a new finding that, until now, has not been present in the empirical literature.

4

Support, Regulation, and Religious Regime as Causes of GRD in the Muslim World

The nature of a government's relationship with the majority religion, in this case Islam, is a significant factor in understanding government-based religious discrimination (GRD). As I show in subsequent chapters, this is also true of other groupings of states, but this relationship is arguably most pronounced in Muslim-majority states. My focus on this factor is not intended to deny the influence of other factors such as societal religious discrimination (SRD), which I also address in this chapter. Rather, I intend to emphasize the importance of this factor in this segment of the world's countries due to its significant explanatory value.

As I discussed in Chapter 1, while there are certainly factors that influence GRD across world regions and majority religions, there are a number of groupings of states with distinct patterns of GRD, and these general causes of GRD manifest differently in each of these groupings. Thus, in this book, I discuss each grouping separately. Each grouping is sufficiently homogeneous based on factors like majority religion, regime, and world region that their patterns of discrimination differ from other groupings but share important commonalities within the same grouping. However, not all groupings are homogeneous based on all of these traits, and there are usually exceptions to most common traits. For example, the Muslim states discussed in this chapter are homogeneous primarily based on majority religion. This is sufficient to make them substantially different from all the other groupings of states analyzed here. Yet there is also significant diversity in GRD and government religion policy in general among these states.

This chapter focuses on fifty-three[1] Muslim-majority countries and autonomous entities (though for simplicity's sake in this chapter I often refer to all of them as countries or states) and the 197 religious minorities included in the Religion and State-Minorities round 3 dataset (RASM3) that are present in these countries.

I argue more specifically that government religion policy, which includes the nature of state-religion bonds, support for religion, and the extent to which governments regulate the majority religion, heavily influences GRD. While this is true for all countries, not just Muslim-majority countries, these fifty-three countries provide a good basis for discussing this more general relationship for at least three reasons. First, I divide government religion policy into seven categories, and this is the only grouping of states with a substantial number of countries in each category. Second, the extent to which these governments regulate the majority religion is diverse, running from some of the most regulatory states in the world to some of the least. Third, the same is true of GRD. There are Muslim-majority states that are among the most tolerant of religious minorities in the world and others that are among the least tolerant. Because of all this, the relationship between government religion policy and GRD is most pronounced and obvious in Muslim-majority states. This makes this grouping of countries an ideal format to develop this concept.

Given this, on the one hand it is impossible to make generalizations about Muslim-majority states. There is perhaps more diversity in all aspects of government religion policy including GRD than in any other grouping of states examined here. On the other hand, patterns can be discerned on levels of GRD in Muslim-majority states. How a government relates to Islam and societal pressures are particularly important in understanding levels of GRD in these states.

Thus, while the actual policies of these states are diverse, they are linked by a common set of relationships between the causes of GRD and GRD itself. In this chapter I demonstrate that those countries most hostile to religion and those most supportive of Islam engage in the most GRD. However, a number of other factors influence GRD in these countries. For example, there are relatively homogeneous subgroupings including several former-Soviet states that are particularly hostile to religion and

---

[1] This count, as is the case with counts of countries belonging to other majority religions, can vary based on counting rules and what exactly is considered a state. See Philpott (2019) for an example of a different count.

engage in high levels of GRD as well as several West-African states that are among the most tolerant of religious minorities in the world. Other influences on GRD in these countries include Islamic ideology and societal religious discrimination (SRD). But other factors that we might expect to have a strong influence, such as democracy, have a weak influence, at most.

STATE-RELIGION BONDS AND RELIGIOUS DISCRIMINATION IN THEORY

Perhaps one of the most basic assumptions in the literature regarding religious discrimination, especially government-based religious discrimination (GRD), is the link between government support for religion and GRD. There are three basic arguments for this link. The first focuses on ideology, beliefs, doctrine, and theology. The second focuses on power politics and interest. The third focuses on identity.

Religions often include exclusive truth claims,[2] usually based on divine revelation. That is, they claim to have a monopoly on the truth and can accept no challenges or contradictions to that truth. Those from within the religion who deny or challenge any aspect of that truth are often called heretics or apostates, and those who are not part of the religious community are the "other." These "others" may be called infidels, heathens, unbelievers, barbarians, or uncivilized, but all of these terms relay the message that those who do not believe the correct beliefs are somehow deficient, incomplete, or even subhuman. While some religions, such as Islam, accept the truth claims of at least some other religions, these religions still generally maintain that their revelations and truths are superior to those of all other religions.

This motivates efforts to bring nonbelievers into the fold. It also can motivate feelings of anger, hate, resentment, enmity, and even fear toward those who will not enter that fold. As Stark (2003: 32) puts it, "those who believe there is only One True God are offended by worship directed toward other Gods." He argues that Judaism, Christianity, and Islam, the three major monotheistic faiths, are particularly intolerant of

---

[2] While this is largely true in that most religions consider their beliefs to be uniquely true, the situation is more complex. For example, a religion could be both exclusive and inclusive. That is, it can hold that its claims are truest and fullest but that it also shares common ground with other faiths, and it can engage in interreligious cooperation. Alternatively, a religion can make strong truth claims and support the religious freedom of other faiths on the very basis of these claims. In addition, secular ideologies can also be no less exclusive.

competition. Many who follow these religions consider their faiths to be the only path to salvation. For those who believe strongly in this interpretation of these religions, allowing nonbelievers to continue to deny the truth is to allow them to be damned for eternity. From this perspective, repressing other religions can be seen as an act of benevolence (Stark, 2001, 2003).

A wide variety of social science literatures commonly recognizes this facet of religion. For example, Jelen and Wilcox (1990: 69) from a comparative politics perspective argue that "religion is often thought to inhibit the development of the tolerance for unorthodox beliefs and practices ... Religion is accused of inculcating ultimate values in its adherents – values which do not lend themselves to compromise or accommodation." Laustsen and Wæver (2000: 719), who focus on international relations, argue that "religion deals with the constitution of being as such. Hence, one cannot be pragmatic on concerns challenging this being." Silberman (2005: 649) argues from a psychological perspective that "once they are constructed, collective meaning systems tend to be viewed within a given group as basic undisputable truths. Accordingly, they are usually held with confidence, and their change or redirection can be very challenging." Sociologists Grim and Finke (2011: 46) argue that "exclusive religious beliefs provide motives for promoting the 'one true faith.' To the extent that religious beliefs are taken seriously and the dominant religion is held as true, all new religions are heretical at best. Thus, established religions will view the new religions as both dangerous and wrong." A large body of survey-based literature links religiosity to intolerance.[3]

Given this, it is probable that states associated with a particular religion will be more likely to discriminate against religious minorities. That being said, the results from this study and others show that GRD is not uniform. That is, states that discriminate tend to discriminate against some minorities more than others (Fox, 2016). This means that regime-level factors cannot by themselves fully explain GRD.

Religious ideology provides a potential explanation for which religious minorities are more likely to be subject to GRD. Some religions, Islam and Judaism in particular, include in their ideologies a hierarchy of alternative beliefs. That is, they have within their theologies criteria that allow them to tolerate certain types of religions more than others. Judaism includes

---

[3] For a survey of this literature, see Wald and Calhoun-Brown (2011: 350–357) and Eisenstein (2008).

the concept of the seven laws of the sons of Noah. Essentially, only Jews who accepted God's covenant are required to follow all the laws of Judaism, but everyone else is required to follow the seven laws that God set down for all man. These laws include (1) to worship a single God (monotheism); (2) not to curse God's name; (3) not to commit murder, (4) adultery, (5) or theft; (6) to establish courts to enforce these laws; and (7) not to eat from a living animal. Thus, other monotheistic faiths in conjunction with a basic set of laws are essentially accepted as legitimate but polytheistic faiths are not.

Classical Islam includes the concept of *Dhimmi* or "peoples of the book." It accepts that there were divine revelations before Mohammed's revelation that created Islam, but these revelations are flawed in some manner. For this reason, religions such as Judaism and Christianity are not banned and are accorded a second-class status in Islamic law. Classically, this includes that these minorities must pay a special tax and are subject to some restrictions but may practice their beliefs. Most interpretations of Islamic doctrine consider religions that are offshoots of Islam such as the Bahai and Ahmadi to be heretical and, therefore, should be banned.[4]

Cesari (2014, 2018) argues that this classical interpretation of Islam is no longer current. The rise of the nation state has caused a fusing of national and religious identity that has caused transformations in how Islam is interpreted. Each Muslim-majority country has adopted an exclusivist national-religious version of Islam to the exclusion of all others. This view of Islam, which has been taken to even greater extremes by groups like Al Qaeda and the Islamic State, sees anyone whose religion is different from their interpretations of Islam as illegitimate. This includes also alternative interpretations of Islam.

Clearly, these theologies are not the sole determinates of GRD in Muslim-majority countries. Historically, these laws have been applied with different levels of strictness and varying interpretations. Peoples of the book have received wildly varying levels of tolerance in different times and places. Groups such as Zoroastrians and Hindus have been considered peoples of the book in some locations where they are indigenous

---

[4] To some extent, the Catholic Church in the Second Vatican Council similarly acknowledges that validity of elements of other faiths, though it is difficult to call this a hierarchy of accepted alternative religions (www.vatican.va/archive/hist_councils/ii_vatican_council/documents/vat-ii_decl_19651028_nostra-aetate_en.html).

even though they are not monotheistic. Also, there are many other motivations to discriminate.

The "power politics" motivation for religious discrimination is discussed extensively in the rational choice literature. Gill (2008) was among the first to discuss the issue, though his focus was on the wider issue of religious liberty. He argues that both politicians and religious institutions follow their rational interests. Religious institutions want religious hegemony in countries where they are a majority. While their motivation may include ideology, hegemony also strengthens the power of the institutions themselves. If everyone in country is required or at least strongly encouraged to be members of the majority religion, this brings in more congregants, more funds, and more influence. In addition, it can bring material support from the government as well as government enforcement of religious precepts.

Politicians, according to Gill (2008), often agree to this monopolistic arrangement because it is also in their interests. Politicians want to stay in power and rule in the most cost-efficient manner. When the national religion lends legitimacy to the government and increases the morality of its congregation, this reduces costs for law enforcement and repressing dissent. This makes the support given to religion a worthwhile investment of resources. In addition, religious institutions often provide social goods such as welfare and charity that the government might otherwise need to provide. One aspect of supporting the majority religion is repressing minority religions. Gill (2008: 45) argues that "hegemonic religions will prefer high levels of government regulation ... of minority religions." In fact, most who address the topic argue that religious monopolies are not possible without repressing religious minorities, including alternate institutions of the majority religion (Casanova, 2009; Froese, 2004: 36; Gill, 2005: 13; 2008: 43; Grim & Finke, 2011: 70; Stark & Bainbridge, 1985: 508; Stark & Finke, 2000: 199; Stark & Iannaccone, 1994: 232).

There are additional reasons that governments who support the majority religion might want to repress minority religions. Religion can be the basis for opposition and political mobilization (Fox, 2018; Wald et al., 2005). This can motivate a government to repress any religion outside its control (Sarkissian, 2015). As governments that support religion generally have significant influence over the religious institutions they support (Fox, 2015), this repression would fall primarily on minority religions.

Yet a central aspect of this body of theory balances this motivation. Repression is costly, and this includes repression of religious minorities. Accordingly, "most authoritarians opt for a strategy of accommodation and cooptation that gives religious actors more leeway than their secular counterparts" (Mantilla, 2016: 2). In fact, there is often a bargaining process between religious minorities and governments where "each side seeks to maximize its interests and discovers such goals are frequently met through collaboration" (Koesel, 2014: 13). Thus, unlike ideology, the power politics explanation for GRD involves complex and cross-cutting motivations.

The final type of argument linking government support for religion and GRD focuses on identity. I argue elsewhere that "theories which focus on religious identity are among the most common found in the political science literature. They are also among the most problematic" (Fox, 2018: 32). Focusing on identity often obscures more complex motives based on ideology and institutional interests, among others. Yet identity can be relevant in this instance.

States often associate with a religion on an identity or cultural level. Religion is clearly linked to many national ideologies (Friedland, 2001: 129–130; Smith, 1999, 2000). That dominant cultures often seek to protect their culture from outside influence is well established in the social sciences literature (Gurr, 1993, 2000; Horowitz, 1985). In this case the religious minority in question is seen as illegitimate because it is foreign or nonindigenous.

While these three reasons why state support for a majority religion might lead to discrimination are not mutually exclusive, they do have different implications for which religions are likely to be targeted or perhaps likely to receive a higher dose of GRD. Religious ideologies target these religions considered most objectionable to the ideology. Religious monopolies target those that are the most significant challenge to this monopoly perhaps due to changing demographics or perhaps due to other political dynamics or perceived political threats. When religious identity is the motivation, religions that are new or perceived as foreign are most likely to be the targets.

A More Complex Approach to State-Religion Bonds and Discrimination

The relationship between a government's level of support for religion and discrimination against religious minorities is complex in two respects. First, the relationship between this support and discrimination is stronger for GRD than it is for societal religious discrimination (SRD). This is logical and straightforward in that one government policy, in this case support for religion, is more likely to be directly related to GRD, which is another government policy, than it is to influence societal actions.

The second element of this complexity is more involved. This is because government support for religion is not simply a scale where some governments support religion more than others. Government motivations for supporting religion and how this support, or the lack thereof, manifests is more complex than a simple continuum from zero support to maximum support.

While there are multiple motives for a government to support a majority religion, they can be divided into positive, neutral, and negative motives. Positive motives can be based on ideology and belief. The government supports religion because the members of the government and many of its citizens are religious and want the state to reflect this in its policies. Even if leaders are not religious, they can believe that religion has a positive influence on society and support it for this reason.

As noted earlier, politicians may find it in their interests to support a religion and form a relationship of mutual support with religious institutions or leaders. I classify this as a neutral motive because from this perspective politicians neither like nor hate religion. Rather, religion is simply a tool to maintain power. In addition, many governments support multiple social institutions for a variety of motivations, and often religion can simply be one of them. For instance, many governments seek non-government providers for social services such as welfare and education. Religious institutions often fulfil this role.

Finally, some governments espouse antireligious ideologies. All these ideologies can be called secular in the sense that any ideology that is not religious, much less antireligious, can be called secular. Philpott (2009) notes that some interpretations of secular are "positive" in that they simply describe what is not religious or differentiate the religious and the nonreligious. However, many secular political ideologies are what Philpott calls "negative" in that they are antireligious. This includes a broad range of ideologies that include Communism, Turkey's Kemalism (in the pre- Erdoğan era), and France's laicite ideology. What they share is a negative view of religion and a desire to keep religion out of the public sphere and in some cases also the private sphere.

What is particularly interesting is that even governments that have this negative approach to religion universally support religion to some extent. The Religion and State round 3 (RAS3) dataset measures fifty-two ways a government might support religion. This includes multiple categories of each of the following: legislating religious precepts as law (including restrictions on women, sex, relationships, and reproduction as well as other religious precepts), financing religion, entanglement between religious and government institutions, government institutions that enforce religion such as religious courts or police, and other forms of support. In 2014, the most recent year of data available, only Japan and Uruguay engaged in as few as two of these types of support. All other countries, whether they have positive, neutral, or negative attitudes toward religion, engaged in three or more types of support. This includes some of the most antireligious states in the world, such as North Korea and Cuba, both with three forms of support, and China, which had eight. This also includes the five Muslim-majority countries, all former-Soviet republics, which maintain a negative attitude toward Islam: Azerbaijan (6), Kyrgyzstan (4), Tajikistan (6), Turkmenistan (11), and Uzbekistan (9).

How is it that these countries that are clearly antireligious, in practice, support religion? Because one of the most common tactics to control religion involves supporting it (Cosgel & Miceli, 2009: 403; Demerath, 2001: 204; Fox, 2015: 65–67; Grim & Finke, 2011: 207). Four of these five former-Soviet republics – all of them other than Azerbaijan – have similar policies that technically support religion but are clearly intended to control it. They all do the following:

- Declare separation of religion and state or secularism.
- Ban religious organizations from influencing politics or the state. This is applied especially to "radical" Muslim organizations.
- Establish Islamic organizations that are fully controlled by the state.
- Use denial of registration to limit, ban, or monitor religious organizations other the state-controlled organization.
- Control, monitor, and restrict both Mosques and religious education.
- Ban any religious activity outside the state-controlled format (Fox, 2018: 36–37).

Thus when controlling religion, these governments also fund it, get involved in religious education, and get entangled in religious organizations, all technically forms of support for religion. Thus, a high score on the RAS3 religious support variable does not necessarily mean that the government is influenced (positively) by a religious ideology.

To make matters even more complex, support for religion is inextricably intertwined with control. This is true even for those states that espouse a religious ideology or otherwise have a positive attitude toward the majority religion. Put differently, "when a government supports a religion, that religion becomes to some degree dependent on the government and more susceptible to government control even if that control was not the original motivation for that support" (Fox, 2015: 65). The regulation, restriction, and control of the majority religion is common among the countries that have official religions and strongly support religion (Fox, 2015: 105–135).

Daniel Philpott (2019) applies all of these concepts to explain variations in religious freedom across forty-seven Muslim-majority countries using Grim and Finke's (2011) data. He divides these countries into three categories. First, religiously free states "are ones whose laws and government policies refrain from coercing or discriminating heavily against individuals and religious communities in their practice of religion. They adhere closely to international human rights conventions in matters of religion" (Philpott, 2019: 50). They are secular but friendly to religion, or "positive" secular states (Philpott, 2009).

Second are secular repressive states, some of which conform largely to my description of secular states that seek to control religion. In the larger sense "secular repressive regimes are secular in the negative sense" (Philpott, 2019: 78). They are the states that follow ideologies that consider religion an impediment to progress, stability, and equality. Essentially, these ideologies are simply incompatible with any religion, including Islam. Accordingly, these regimes

did not discover Islam to be a threat. Rather, they proffered a vision by which Islam could only be a threat. Following Enlightenment philosophers, they thought that they had on their side pure reason, that their conclusions were ones at which any rational person would arrive were he or she unshackled from superstition, hierarchy, and ignorance.

(Philpott, 2019: 110)

Some regimes may also consider religion a source of potential political opposition (Sarkissian, 2015).

Third, religiously repressive states are those that are linked to some interpretation of Islam. Not all of these states actively seek to repress religious minorities as a matter of religious belief. However, the structure of government that is set up when a state enforces Islam within its borders has this inevitable result. "The vigorous enforcement of religious speech and behavior through law and policy in a quest for a thoroughly Islamized environment, though, frequently involves the restriction of faiths other than Islam as well as dissenters within Islam. Often, the restriction is harsh" (Philpott, 2019: 121). That being said, some states do repress other religions for theological reasons. For example, the practice of any religion other than Islam is illegal in Saudi Arabia.

Durham (1996) makes a similar argument. He argues that religious freedom is most absent in the most religious states and those that are the most hostile to religion while states that are more neutral toward religion have the greatest religious freedom. Essentially this is a U-shaped relationship. Durham divides regimes into seven categories: (1) established churches, (2) endorsed churches where the state has no official religion "but acknowledge that one particular church has a special place in the country's traditions" (Durham, 1996: 20), (3) cooperationist regimes where multiple religions, but not all religions, benefit from preferential treatment, (4) accommodationist regimes that have separation of church and state but benevolent neutrality toward religion, (5) separationist regimes that have separation of church and state and are slightly hostile toward religion, (6) inadvertent insensitivity where there is little distinction between regulation of religious and other types of institutions, and (7) states that are overtly hostile to religion and persecute it. Durham (1996) argues that religious freedom is greatest in accommodationist regimes and lowest in states with established churches and those hostile to religion.

These arguments contain essential insights into patterns of religious discrimination in the Muslim world as well as everywhere else. However, I posit they lack the precision necessary to fully explore the relationship between different types of religion-state arrangements and GRD for two reasons. First, they conflate the treatment of the majority religion and minority religions. As Philpott (2019) and Durham (1996) are examining religious freedom in the larger sense that includes freedom of religion for the majority religion as well as for minority religions, this is appropriate for their analyses. However, both give far more attention to the relationship between the state with the majority religion or with religion in general than to the relationship between the government and minority religions. Second, I posit that it is possible to create a better and more useful categorization of government religion policy.

Classifying Government Religion Policies

The Religion and State round 3 (RAS3) dataset has a thirteen-category classification system for types of government religion policy that I simplify into seven categories for the purposes of the analysis and discussion in this book. The first category is states that are hostile to religion. This category is basically the same as Philpott's (2019) secular repressive category. While RAS3 can differentiate between these states along lines similar to

Durham's (1996) categorization, in 2014 only fifteen states worldwide including five Muslim-majority states fit into these categories. This is too few states to address these distinctions using quantitative methodology. Thus this category includes states that Durham (1996) might have classified as separationist such as France and those that are overtly hostile to religion such as North Korea. Previous analyses of RAS and RASM show that states that heavily regulate all religion also engage in GRD (Fox, 2008, 2015, 2016). That is, those states most hostile to religion still subject minorities to an extra dose of GRD.

This brings up an interesting question. Why would states hostile to religion engage in GRD, which is defined here as restrictions placed on minority religious practices and institutions that are *not* placed on the majority religion? One would expect these states to repress all religions equally or even focus repression on the majority religion, which is likely the religion to be seen as the most in need of state control because it is the largest religion in the country. One possible explanation is that despite hostility to religion in general, on some level these states still prefer the majority religion over minority religions. That is, while they are hostile to the concept of religion, the majority religion, while objectionable, is less intolerable than minority religions. This is likely at least in part a product of identity and in-group, out-group dynamics. This would be especially the case for minorities considered nonindigenous to the state. Sarkissian (2015) and Durham (1996) argue that many states hostile to religion are hostile because they fear religion as a potential basis for organizing against the state. From this perspective, religions other than one's own may be less familiar or perceived as more threatening (Sandal & Fox, 2013). This may also contribute to a link between high levels of regulation of the majority religion and GRD.

Another possible reason is that a state's secular antireligious ideology is not the only potential motivation for GRD. As I discuss throughout this study, there are many potential motivations. I argue that when one of these additional motivations is among the causes of GRD against a minority, if a state has an antireligious ideology, this enhances the influence of the additional motivation. For example, if a government considers a religious minority to be nonindigenous and illegitimately encroaching on the state, that state's antireligious ideology can combine with this motivation to intensify GRD against that minority. That is, the state's negative attitude toward religion may be at least partially latent with regard to GRD, but other motivations for GRD can open the floodgates.

The second category of government religion policy is neutral states. While this category is similar to Philpott's (2019), my criteria for being included in this category are more precise. This category includes states that largely maintain separation of religion and state but have a positive attitude toward religion such as the United States, much like Durham's (1996) accommodation category. In practice, no state fully adheres to separation of religion and state, as all of them support religion to some extent, but these states have levels that are lower than those in the other categories. This category also includes states that support religion, but support all religions mostly equally. This is a different form of neutrality based on equality rather than separation of religion and state. However, some would argue that this form of neutrality is also a kind of separation of religion and state or even secularism (Finke, 2013; Madeley & Enyadi, 2003).

Third are states that support multiple religions over all other religions. That is, there is a tiered system where the top tier is populated by at least two religions. It is essentially the same as Durham's (1996) cooperationist category.

The fourth classification of government religion policy is states that have no official religion but otherwise behave as if they have one. That is, they support one religion more than all others without declaring an official religion. This is similar to Durham's (1996) endorsed churches category.

Where I diverge to the greatest extent from Philpott (2019) and Durham (1996) is that I divide states with official religions into three categories. This is because not all official religions are the same. Accordingly, I call the fifth category active official religions. These states have official religions and actively support them. However, state control of these religions is limited, especially compared to the other two categories of official religion. Thus, the institutions of the official religion tend to have some measure of independence, though it is rarely complete independence.

Sixth is the official religion positive control category. These states declare an official religion and support it but substantially control the institutions of that religion. While on the surface there are some similarities between this category and those states hostile to religion, there are two key distinctions. First, none of the hostile states declare an official religion. Rather, most of them explicitly declare separation of religion and state or that they are secular. Second, while many hostile states, including the Muslim-majority states, Kyrgyzstan, Tajikistan, Turkmenistan, and

Uzbekistan, maintain official religious organizations, the sole purpose of this policy is control. In the cases of official religion positive control states, there is a motivation to control but there is also a motivation to support. This is borne out by the RAS3 data. Twenty-one of the fifty-two types of support in RAS3 involve legislating religious precepts. States in this category legislate a mean of 7.46 types as opposed to 0.67 types for the hostile states. This is further evidence of the deep but complex relationship between control and support.

Why would states that are favorable to religion seek to control it? There are at least two possible motivations. It can involve ideological purity. That is, the state may favor a certain interpretation of the majority religion and seek to make sure that all religious institutions remain true to that interpretation. It can also involve marginalizing the political influence of religious institutions. That is, it is possible for political leaders to be supportive of religion but not want religious institutions and religious leaders to challenge their power. Religious institutions and leaders can support opposition to the government or even become that opposition. They can also attempt to dictate policy to the government on a wide range of issues. Maintaining control over religious institutions can be a strategy to prevent this from happening and, in addition, ensure that the religious institutions actively support the regime. These two motivations are not mutually exclusive.

On a more basic level, as I argued earlier, control and support are deeply connected. This is not just a motivation; it is also a dynamic. For example, if a religion receives a substantial portion of its funding from the government, this automatically gives the government more influence over that religion, its institutions, and its clergy. To the extent that a religious institution is dependent on government financial support, it is also more difficult to refuse requests or demands from the government. To do otherwise would risk this support (Fox, 2015). These levers of power exist whether or not they were intended when the government began to support religion and can be pulled at any time. Kuhle (2011) argues that is was precisely due to this form of control that governments in Nordic states have successfully forced their national churches to change their stances on issues like female clergy and gay marriage.

The final category is states with mandatory religions. All eleven countries in this category worldwide are Muslim-majority and declare a brand of Islam the official religion. These states support religion, on average, much more strongly than the other categories as well as seek to control it.

What makes them distinctive is the extent to which Islam is mandatory. In Saudi Arabia and the Maldives observing Islam is mandatory for all residents, and it is not possible to be a citizen if one is not a Muslim. In the other countries, observing Islam is mandatory for Muslims only, though some aspects of Islam may be imposed on even non-Muslims in public spaces. These countries regulate religion even more strongly than do those in the previous category, likely for the same reasons. However, I posit that making the majority religion mandatory constitutes a deeper level of connection between a government and that majority religion. It also inevitably results in restrictions on minority religions. As discussed in more detail in Chapter 2, several of the types of GRD included in RASM3 explicitly involve enforcing aspects of the majority religion on members of minority religions.

As shown in Table 4.1, mean levels of religious support in Muslim-majority states conform well to these seven categories of state-religion relationships. It is lowest in neutral states and highest in states with mandatory official religions. Interestingly, it is slightly higher in states hostile to religion than in neutral states. This is likely due to the use of support as a form of control.

It is important to emphasize that thirty-six of the fifty-two (69.2 percent) Muslim-majority states in this study give preference to Islam above all other religions. Also, as noted earlier, the eleven Muslim-majority states in the mandatory official religion category are the only states in this category worldwide. Thus, the proportion of Muslim-majority states that are deeply connected to a single religion is higher than found in any other religion. However, this is an issue of distribution across categories. I posit that states in each category will behave similarly across different religions.

In sum, like Philpott (2019) and Durham (1996), I expect a U-shaped relationship between GRD and these forms of support for religion. States hostile to religion and states with mandatory religions will have the highest levels of GRD, and states with neutral policies will have the lowest levels.

Support, Regulation, and Control

This classification system is based on support, neutrality, and hostility to religion. It is also based on control. As discussed earlier, those countries that most strongly support a religion are often among those that are most likely to seek to regulate and control that same religion. On the other side

TABLE 4.1 *Mean levels of religious support, religious regulation, SRD, and GRD in Muslim-majority states in 2014 controlling for official religion*

| | Official religion policy | | | | | | |
	Hostile	Neutral	Multiple religions preferred	One religion preferred	Active official religion	Official religion: Control	Official religion: Mandatory
Religious support	7.20	6.40	11.67	16.25	18.50	20.08	32.55
Regulation of the majority religion	46.80	5.60	12.67	18.75	12.50	20.74	26.91
SRD	0.89	0.15	3.79	4.61	6.00	4.83	4.96
GRD	14.11	0.08	5.72	8.57	5.47	14.39	21.73
No. of countries	5	5	6	7	6	12	11
No. of minorities	19	13	29	28	21	36	51

For religious support and regulation of the majority religion the unit of analysis is a country. For SRD and GRD the unit of analysis is a minority.

of the spectrum, those countries that are most hostile to religion are also likely to significantly regulate the majority religion and one of the most effective tactics to control religion is to support it (Fox, 2015).

I posit that countries that most strongly regulate and control the majority religion are also more likely to engage in GRD. Among states that support a single religion, regulating and controlling religion represents a complex set of motivations. It can involve fear of religion's political power. This fear can also apply to minority religions and perhaps be even magnified if the minority groups are also considered outsiders. That is, the religion of the "other" can be seen as more threatening than one's own religion. It can also represent the extent to which the government is intertwined with the majority religious institutions. This, in turn, can be a motivation for supporting a religious monopoly, and one way to support a religious monopoly is by restricting religious minorities.

Among states that are hostile to religion, as I discussed earlier, one would think that this hostility would be applied equally to all religions including the majority religion. Yet, as I document both in this chapter and subsequent chapters, religious minorities in these countries experience significant levels of GRD, which is specifically defined here as restrictions that are placed on minorities that are *not* placed on the majority religion. As I noted earlier, states that are hostile to religion may be motivated to engage in GRD for several reasons, including that they seek to regulate religion in general but might see minority religions as needing additional limitations. Minority religious institutions are often less understood by the majority in comparison to their own religious institutions. Minority religious institutions are also, understandably, likely to be resistant to interference by members of another religion. Finally, other motivations for discrimination might be amplified by the government's hostility to religion. This combined with a government that sees a need to regulate all religion within its borders can lead to restrictions on that religious minority.

As shown in Table 4.1, the RAS3 measure for government regulation of religion in general, and this explicitly includes the majority religion (the measure includes twenty-nine components each measured on a scale of 0–3) is highest for governments hostile to religion. For all other states it, for the most part, increases as the state becomes more closely connected to religion. The only exception is that it is lower in states with active official religions than in states that have no official religion but prefer Islam over all other religions. I discuss this phenomenon in more detail later in this chapter.

STATE-RELIGION BONDS AND RELIGIOUS DISCRIMINATION IN MUSLIM-MAJORITY STATES IN PRACTICE

The argument that state-religion relationships influence levels of GRD in Muslim-majority states is born out in Table 4.1 which shows that GRD is highest in states that are the most hostile to religion in general and those states most closely linked to Islam. While this general pattern is robust, as shown in Tables 4.2a and 4.2b, there is considerable variance and nuance within this pattern in at least two respects. First, levels of GRD vary considerably within most of these states. Second, there is a regional component to many of the groupings of states into my typology of state-religion relationships. The first of these observations I address later in this chapter. The latter I address here using a category-by-category approach.

Hostile States

All five Muslim-majority states that are hostile to religion are former-Soviet states. This is perhaps not surprising, as Communism is one of the modern ideologies that is most hostile to religion in general, and all of these states other than Kyrgyzstan are autocracies that retain many elements of the Communist regimes that preceded them. In 2010 Kyrgyzstan, after a revolution that deposed President Kurmanbek Bakiyev, adopted a new constitution that set it on the path to become more democratic. However, this did not result in a lowering of its regulation of both Islam and minority religions, which was its policy while it was a more autocratic state until 2010.

Kyrgyzstan's policy is typical of the policy of these states toward religious that I outlined in general terms earlier in this chapter. The 2008 *Law on Freedom of Religion and Religious Organizations in the Kyrgyz Republic* reiterates the country's constitutional stance that it is secular and bans all proselytizing. Distribution of religious material is restricted to buildings owned by the religious group or specifically designated public places. The law also requires all religious organizations, including schools, to register with the State Commission for Religious Affairs. Unregistered religious organizations may not legally operate. The government denies registration to about 25 percent of religious organizations that apply including Muslim groups deemed extremist or separatist, and "nontraditional" religions. Also, groups with less than 200 members may not register.

TABLE 4.2A *Levels of SRD and GRD in 2014 in Muslim-majority states*

		SRD			GRD	
		1990	2014	Avg.	1990	2014
Hostile						
Azerbaijan	Jews	0	0	0.08	0	2
	Orthodox Christians	5	1	0.83	11	12
	Other Christians	5	6	5.99	15	16
	Sunni Muslims	1	2	1.71	8	12
Kyrgyzstan	Bahai	0	0	0.00	2	9
	Buddhists	0	0	0.00	2	9
	Jews	0	0	0.12	2	9
	Orthodox Christians	1	1	1.17	2	9
Tajikistan	Other Christians	1	1	1.66	4	24
	Christians	1	1	1.25	4	8
	Shi'a Muslims	0	0	0.00	1	2
Turkmenistan	Catholics	1	1	1.00	1	11
	Muslims, Shia	0	0	0.00	2	19
	Orthodox Christians	0	0	0.00	0	6
	Other Christians	1	1	1.00	7	27
Uzbekistan	Protestants	1	2	1.12	6	26
	Christians	1	1	1.16	25	32
	Jews	0	0	0.28	8	9
	Shia Muslims	0	0	0.00	19	26

		SRD			GRD	
		1990	2014	Avg.	1990	2014
Chad	Animist	0	0	0.00	0	2
	Bahai	0	0	0.00	0	2
	Christian	0	1	0.64	0	2
	Faid al-Djaria Sufi Muslim	0	0	0.00	0	8
Kazakhstan	Catholics	0	0	0.00	1	1
	Jews	1	1	1.21	1	1
	Non-Sunni Muslims	1	1	1.00	3	32
	Orthodox Christians	0	0	0.00	1	1
	Protestants	2	6	2.53	3	32
Kosovo	Catholics	1	1	1.00	0	0
	Jews	3	3	3.14	0	0
	Orthodox Christians	17	17	17.57	3	5
	Protestants	1	1	1.14	2	2
Lebanon	Buddhists	0	0	0.00	8	8
	Druze	0	0	0.00	2	2
	Hindus	0	0	0.00	8	8
	Maronite Christians	3	5	3.24	2	3
	Orthodox Christians	2	4	2.52	2	3
	Other Christians	2	2	2.28	10	10
	Shi'i Muslims	0	8	1.68	2	2
	Sunni Muslims	0	8	1.68	2	2

(continued)

TABLE 4.2A (continued)

		SRD			GRD	
		1990	2014	Avg.	1990	2014
Neutral						
Burkina Faso	Animists	0	0	0.00	0	0
	Christians	0	0	0.04	0	0
	Shi'i Muslims	0	0	0.00	0	0
Mali	Animists	0	0	0.00	0	0
	Bahai	0	0	0.00	1	1
	Christians	0	0	0.24	0	0
Niger	Animists	0	0	0.36	0	0
	Christians	0	0	0.00	0	0
Senegal	Animists	0	0	0.00	0	0
	Christians	0	2	0.68	0	0
Sierra Leone	Animists	0	0	0.04	0	0
	Bahai	0	0	0.00	0	0
	Christians	0	0	1.76	0	0
Multiple religions supported						
Albania	Catholics	0	0	0.04	1	2
	Non-Sunni Muslims	0	0	0.28	1	2
	Orthodox Christians	0	0	0.52	1	3
	Protestants	0	0	0.00	1	3

		SRD			GRD	
		1990	2014	Avg.	1990	2014
Nigeria	Animists	0	0	0.00	3	4
	Christians (north)	17	18	17.60	8	15
	Shia Muslims	16	17	16.60	3	7
	Sunni Muslims (south)	16	17	16.60	3	4
One religion preferred						
Cyprus, Turkish	Christians	4	4	4.16	7	8
Gambia	Ahmadi Muslims	0	1	0.04	0	0
	Animists and Witchcraft	0	0	0.00	1	1
	Bahai	0	0	0.00	1	1
	Christians	1	1	1.04	1	1
Guinea	Animist	0	0	0.00	1	0
	Christian	1	2	1.32	3	1
	Non-Sunni Muslims	0	0	0.00	0	0

TABLE 4.2B *Levels of SRD and GRD in 2014 in Muslim-majority states*

Country	Group	SRD 1990	SRD 2014	SRD Avg.	GRD 1990	GRD 2014
Indonesia	Ahmadi Muslims	6	10	7.48	21	24
	Animists	0	0	0.08	24	20
	Buddhists	1	2	1.20	10	13
	Christians	17	19	18.52	11	15
	Confucians	0	0	0.00	18	10
	Hindus	1	1	1.16	9	9
	Shia Muslims	5	9	6.36	22	24
Sudan	Animists	13	6	12.20	19	17
	Christians	15	13	15.16	27	32
	Muslims, Shi'i	2	2	2.00	2	3
Syria	Christians	3	3	3.00	3	4
	Druze	0	0	0.00	3	3
	Shia Muslims	0	0	0.00	1	1
Turkey	Alevi	0	0	0.04	12	12
	All other Christians	16	16	16.08	16	16
	Jews	9	11	10.36	8	8
	Orthodox Christians	10	10	10.28	12	12
Zanzibar	Bahai	1	1	1.00	0	2
	Christians	12	17	12.84	0	3
	Hindu	1	1	1.00	0	0
Libya	Buddhists	0	0	0.00	8	8
	Christians	2	16	3.8	14	17
Somalia	Christians	6	10	8	10	10
Official religion: Positive control						
Algeria	Catholics	4	4	6.08	16	24
	Jews	2	4	4.12	17	23
	Protestants		5	6.28	17	27
Bahrain	Buddhists	1	1	1	6	6
	Christians	4	4	4.12	7	7
	Hindus	1	1	1	4	4
	Shi'i Muslims	8	10	8.36	8	14
Comoros	Animists	0	0	0	0	5
	Christians	6	6	6.64	20	23
	Shi'i Muslims	3	3	3.04	0	6
Egypt	Bahai	1	1	1.16	27	27
	Christians (Coptic)	43	47	44.08	21	23
	Jews	6	6	6	14	14
Jordan	Bahai	1	1	1	16	16
	Christians	4	6	4.68	14	19
	Druze	0	0	0	13	13

(continued)

TABLE 4.2B (continued)

		SRD			GRD	
		1990	2014	Avg.	1990	2014
Active official religion						
Bangladesh	Ahmadis	7	7	7.12	0	2
	Animists	0	0	0.00	0	0
	Buddhists	3	3	3.20	1	1
	Christians	5	5	5.08	0	0
	Hindus	14	13	12.32	1	1
	Shi'i Muslims	0	0	2.00	1	0
Djibouti	Bahai	2	2	2.00	0	0
	Buddhists	2	2	2.00	0	0
	Christians	5	6	5.04	0	0
	Shi'i Muslims	2	2	2.00	0	0
Iraq	Christians	4	28	15.04	11	7
	Shi'i Muslims	0	0	0.00	37	37
	Sunni Muslims	0	16	16.00	1	5
	Yadzis	0	14	14.00	3	5
Kurdistan	Christians	2	2	2.27	8	7
(Iraq)	Shi'i	0	0	0.00	3	2
	Yazidis	0	0	0.18	7	7
	Zoroastrians	0	0	0.00	7	6

		SRD			GRD	
		1990	2014	Avg.	1990	2014
Mauritania	Shi'i	0	0	0	1	0
	Animists	0	0	0	4	6
	Christians	0	0	0.08	10	16
Morocco	Christians	4	4	4.16	15	20
	Jews	2	4	2.24	3	3
	Shi'i Muslims	2	2	2	16	20
Palestinian Authority	Christians	19	16	15.77	11	11
Tunisia	Bahai	1	1	1	18	19
	Christians	2	9	3.28	12	13
	Jews	2	12	3.76	10	11
UAE	Bahai	0	0	0	19	19
	Buddhist	0	0	0	20	20
	Christian	1	1	1	18	18
	Hindu	0	0	0	19	19
	Shi'i Muslims	0	0	0	19	1
Western Sahara	Christians	4	4	4.04	15	20

TABLE 4.2C *Levels of SRD and GRD in 2014 in Muslim-majority states*

		SRD			GRD	
		1990	2014	Avg.	1990	2014
Yemen	Christians	1	3	2.16	12	14
	Hindus	0	0	0.04	11	12
	Jews	7	13	9.56	8	9
	Shi'i Muslims	0	6	2.64	12	16
Official religion: Mandatory						
Afghanistan	Bahai	1	1	1	11	16
	Christians	13	15	13.34	7	17
	Hindus	5	7	6.04	11	16
	Muslims, Shi'i	1	2	1.17	4	0
	Sikhs	6	8	7.13	11	16
Brunei	Animists	2	3	2.08	21	27
	Bahai	2	3	2.08	22	29
	Buddhists	2	3	2.08	21	27
	Christians	2	3	2.08	21	27
	Confucians	2	3	2.08	21	27
	Hindus	2	3	2.08	21	27
Gaza	Orthodox Christians	13	15	13.1	10	10
Iran	Bahai	20	21	20.2	50	52
	Christians	1	1	1.08	35	35
	Jews	2	5	5.08	13	13
	Sunni Muslims	2	2	2.04	18	18
Kuwait	Bahai	1	1	1	20	21
	Christians	5	5	5.04	21	22
	Hindus	1	1	1	21	22
	Shi'i	5	5	5.16	7	9
	Sikh	1	1	1	21	22

		SRD			GRD	
		1990	2014	Avg.	1990	2014
Malaysia	Bahai	0	0	0.04	13	15
	Buddhists	1	2	0.16	9	11
	Chinese Religions	0	0	0	9	11
	Christians	0	5	0.4	15	20
	Hindus	0	0	0.08	14	16
	Shi'i Muslims	2	2	2	22	30
Maldives	Buddhists	0	0	0.08	38	38
	Christians	0	0	0.04	38	41
	Hindus	0	0	0.08	37	37
Oman	Bahai	0	0	0	15	18
	Buddhists	0	0	0	16	19
	Christians	0	0	0	11	13
	Hindus	0	0	0	11	13
	Shi'i Muslims	1	1	1	2	2
	Sikhs	0	0	0	11	13
Pakistan	Ahmadis	29	29	29.04	33	36
	Bahai	1	1	1	10	10
	Christian	35	35	35.12	15	15
	Hindus	23	23	23	18	19
	Shi'i Muslims	20	20	20.04	16	16
	Sikhs	8	8	8.04	3	4
Qatar	Bahai	0	0	0	22	22
	Buddhists	0	0	0	22	22
	Christians	0	0	0.08	24	23
	Hindus	0	0	0	22	22
	Shi'i Muslims	0	0	0	4	4
Saudi Arabia	Buddhists	4	4	4	40	40
	Christians	6	6	6	43	45
	Hindus	4	4	4	40	40
	Shi'i Muslims	4	5	4.08	40	40

Denial of registration and the 200-member minimum results in severe restrictions on many small religious Christian groups as well as groups often considered cults like Jehovah's Witnesses (which are denied registration in many parts of the country), Mormons, Scientologists, Hare Krishnas, and the Unification Church. These groups may not buy or rent places of worship. The government often raids meetings held in private homes and uses a law against proselytizing to minors to prevent them from bringing children to religious services. Other groups like Jews, Bahai, Buddhists, and Orthodox Christians register successfully (Corley, 2011, 2013; Vennard, 2010). This pattern of elevated restrictions against Christian minorities is common to all five Muslim-majority states in this category.

Arguably, this targeted persecution of certain Christians has a cultural rather than a religious basis. While each of the nineteen minorities in these states experience GRD, in all of them, the minorities that experience the highest levels of GRD are Christian groups, but this applies to a subset of Christian groups. Those Christian groups that the government considers indigenous to the country experience levels that are considerably lower than those perceived as nonindigenous, particularly US-based Protestant organizations and Jehovah's Witnesses. For example, Orthodox Christians in Azerbaijan, Tajikistan, and Turkmenistan all experience lower levels of GRD than other Christians in the same country. Thus, this likely has more to do with protection of national culture and identity than religious ideology.

Neutral States

All five neutral Muslim-majority states – Burkina Faso, Mali, Niger, Senegal, and Sierra Leone – are located near each other in Western sub-Saharan Africa. This indicates a strong regional trend. In these states GRD is practically nonexistent. The only exception is that Mali does not allow the Bahai to register but this has not otherwise prevented them from engaging freely in religious practices.

The obvious potential explanations for this regional concentration of tolerant Muslim-majority states that maintain separation of religion and state include demographics and religiosity. Philpott (2019) demonstrates that these countries have a wide range of demographics and include both states with large Muslim majorities and states where the majority is far narrower, as do Muslim-majority states that are more religiously repressive. In addition, these states have unusually high levels of religiosity yet remain tolerant of minorities. Thus, these factors cannot explain this regional phenomenon.

Philpott (2019) argues that the explanation for the low levels of GRD in these specific states is cultural and related to specific interpretations of Islam. While many of these states have less tolerant Muslim organizations that push for more restrictive laws, these organizations have been unsuccessful because the majority continues to support tolerance. Philpott (2019) argues that this has to do with five interrelated factors. First, these countries have long-standing traditions of tolerance. "Christians and Muslims celebrate one another's holidays; marry one another and create interreligious extended families; sometimes attend one another's prayers; and even display tolerance for conversion to the other's faith" (Philpott, 2019: 63). Second, a tolerant brand of Sufism is popular in the region. "Sufis are … known for their tolerance. Where they have conquered, they have taken on local practices and traditions. Their teachers stress the presence of God within every human being, respect for other religious traditions, and the free character of faith, all of which favor a political theology of religious freedom" (Philpott, 2019: 64). Third, there is an element of syncretism in West African Islam, which can blur the lines between religions.

Fourth is a history of tolerance. Islam came to West Africa not through conquest but with Muslim traders and teachers who migrated to the region. At first, they were a minority who were dependent upon the tolerance of the local rulers. When, eventually some rulers began converting to Islam, they applied this tradition of tolerance, from which Islam had previously benefitted, to religious minorities. While at various points in history jihadist movements tried to impose a less tolerant version of Islam in the region, they were consistently defeated (Philpott, 2019).

Fifth, these countries were all under the control of European colonial powers from the late nineteenth century and became independent between 1950 and 1970. All of these countries had arrangements where the European governments supported local governments that included religious freedom arrangements for the locals as well as for Christians. This helped establish a tradition of European-style secularism combined with religious freedom. As I discuss in the next chapter, it is arguable that with regard to religious tolerance, the students have surpassed their teachers.

States That Support Multiple Religions

These six states are not regionally concentrated but have in common religious policies where the state gives roughly equal support to at least two religions, including Islam. All but two of the minorities – Catholics and Jews in Kosovo – experience at least some GRD, but in most cases levels of GRD are low. Nevertheless, in all of these countries other than Albania, at least one religious minority is subject to GRD considerably higher than other minorities in that country.

In some cases, this differential GRD can be traced directly to the government's support of some religions but not others. Kazakhstan gives preference to five religions "traditional" to the country: Sunni Hanafi Islam, Russian Orthodoxy, Roman Catholicism, Lutheranism, and Judaism. The government severely restricts other religions, particularly non-Sunni Muslims and non-Lutheran Protestants. Lebanon's government similarly gives preferential treatment to some religions. However, this is done through a consociational arrangement where many religious groups are formally included as part of the government and given autonomy on religious matters within their community. Groups such as Buddhists, Hindus, and Christian groups not included in the arrangement experience higher levels of GRD.

In other cases, the reason is more country-specific. In Chad, the government bans Al Faid al-Djaria, a Sufi group that operates in the Kanem, Lake Chad, and Chari Baguirmi areas, because the government deems some of their customs un-Islamic. These include the incorporation of singing, dancing, and the intermixing of sexes during religious ceremonies. Thus, this appears to be government support for doctrinal orthodoxy in Islam. In Kosovo levels of GRD are generally low, but GRD against Orthodox Christians is slightly higher, likely as a result of past tensions with Serbians.

In Nigeria, the north is majority Muslim and the south is majority Christians. So, effectively, Christians are a minority in the north and Muslims in the south. While Muslims in the south experience no more GRD than other religious minorities in the country, Christians in the North have been subject to high levels by the regional governments, many of which impose elements of Islamic law on the entire population in their region. Thus, while this split-government policy in some ways supports multiple religions, in others it is more akin to those that support one religion more than others.

States That Prefer One Religion

These eight countries do not declare an official religion, but in practice support Islam more than other religions. Despite this overt preference for Islam, there is considerable diversity in levels of GRD among these states.

Four of them engage in relatively low levels of GRD. The Gambia and Guinea behave similarly to the five West African Muslim-majority states that are neutral on issues of religion. These two states are in the same region of West Africa. This suggests that this low GRD is due to the regional cultural phenomena I described earlier when discussing these states. Zanzibar, a Muslim-majority self-governing island that is part of Tanzania, also engages in low levels of GRD.

Syria was included in RASM3 until 2012 when the civil war began, which basically undermined all political intuitions and civil society. Before the civil war Syria also engaged in low levels of GRD. Syria, Turkey, and Lebanon are the only three Middle Eastern countries not to have an official religion, though the president of Syria is required to be a Muslim. The low levels of GRD in Syria are likely due to a unique religion-state relationship. While the state strongly supported Islam as well as had significant levels of control over Islamic institutions, its outlook under President Bashar al-Assad and his father, who was president before him, was basically secular and based on the Socialist Ba'th Party. In addition the government was largely run by members of the Alawite sect of Islam, which many Muslims consider heretical. Thus, the government's support for Islam was arguably intended for the dual purpose of preventing Islam from becoming a basis for opposition and lending legitimacy to the regime. That being said, in the long run, it failed on both accounts.

The other four countries in this category engage in higher levels of GRD against most of their minorities. Sudan's official religion was Islam until 2005 when it changed its constitution as part of a peace agreement with the non-Muslims in its southern region that has since become the independent country of South Sudan. However, in practice Sudan's religion policy remained basically the same after 2005. It supports Islam to the extent that it enforces elements of Islamic law in much of the country. This enforcement includes applying Islamic law to religious minorities, which inevitably not only leads to GRD, it usually constitutes GRD. Christians living in Sudan experience levels of GRD higher than any other group in this category of states.

In Indonesia, all seven religious minorities experience moderate to high levels of GRD. Ahmadi Muslims and Shi'i Muslims experience the highest levels and are often singled out for types of GRD not applied to other groups. This is heavily influenced by theological motivations. For example, some provinces require Ahmadi Muslims to renounce their faith in order to get married or go on the pilgrimage to Mecca. Also, non-Sunni

Muslims are often prosecuted under blasphemy laws for following "deviant" teachings.

Until 2010 Turkey was coded by RAS3 as being hostile to religion. This changed due to a number of policy changes that were applied incrementally beginning in 2002 with the rise to power of Recep Tayyip Erdoğan and the AKP party. However, GRD has changed little in Turkey during the 1990–2014 period. This indicates that the roots of GRD in Turkey may be more rooted in national culture than in the government relationship with religion. Alternatively, it may simply be a continuation of the high levels of GRD that are typically found in countries hostile to religion.

Given all of this, in the absence of an official religion, favoring a single religion over all others has the potential to result in GRD, but it does not necessarily result in high levels of GRD. The extent and nature of this support is important. Indonesia and Sudan support Islam more strongly than all other countries in this category. In particular, these countries have the highest levels of legislating and enforcing aspects of Islam on the populace. As I noted earlier, enforcing a majority religion is closely related to GRD and often constitutes GRD if the majority religion is also enforced on religious minorities.

The RAS3 dataset measures the presence of twenty-one aspects of religious law or doctrine a country might legislate. Sudan legislated sixteen of these categories, and Indonesia legislated fifteen. In contrast, no other state in this category had more than nine, while Gambia and Guinea, the most tolerant states in this category, legislated three and two, respectively. However, a lack of this type of legislation does not guarantee an absence of GRD. Turkey legislated none of these twenty-one types of laws but still engaged in substantial levels of GRD.

Enforcing religious doctrine as national law is a sign of a deep commitment by a state to a religion. While GRD is likely in states with this type of connection to their majority religion, an absence of this connection does not necessarily mean there will be no GRD because GRD has multiple causes. In Turkey, for example, SRD is considerably higher than in The Gambia and Guinea. This may explain the substantial levels of GRD in Turkey but low levels in The Gambia and Guinea.

States with Active Official Religions

States with active official religions are those that declare an official religion but allow the majority religious institutions a considerable level of independence from the state. Like the previous category, levels of GRD vary considerably among the six Muslim-majority countries in this category. Djibouti, which is located in the same region of West Africa as the other seven particularly tolerant African Muslim-majority states, engages in no GRD against any minority included in the RAS3 dataset. Thus, in this case the region's culture and tolerant approach to Islam is evidently a more important determining factor for GRD than the state's declaration of an official religion. It engages in six of the twenty-one potential ways a country might legislate religion, including various aspects of family and inheritance law as well as restrictions on abortion and the LGBTQ community. Bangladesh has even lower levels of this form of support for religion. It uses Islamic law for inheritance and restricts abortion and the LGBTQ community. It engages in low levels of GRD against three of the seven religious minorities in the country and none against the other four.

Iraqi Kurdistan is a relatively new self-governing entity, yet it engages in moderate levels of GRD against most of its religious minorities. To some extent, the GRD in Iraqi Kurdistan is a legacy of Iraqi law, which carried over into the autonomous region's government. This is slowly changing. For example, until 2012 Islamic education was mandatory in all public schools, even for religious minorities. This requirement was eliminated and replaced with a course in world religions.

While Iraq's Shi'i Muslims are coded as experiencing high levels of GRD, this is because under the post-Saddam government they are no longer the religious minority, and the coding represents the Saddam Hussein era when effectively Iraq's Sunni minority ruled Iraq. Numerical minorities that effectively control a government are considered the political majority in RASM3.

The only other example of substantially high GRD among these states is Libya's Christian minority. Until Qaddafi's fall as leader of Libya in 2011, RASM3 coded Libya as a state with a state-controlled version of Islam. Many of the substantial number of policies supporting and legislating Islam remain in effect since then. However, as the new government does not possess the resources to fully control all of Libya, much less Islamic institutions within the country, it was moved to this category from that point onward. Thus, these high levels of GRD are associated with a policy developed under a different type of regime.

Mean levels of GRD for these states are substantially lower than for states with no official religion but prefer a single religion and are at about the same levels as states that prefer multiple religions. I posit the key issue is the regulation of the majority religion. States with "active" official religions are placed in this category precisely because, despite their support for religion, they engage in lower levels of regulation than other states with official religions. Although support entails a certain amount of implied control, these states engage in less overt control of the majority religion. As regulation and GRD are related, this general approach to religion results in lower levels of GRD.

In contrast, states that have no official religion but prefer one religion are all included in the same category. To break these eight states up unto multiple categories would result in at least one of the categories having too few countries. Thus states like Indonesia, Sudan, and Turkey that heavily regulate religion and also engage in high levels of GRD against at least some minorities are included in the same category as states like The Gambia and Guinea, which engage in lower levels of both regulation and GRD. Yet this link is not absolute. For example, Syria (pre–civil war) had levels of regulation higher than any other state in the preferred religion category but relatively low levels of GRD. This is further evidence that while an important influence on GRD, regulation of the majority religion is not always the determining factor.

States with Official Religions That Seek to Control Those Religions

These states substantially support the majority religion but also engage in significant levels of control. For the purposes of defining this category, control is not measured by the RAS's general regulation index but rather focuses more specifically on whether the government controls the majority religion's institutions. In most cases, this involves the power to appoint some or all clergy as well as other forms of control. Other than Mauritania, all of the Muslim-majority countries in this category are in the Middle East, so there is a strong regional component to this style of religion policy.

Unlike the one religion preferred and active official religion categories, the states in this category are largely consistent on GRD. All of them engage in levels of GRD of ten or higher against at least one religious minority and only four of the thirty-six minorities in these countries experience GRD lower than five – Hindus in Bahrain, Shi'i Muslims in Jordan and the UAE, and Jews in Morocco. None of these minorities experienced no GRD between 1990 and 2014. These governments, on average, both more strongly support and regulate Islam than all of the categories previously discussed.

Mean levels of GRD in these states are similar to those in states that are hostile to religion but for different reasons. Like states hostile to religion, they seek to regulate and control religion but unlike hostile states, they have a positive attitude toward religion. The rulers are religious, or at least profess to be religious, and see religion as something that can have a positive influence in society if managed properly. However if it is not managed properly, it has the potential to be a source of political opposition and perhaps a negative force in general. In essence, these governments like religion as long as it is "good" religion and not "bad" religion from their perspective. While this is part of the motivation for GRD, the ideological, structural, and identity-based links between state support for religion and GRD discussed at the beginning of this chapter also apply.

Yemen provides a good example of this phenomenon. Until 2001, Yemen was coded by RAS3 as having an active official religion. While Yemen has dealt with multiple insurgencies over its history, the Al Qaeda insurgency, which began in 1998, had a lasting impact on its religion policy. The government during this period also experienced multiple insurgencies and opposition movements by Shi'i groups as well as Sunni groups in the South. In 2001, the government began an escalating crackdown on Al Qaeda. This also resulted in policy changes that moved it to the official religion positive control category. In 2001, the government authorized the implementation of unifying the curriculums of all publicly funded schools. By 2006 this was being applied also in private schools. This is a move often taken by governments that fear opposition groups using their interpretation of religious ideology to legitimize their opposition. In fact, in 2004, Yemen's Minister of Religious Endowment stated that the government intends to eradicate teachings encouraging religious extremism and sectarianism and has formed a special government committee to further revise all religious school curricula in order "to make sure that they conform with the constitution, and national and religious ideology of the state and do not undermine national unity" (United Press International, 2014). The government began training religious teachers in its official version of Islam and in 2007 closed over 4500 "unlicensed" schools and replaced them with schools under the control of the Ministry of Endowments and Religious Guidance.

Yemen's government also began restricting the number of hours Mosques can be open to the public and in 2003 dismissed imams who preached against the regime. After that, it began appointing imams to some Mosques. New Mosques may not be built without government permission. The government monitors sermons in Mosques for political content and bans political activities in Mosques.

What is interesting is that these increasing efforts to control Islam seem to be directly linked to the increasing threat of opposition groups that follow radical Islamic ideologies, though these efforts have not been successful in eradicating this opposition. Nevertheless, the government still maintains Islam as its official religion and supports it. Article 2 of Yemen's constitution declares Islam as the official state religion. Sharia is enshrined as "the source of all legislation" and dictates legislation on women's rights, inheritance laws, family law, and criminal justice. Conversion away from Islam is banned as is proselytizing by non-Muslims and blasphemy. Homosexuality is punishable by death. The state collects a mandatory Zakat tax (Islamic tax) for charitable purposes, which it uses to fund charities and Islamic institutions (Yemini Constitution, 1994).

Thus, Yemen supports Islam but only the forms of Islam it considers theologically appropriate and nonthreatening to the state. As a result, it strongly regulates Islam and exercises substantial control over Islamic institutions. This combination of regulating religion and its commitment to Islam is likely a significant influence on GRD levels in the country. That GRD against all minorities in Yemen increased after regulation increased is consistent with this understanding of Yemen's religion policy.

States with Mandatory Official Religions

Like the previous category, these states both support and regulate religion though this support and regulation is on average considerably higher. That being said, what most differentiates these states from the others is that all of these states make Islam mandatory for Muslims, and some of them make observing aspects of Islam mandatory also for non-Muslims. This enforcement of Islam is present in states in the previous category but is generally limited to the use of Islamic law in family law and inheritance and sometimes criminal law as well as bans on eating in public on Ramadan, blasphemy, apostasy, conversion away from Islam, alcohol, premarital sex, abortion, and homosexuals.

States classified as having mandatory religions also have these types of policies. However, these policies are more likely to be present and enforced more strictly than in other countries. In addition, the enforcement of Islam is more all-encompassing. In Saudi Arabia, Kuwait, and the

Maldives, for example, all citizens must be Muslim. Malaysia's constitution states that all ethnic Malays are Muslims, but the country does not ban non-Muslims from citizenship. Saudi Arabia and the Maldives ban any public non-Muslim religious activities. The Maldives even regulates the nature of Islamic prayer. Performing the Islamic ritual *namaz* prayer in a non-government-approved way or possessing Islamic religious materials not approved by the government can lead to arrest (Larson, 2009). Afghanistan, Brunei, Gaza, Iran, Qatar, Saudi Arabia, and some local governments in Malaysia require women to wear traditional Islamic head coverings in public. Brunei, Malaysia. Gaza, Iran, and Saudi Arabia have police forces or other government agencies whose sole purpose is to enforce Islamic law.

It is also worth emphasizing that no non-Muslim-majority states fit into this category. These eleven states, all of which are located in the Middle East or non-former-Soviet Asia, are the only ones in the world with this type of religion-government relationship.

Levels of GRD in these countries are higher than for any other category of Muslim-majority state. Shi'i Muslims in Afghanistan are the only minority that does not experience GRD, likely because most of them are ethnic Hazaras who live in a region where they are the majority. In these states, the relationship between regulating Islam and GRD applies. For example, Iran and Saudi Arabia score highest worldwide on both regulating Islam and GRD. They are also among the strongest supporters of Islam, confirming the relationship between support and control of religion.

In sum, government policy toward the majority religion has significant explanatory power to predict GRD among Muslim-majority states. This includes the nature of state-religion bonds and the extent to which the government regulates Islam. While these two factors are related, they do not fully determine one another. As I demonstrate in later chapters, this dynamic is not unique to Islam.

There are also regional factors that play a role. The most hostile states are former-Soviet. The most tolerant states are largely, though not exclusively, concentrated in West Africa. The states that most strongly support Islam are concentrated in the Middle East and non-former-Soviet Asia.

PATTERNS OF SRD AND GRD AGAINST SPECIFIC MINORITIES

The regime-level factors analyzed until now in this chapter provide insight into the causes of GRD but cannot explain a major element of this GRD.

As presented in Tables 4.2a, 4.2b, and 4.2c, nearly all of these states that discriminate, discriminate unequally. That is, some minorities experience more GRD than others. Regime-level factors cannot explain this. In this section, I examine three possible motives for this differential GRD: Islamic ideology, threat perception, and societal religious discrimination (SRD).

As discussed in detail earlier in this chapter, classical Islamic ideology has categories of minorities that are subject to different levels of tolerance. Peoples of the book are tolerated to a point, heretical offshoots of Islam are not, and many religions that fall into neither category are not considered legitimate but are not quite the same as the heretical offshoots. Yet, regardless of theological motivations, in practice some minorities may seem to pose a greater threat than others. Finally, as argued in Chapter 3, I posit that SRD is a cause of GRD, but it is likely that a trigger is required for this relationship to manifest.

Theology versus Threat Perception as Explanations for SRD and GRD

Figure 4.1 presents levels of SRD for each minority group between 1990 and 2014. The categories of minorities included are all those present in at least ten Muslim-majority countries. Clearly, classic Islamic ideology is not the primary driving force behind this form of discrimination because Jews and Christians, the type of minority that is theologically tolerated, are subject to the highest levels of SRD. However, Cesari's (2014, 2018) argument that there is now a general theological hostility to all minorities is an incomplete explanation because it cannot account for the different levels of SRD against different minorities.

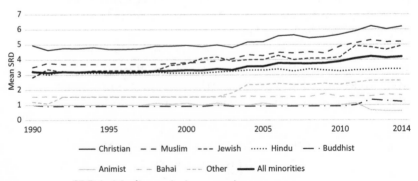

FIGURE 4.1 SRD in Muslim-majority countries, 1990–2014

This means that societal actions toward religions minorities seem to be driven more by threat perceptions. Jews are often associated with Israel, which is considered by many Muslims to be a significant threat to Islam and has been the cause of considerable anti-Semitism among Muslims (Lassner & Troen, 2007; Lewis, 1999). This result for Jews may also be related to more classic anti-Semitism similar to the anti-Semitism found in the West.

Many Muslims perceive the Christian West as a significant threat to Islam (Blaydes & Linzer, 2012; Ciftci & Tezcur, 2016; Huntington, 1996; Mostafa & Al-Hamadi, 2007). This is likely due to world politics where the West is perceived as the world powers that collectively oppressed Islam through colonialism and is currently the obstacle to Islamic power in the world. Miles (2004) argues that many Muslims believe that since the defeat of the Ottomans at the gates of Vienna in 1683, Muslims have experienced a series of defeats and humiliations. To those Muslims who see the world this way, Christians are the enemy in a centuries-old war. Also, Christian missionaries are a source of considerable agitation in many Muslim-majority countries (Fox, 2016). However, most of the other religions listed in Figure 4.1 do not actively proselytize.

Yet Muslim minorities also experience high levels of SRD. This likely reflects Sunni-Shi'i tensions, which often have complex sources that are at least partially theological.

In contrast, the results for GRD in Figure 4.2 show that Hindus, Buddhists, and Bahais experience the highest levels of GRD. Bahais are considered by many Muslims to be a heretical sect, while Hindus are polytheists, and Buddhists are in most Muslim-majority countries not considered a people of the book that is deserving of tolerance. Thus,

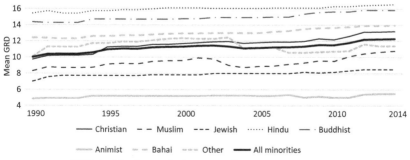

FIGURE 4.2 GRD in Muslim-majority countries, 1990–2014

governments seem to be more influenced by formal Islamic theology on religious minorities than are societal actors. Interestingly, Animists, a polytheistic type of religion, experienced the lowest levels of GRD. This result is largely due to where Animists are located. Eight of the fifteen Animist minorities are located in the West African region that is the most tolerant grouping of Muslim-majority states. Among these eight countries, only Gambia and Chad discriminate at all against Animists with a scores of 1 and 2, respectively. The mean level of GRD for the other seven countries in 2014 is 11.29. Thus, in the case of GRD against Animists, regional culture seems to overshadow theology.

Also, it is noteworthy that both GRD and SRD have been increasing over time. For SRD this was statistically significant for all groups combined as well as for Christian, Jewish, and Muslim minorities. For GRD this was statistically significant for all groups combined as well as all minorities other than Jews and Animists.

SRD as a Cause of GRD

This section analyzes the causes of GRD using both a bivariate and multivariate analysis. While it focuses on SRD as a cause of GRD, the analysis includes multiple potential causes. The findings confirm a strong connection between government religion policy and GRD. SRD is a cause of GRD but only for some minorities. In Muslim-majority states, SRD causes GRD for Christian and Bahai minorities. I posit that this is due to a threat perception trigger for Christians and a theological trigger for the Bahai.

A cross tabulation of SRD and GRD in these counties in 2014 presented in Table 4.3 shows no discernable pattern. However, it is possible that this pattern can emerge when controlling for other factors.

Table 4.4 presents a multivariate analysis of the causes of GRD. It also applies these factors to explain SRD, though with considerably less success. It includes the following independent variables:

- The minority's proportion of the population expressed as a percent. There is some debate on how this influences discrimination in general. On the one hand larger minorities may be perceived as a greater demographic threat to the majority and, accordingly, attract more discrimination. On the other hand, smaller minorities are likely to have less political power, which can make them more vulnerable to

TABLE 4.3 Cross tabulation of SRD and GRD in Muslim majority states in 2014

SRD score \ GRD score	0	1	2	3	4	5	6	7	8	9	10	11	12	13	14	15	16–20	21–25	26–30	30+
0	@@@@ @@@ CCCCM MMMX	CCM M XX @	CMM MM J## X	CC #	M@	@	C@# #	Mb*		XbJ	#	#	X#	C*##		X	CM@b b**X XX	Cb*X	M	CMbX
1	CM*	JC	CCMX		X		b		C	C*	X	C	C				CXX	C*X#	CX	CCM
2	CMb	C		M	C		CM			C	b	M	M	b			MM		CM	CM
3	J	b							C						C				Cb*@X	
4	C			CJ					C	M							CC	CJ		B*
5	C			C													CC	C	C	M
6	C														J		CCM@			CC
7			M														*			
8		M	MM		#				J				J				#			
9										J								M		
10											C			C				M		
11												C		C	M					
12									J			J								
13	*									J										C
14									J											
15											C	C					C			
16								M				C					C			
17				C	M			M												
18								C								C				
19																C				
20																	M			
21+								C								C	*			CMX

C = Christian, M = Muslim J = Jewish, b = Buddhist, * = Hindu, @ = Animist, X = Bahai # = Other.

125

TABLE 4.4 *Multivariate analysis predicting GRD and SRD in Muslim-majority states*

| | GRD | | | | | | | | | | | | SRD | |
| | Model 1 | | Model 2 | | Model 3 | | Model 4 | | Model 5 | | Model 6 | | Model 7 | |
	Beta	Sig.	Beta	Sig.	Beta	Sig.	Beta	Sig.	Beta	Sig.	Beta	Sig.	Beta	Sig.
Minority percent	0.017	.789	0.006	.908	0.020	.745	0.001	.986	0.022	.717	-.011	.869	-0.022	.785
Polity	0.122	.087	0.104	.136	0.105	.135	0.145	.036	0.144	.036	.074	.295	0.113	.214
Regime durability	0.210	.002	0.219	.001	0.220	.001	0.241	.000	0.243	.000	.243	.000	-0.067	.429
Per capita GDP (log)	0.022	.770	0.036	.621	0.036	.622	0.051	.481	0.051	.482	.182	.013	-0.096	.313
Population (log)	-0.035	.610	-0.065	.340	-0.062	.362	-0.060	.375	-0.059	.389	.156	.009	0.182	.038
Religious support	0.353	.000	0.324	.001	0.325	.001	0.311	.001	0.313	.001	–	–	0.191	.129
Regulation of the majority religion	0.384	.000	0.394	.000	0.392	.000	0.399	.000	0.397	.000	.207	.000	-0.051	.657
Regime hostile to religion	0.019	.820	0.018	.824	0.019	.814	0.011	.889	0.012	.883	-.081	.167	-0.002	.986
Regime neutral to religion	0.008	.892	0.032	.589	0.030	.611	0.023	.688	0.021	.715	-.270	.000	-0.147	.055
Official religion: control	0.127	.050	0.118	.064	0.118	.065	0.137	.031	0.136	.033	-.456	.000	0.061	.458
Official religion: mandatory	0.181	.050	0.171	.058	0.169	.062	0.160	.079	0.154	.091	–	–	0.078	.508
Violent and semiviolent minority actions	0.006	.923	–	–	-0.027	.666	–	–	-0.044	.488	-.048	.486	0.222	.006
SRD	–	–	0.145	.010	0.150	.009	–	–	–	–	–	–	–	–
SRD Christian	–	–	–	–	–	–	0.108	.034	0.114	.028	.129	.020	–	–
SRD Muslim	–	–	–	–	–	–	0.088	.105	0.102	.079	.081	.192	–	–
SRD Buddhist	–	–	–	–	–	–	-0.021	.672	-0.021	.684	.024	.651	–	–
SRD Jewish	–	–	–	–	–	–	-0.056	.279	-0.054	.295	-.035	.520	–	–
SRD Hindu	–	–	–	–	–	–	0.015	.766	0.016	.758	.001	.980	–	–
SRD Animist	–	–	–	–	–	–	0.056	.256	0.056	.259	.084	.107	–	–
SRD Bahai	–	–	–	–	–	–	0.208	.000	0.209	.000	.219	.000	–	–
SRD Other	–	–	–	–	–	–	-0.022	.666	-0.020	.685	-.042	.430	–	–
DF	196		196		196		196		196		196		196	
Adjusted R²	.501		.519		.517		.550		.549		.470		.184	

discrimination (Fox, 2016). This data is taken from the RCS dataset (Brown & James, 2017).

- Democratic regimes are generally argued to be more tolerant of religious minorities. I discuss this relationship in more detail in Chapters 5, 7, and 9. I use the Polity score to measure democracy.[5]
- I use the number of years since the last change in the Polity score to measure a regime's durability. When regimes are unstable or in transition conflict and discrimination can be more common (Gurr, 1993, 2000). On the other hand stable and more established regimes may have more resources to engage in discrimination.
- I use the log of per-capita GDP to measure economic development.[6] Past studies have shown that more developed countries engage in higher levels of GRD, perhaps because they have more resources to do so (Fox, 2008, 2015, 2016).
- I control for the country's population using the log of the population[7] because the political dynamics of large and small countries may be different.
- I control for official government religion policy, support for religion, and the regulation of the majority religion using the variables descried in this chapter's discussion. All of these variables are from the RAS3 dataset and integrated into RASM3.
- RASM3 includes a variable including five types of violent or semiviolent actions that can be taken by a minority group against the majority, which I describe in Chapter 3. This is because such actions may provoke a discriminatory reaction.
- I control for SRD using the RASM3 variable, which, as discussed in Chapters 2 and 3, is posited to cause GRD. As I discuss next, the controls for SRD are complex.

This analysis includes seven models. Model 7 uses SRD in 2014 as the dependent variable with all the independent variables described earlier other than SRD. This is to examine whether the causes of GRD and SRD are similar.

Models 1 to 6 use GRD in 2014 as the dependent variable using all the controls discussed earlier, though not all of them in all the models. Model

[5] See Jaggers and Gurr (1995).
[6] These are taken from the World Bank at https://data.worldbank.org/.
[7] These are taken from the World Bank at https://data.worldbank.org/.

1 is a baseline using all variables other than SRD. Model 2 adds SRD (using the average score from 1990–2014 to account for SRD previous to the GRD as a cause). However, it drops the violent and semiviolent actions variable as there is a strong relationship between these two variables. Model 3 adds this variable back into the test. Models 4 and 5 repeat models 2 and 3 but using minority-specific versions of the SRD variable.[8] As I discussed in Chapter 3, the relationship between SRD and GRD can exist for some minorities but not others. This is because its potential often needs a trigger to unlock it. This requires an analysis of whether SRD and GRD are correlated for each minority individually. Model 6 drops the variables for support and regulation of religion because these variables are associated with the variables for official government policy.

All models use four dummy variables for the various official religion policies excluding preferred religion and active official religions. These were excluded because when using a series of dummy variables to measure categories on a larger variable in which each unit of analysis is included exactly once, some categories must be excluded. These two variables contain a sufficient number of cases to meet this requirement and have similar levels of many of the other variables.

The multivariate analysis supports the argument that how a government relates to the majority religion strongly influences GRD. Both support for religion and regulation of the majority religion significantly predict GRD in all models where they are included. The variables measuring official religion policy also significantly influence GRD. That they become more significant in model 6 where support for religion and regulation of the majority religion are dropped emphasizes that official religion policy is strongly related to these factors. That they remain significant in models 1 through 5 shows that they still have independent explanatory value.

SRD is significant in some manner in all the models in which it is included. The general SRD variable is significant in models 2 and 3, replicating the results from Grim and Finke (2011) who found a link between societal discrimination and religious freedom in a country. However, the results in models 4, 5, and 6 show that this relationship exists

---

[8] This is accomplished by setting the variables at 0 for all cases not involving the specific minority, and the SRD score remains as is for those cases that do involve that minority. These variables were calculated by multiplying a dummy variable for the minority in question with SRD.

only for Christian and Bahai minorities. This is consistent with the argument that the relationship between SRD and GRD requires a trigger of some sort to activate it.

In the case of the Christians, as noted earlier, there are two potential triggers. First, many Muslims perceive the Christian West as the enemy and associate Christian minorities with this perceived enemy. Second, Christians are among the most active proselytizers worldwide. That forty-two of the fifty-two (79.8 percent) Muslim-majority countries examined here limit non-Muslim proselytizers in some manner is indicative of this hostility to proselytizing. Both of these triggers can be put into the general category of perceived threats. The likely trigger for the Bahai is their heretical status according to Islamic theology. Governments that might be tolerant of other minorities are evidently more willing to give in to societal pressures regarding a minority that they consider to be a heretical offshoot of Islam. It is likely that this relationship exists for other sects considered heretical by many Muslims such as the Ahmadis, but there are too few cases of these other minorities to test this proposition.

The variables that are not consistently correlated with GRD are as interesting as those that are consistently correlated. Democracy, as measured by the Polity index, is significant only in models 4 and 5. This is important because it is generally assumed that democracies are more tolerant than nondemocracies. Among Muslim-majority states, the causal aspect of this relationship is inconsistent. There are few true democracies in the Muslim world, but Albania, Kosovo, Indonesia, Turkey, and Comoros all score 8 or 9 on a scale of −10 to 10 on the Polity Index and their average scores for support for religion and regulation of the majority religion are lower than other Muslim-majority states.[9] Thus, for these countries, much of democracy's influence on GRD is indirect. That is, it influences elements of government religion policy, which, in turn, influence GRD.

Minority characteristics other than the religion of the minority do not seem to influence GRD. Whether the minority engages in violent actions and the size of the minority are not significantly correlated with GRD in Muslim-majority states.

Regime durability, in contrast, strongly predicts GRD with stable regimes engaging in more GRD. This means that given time and stability

---

[9] These five states score a mean of 14.40 for support and 15.40 for regulation as opposed to 19.31 and 21.48, respectively, for the other forty-eight Muslim-majority states.

Muslim-majority regimes will increasingly discriminate against religious minorities.

The results for SRD as a dependent variable can be better described as a lack of results. The only two variables to predict SRD significantly are the country's population size and if the minority engages in violent or semiviolent actions against the majority. More populous countries have higher levels of SRD. Perhaps this is because in more populous countries members of different groups are less likely to know each other personally. That SRD is more common against minorities that engage in violence is logical. However, only 10.2 percent of minorities in these countries engaged in violent or semiviolent actions against the majority at some point between 1990 and 2014, but 72.6 percent experienced SRD during the same period. Thus, this explanation cannot explain most SRD in these countries.

CONCLUSIONS

It is unwise to generalize about Muslim-majority states and GRD because Islam is a diverse religion with a long history. There are regional and doctrinal differences as well as different histories across groups of Muslims. As shown here, there are Muslim-majority states that are among the most tolerant in the world of religious minorities. Yet others are among the least tolerant.

That being said, there are patterns that emerge when examining the causes of GRD in Muslim-majority states. These patterns overlap with world region indicating that regional history and culture is significant. West Africa has a grouping of extremely tolerant Muslim-majority states, many of which remain neutral on the issue of religion. In addition, several of those that support Islam are nevertheless tolerant of religious minorities. Several former-Soviet states are hostile to Islam and are among the strongest regulators of Islam, or any religion for that matter, in the world. Nearly all Middle Eastern states declare Islam their official religion. Most of them are in the two categories of states that are most strongly connected to religion and engage in the highest levels of GRD.

Taking a broader view, the combination of a country's official religion policy, the extent to which it supports religion, and the extent to which it regulates and controls the majority religion all significantly influence GRD. However, as these are country-level factors, they cannot explain why the countries that discriminate do so differently against different minorities. The extent of SRD provides some explanation for this, but

SRD proves significant only in relation to Christian and Bahai minorities. The former is likely triggered by perceptions of a global struggle between Muslims and Christians as well as Christian proselytizing. The latter is likely triggered by the belief that the Bahai are a heretical offshoot of Islam. Both of these can be considered existential threats. Islam's doctrinal differential tolerance for different religions can also explain some of this variation.

It is interesting that there is no SRD-GRD link for Jews. Jews, due to their association with Israel, could be considered existential threats by regimes in Muslim-majority states. That this phenomenon does not trigger the SRD-GRD link has at least three potential explanations. First, most Jewish minorities in Muslim-majority states are very small. This is because most Jews who lived in Muslim countries were expelled after the creation of the state of Israel, and few remain. Second, most of the remaining Jewish populations are indigenous and predate the formation of the state of Israel, so it is possible they are not strongly associated by the regime with the Israeli threat. Third, it is possible that these regimes do not consider Israel an existential threat.

Population size of the minority is not a factor. The extent to which minorities engage in violence against the majority is also, surprisingly, not a direct influence. However, as it influences SRD, it is an indirect influence.

That democracy is, at most, a weak influence on GRD in Muslim-majority countries is perhaps even more surprising, given that there is an expectation that democracies are more tolerant of minorities than non-democracies. While democracy is correlated with aspects of religion policy that influence GRD (Fox, 2015), given that there is still a wide variation of government religion policies among democracies, this is a tenuous and indirect link between democracy and GRD at best. This weak correlation between democracy and tolerance is a theme that is found in other world regions, and I discuss it more comprehensively in subsequent chapters.

5

Non-Orthodox Christian-Majority Democracies in the West and Europe

This chapter focuses on Western democracies and those former-Soviet Christian-majority democracies that do not have Orthodox Christian majorities. As this is a somewhat awkward label for a group of states, I refer to them in this chapter as European and Western non-Orthodox Christian-majority democracies (EWNOCMD). For operational purposes I define democracy here as any state that scores 8 or higher on the Polity index which measures countries on a scale of −10 (most autocratic) to 10 (most democratic) (The Polity Project, 2018). I include countries with no polity score if the Freedom House democracy index determined them to be "free" (Abramowitz, 2018).

This grouping of states consists of twenty-four Western democracies and nine democracies in the former-Soviet bloc. These states share a world region, a democratic regime, and a Christian majority, though there is some religious heterogeneity due to denominational differences within Christianity. Many of them are joined into a common framework by organizations such as NATO and the European Union. They also share a common history and culture. I exclude the Orthodox-majority countries from this grouping because, as I demonstrate in Chapter 6, these states have patterns of discrimination that are considerably different from those of EWNOCMD states.

Even when focusing on this relatively homogeneous group of states, the causes of discrimination are complex. There is no single cause that can explain all types of discrimination. Rather, there are multiple and sometimes crosscutting influences on levels of discrimination. Also, the combination of causes and influences on discrimination as well as patterns of discrimination can be different for different types of minorities.

Among the EWNOCMD countries, I argue that six factors influence government-based religious discrimination (GRD). (1) States with neutral religion policies engage in less GRD, but there is no discernable difference in GRD levels among the countries with nonneutral policies. (2) Muslim minorities, when perceived as a security threat, experience higher GRD. (3) Societal religious discrimination (SRD) can be a cause for GRD but only for Muslim minorities. (4) Secular ideologies can result in policies that restrict some religious practices, especially for Jews and Muslims. (5) Anticult policies often explicitly restrict religions perceived as cults. (6) Many countries restrict religious minorities that they see as foreign or not part of the national culture. While anti-Semitism is an important factor in predicting SRD, it has no discernable influence on GRD in these countries. However, in other parts of the world, there is a link between anti-Semitism and GRD.

In this chapter, I also consider the assumption that Western liberal democracies ideologically support religious freedom in theory and provide it in practice in light of the fact that no country examined in this chapter other than Canada fails to engage in at least some GRD. This, combined with findings in Chapters 7 and 8 that Christian-majority countries in the developing world, whether or not they are democratic, have lower levels of discrimination than do EWNOCMD states call into question these basic assumptions regarding the nature of liberal democracy.

STATE-RELIGION BONDS AND RELIGIOUS DISCRIMINATION

In Chapter 4, I demonstrated a strong link between government religion policy and GRD among Muslim-majority states. This link is present in EWNOCMD states but manifests differently and arguably less robustly. As shown in Tables 5.1, 5.2a, and 5.2b, while the U-shaped pattern where those states most supportive of and most hostile to religion engage in higher levels of GRD holds, this "U" is less pronounced. Part of this may be because these states have a narrower range of diversity in their government religion policies.

The one pattern that is similar to Muslim-majority states is that the five states that have neutral policies have low levels of GRD. Among the twenty-nine religious minorities in these countries, only eight are subject to any GRD. Only two of these score higher than 1. Muslims in the US score 2 because since 2002, just after the September 11, 2001, attacks,

TABLE 5.1 *Mean levels of religious support, religious regulation, SRD, and GRD in EWNOMD states in 2014 controlling for official religion*

| | Official religion policy | | | | | |
	Hostile	Neutral	Multiple religions preferred	One religion preferred	Active official religion	Official religion: Control
Religious support	6.00	6.40	9.67	10.25	11.00	17.00
Regulation of the majority religion	11.00	1.60	5.42	3.00	4.67	17.00
SRD	6.33	3.76	3.79	2.28	2.79	2.75
GRD	3.83	0.41	3.56	3.29	2.91	4.75
No. of countries	1	5	12	8	6	1
No. of minorities	6	29	48	35	24	4

For religious support and regulation of the majority religion the unit of analysis is a country. For SRD and GRD the unit of analysis is a minority.

many local governments began making it difficult to open mosques, and both the national government and many local governments began surveillance programs on Muslims. Muslims in the Netherlands scored 3. This is mostly because of government monitoring of and restrictions on imams. The state monitors imams who preach intolerance or support for the Islamic State. The government requires all imams and other spiritual leaders recruited in Islamic countries to complete a year-long integration course before permitting them to practice ("Muslim Clerics," 2014). In addition, Dutch courts do not consider it discrimination when employers refuse to hire or fire employees who do not conform to "reasonable" expectations even if the reason for the refusal is religious. This includes expectations, such as shaking hands with the opposite gender in meetings, adhering to work schedules, attire issues, or trimming one's beard to fit company policy. The government may reduce the social assistance bene-fits of those who are unemployed due to this type of issue (European Commission against Racism and Intolerance, 2013; US Department of State, 2009).

There is little difference in the mean scores for the various countries in the multiple religion preferred, one religion preferred, and active official religion categories. These categories also constitute twenty-six of the thirty-three EWNOCMD countries. Yet there is variation. Most of them engage in at least moderate levels of GRD against at least one minority. However, eight states – Andorra, Estonia, Finland, Lithuania, Luxembourg, Malta, Poland, and Slovenia – engage in levels of GRD no higher than 2 against any minority. As this includes at least two states in each of the three categories, government religion policy does not explain this phenomenon. However, it can be said that all these states, other than Finland, are either among the smallest states in the region or located in the former-Soviet bloc. While this result is consistent for Europe's smallest states, other former-Soviet bloc countries such as Croatia, the Czech Republic, and the Slovak Republic engage in high levels of GRD against at least some of their religious minorities.

France is the only country among the EWNOCMD states that is hostile to religion. France has higher levels of GRD than the mean for the states in the multiple religion preferred, one religion preferred, and active offi-cial religion categories. However, several states in these categories, includ-ing Germany and Sweden, have levels of GRD comparable to France. Similarly, the only country among the EWNOCMD states that has an official controlled religion is Denmark. Like France, while its mean levels of GRD are relatively high, its score is similar to several of those in other categories. Given this, the key difference in government religion policy among these states is whether or not a state is neutral toward religion.

One possible explanation for this is that among the nonneutral EWNOCMD states – those that either are hostile to religion or support it – have levels of hostility or affinity to religion that are less pronounced than found in many Muslim-majority states. Comparing the results in Table 5.1 to the same scores for Muslim-majority states on Table 4.1 shows that for all variables in all nonneutral categories the scores are as high or higher for Muslim-majority states. Put more generally, when government polices engage with religion, this engagement tends to be more intense in Muslim-majority states as compared to EWNOCMD states. This suggests that there is a deeper connection between religion and politics on Muslim-majority countries than in EWNOMCD states.

PATTERNS OF DISCRIMINATION WITHIN EWNOCMD STATES

While government religion policy provides at best an incomplete explanation for difference in GRD between EWNOCMD states, discrimination within EWNOCMD states – that is, which minorities are likely to experience higher GRD and SRD – follows more concrete patterns. Figure 5.1 shows mean levels of SRD over time. This analysis looks at Christian, Muslim, Buddhist, and Jewish minorities as well as all other minorities in a single "other" category because no other minority living in this grouping is present in a sufficient number of states for meaningful analysis as a separate category.

Jewish minorities, by far, experience the highest levels of SRD in these countries. In 2014, SRD against Jews was well over double the mean and 51.7 percent higher than Muslims, who experienced the next highest levels of SRD. The gap between Muslims and all non-Jewish minorities is even more profound than the gap between Muslims and Jews. The "other" category experienced the third-highest levels of SRD, and these levels were approximately one-fifth and one-third of those experienced by Jews and Muslims, respectively, in 2014.

Australia provides a good example. Since 2008, anti-Semitic incidents have been particularly high. In any given year, this includes hundreds of instances of vandalism, harassment, and threats of violence. One of the most notorious incidents involved a gang of youths who traumatized Jewish kids on a school bus in Sydney in August 2014 with anti-Semitic slurs and threats to slit their throats. Six minors were arrested after the incident. There were also multiple reports of physical attacks and arson.

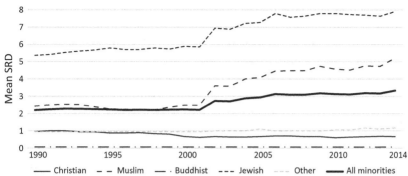

FIGURE 5.1 Mean levels of SRD 1990 to 2014 in EWNOMD states
Significance of change between 1990 and marked year for all minorities <.05 in
2003, <.1 in 2002 and 2004, <.001 in 2005–2014
Significance of change between 1990 and marked year for Muslims <.05 in
2002 and 2003, <.01 in 2004 and 2005, <.001 in 2005–2014
Significance of change between 1990 and marked year for Jews <.05 in
1992–1995 and 1999–2001, <.01 in 2002–2005 and 2010, <.001 in 2006–2009
and 2011–2014
Significance of change between 1990 and marked year for "other" minorities
<.05 in 2012
Significance of difference between Christians and all other groups <.05 in
1990–1998, <.01 in 1999, <.001 in 2000–2014
Significance of difference between Muslims and all other groups <.05 in
2010–2014
Significance of difference between Buddhists and all other <.001 in 1990–2014
Significance of difference between Jews and all other groups <.001 in 1990–2014
Significance of difference between "other" minorities and all other group <.05 in
2007–2014

In addition, anti-Semitic behavior in public was common. For example, in April 2012, Cardinal George Pell, Archbishop of Sydney, made disparaging comments about Jews during a public debate. In August 2012, a popular radio host made a Holocaust-related joke on the air. Also, a Jewish man won a compensation claim after being the victim of anti-Semitic bullying and harassment while employed at the Taxation Office in 2009 (Anti-Defamation League, 2013; Goldberg, 2014; World Jewish Conference, 2009).

Incidents against Muslims were present but less common. There were multiple reports of discrimination, especially in employment, against Muslim women wearing Hijabs or other Islamic dress. There were reports of vandalism, but far less than against Jews. However, a police raid against suspected terrorists in 2014 resulted in a backlash of hate crimes against Muslims including vandalism, verbal abuse in public, and anti-Muslim social media comments (Doorley, 2014; Kozoil & Abdallah, 2014; US Department of State, 2009; WAToday, 2014). There were no reports of SRD against other religious minorities in Australia.

Patterns of change over time differed across groups in EWNOCMD states. Levels of SRD against Buddhists and "other" groups remained mostly stable over time. Levels of SRD against Christian minorities dropped to 69.6 percent of their 1990 levels by 2014. Levels of SRD against Jews and Muslims both jumped in 2002 and continued to rise thereafter. By 2014 levels of SRD against Jews and Muslims increased by 47.5 percent and 115.0 percent, respectively.

The rise of SRD against Muslims in the Netherlands is one of the more dramatic examples. Until after the events of September 11, 2001, levels were relatively low. After this, incidents of harassment began to increase. The catalyzing instance of physical violence against Muslims occurred in November 2004 following the killing of Dutch filmmaker and critic of Islam Theo van Gogh by a Dutch Muslim extremist. Following the killing, there were numerous minor incidents including physical violence. There were also waves of arson attacks against Mosques following both the September 11 and van Gogh attacks. The founding of Geert Wilders's anti-Muslim Freedom Party resulted in an additional escalation. The first incidence of local opposition to building a Mosque occurred in 2007. SRD against Jews in the Netherlands also rose during this period, but the causes are less obvious. However, it is likely that the extreme right-wing organizing activity against Muslims spurred by the van Gogh attacks is also at least partially responsible for increased attacks against Jews.

On a more general level in EWNOCMD states, this rise was driven by a rise in a significant number of categories of SRD. Seventeen of the twenty-seven categories of SRD rose substantially against both Jews and Muslims between 1990 and 2014. Some categories of SRD also became more common for only one of these minorities. Publications circulated against a minority and harassment so severe that it caused a substantial number of the minority to leave the region rose against Jews only. There was also a substantial rise in societal efforts to prevent the opening of mosques but not synagogues. The other seven types of SRD were at zero or levels near zero for both minorities for the entire period. This rise was also widespread across countries. SRD rose against Jews in twenty-four of thirty-three countries but dropped in Croatia, the Czech Republic, and

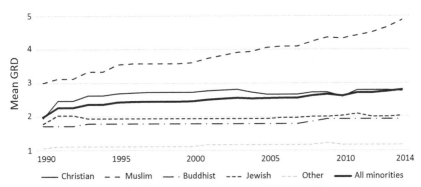

FIGURE 5.2 Mean levels of GRD 1990 to 2014 in EWNOMD states
Significance of change between 1990 and marked year for all minorities <.05 in
2001, 2004–2007, and 2010, <.01 in 2002–2003, 2008–2009, and 2011–2013,
<.001 in 2014
Significance of change between 1990 and marked year for Christians <.05 in
1997–2003
Significance of change between 1990 and marked year for Muslims <.05 in
2003–2007, <.01 in 2008–2011, <.001 in 2012–2014
Significance of difference between Muslims and all other groups <.05 in
2011–2014

Estonia. It rose against Muslims in twenty-two countries but dropped in
Croatia.

Thus, this rise in SRD against Jews and Muslims in EWNOCMD
countries was both broad and deep with one important exception, the
East-West divide. SRD against Muslims and Jews rose considerably in
Western democracies but not in the former-Soviet states. In former-Soviet
states, SRD against Jews remained high throughout the study period but
rose only by 9.6 percent compared to a 77.8 percent rise in Western
democracies. SRD against Muslims increased by 156.6 percent in Western
democracies but dropped by 35.1 percent in the former-Soviet states.
Thus, it is precisely in long-standing liberal democracies where SRD
increased.

As shown in Figure 5.2, patterns of GRD are different. Muslims, by
far, experience the highest levels of GRD. In 2014 GRD against Muslims
was 87.0 percent higher than against Christians, who experienced the
second-highest levels of GRD. Levels of GRD against all other categories
of religious minority were substantially lower than those against Christians and at similar levels to each other. While overall, GRD increased
over time with statistical significance, this was mostly driven by increases
against Christian and Muslim minorities.

This phenomenon of increasing GRD against Muslims is robust. Unlike SRD, which jumped in 2002 then continued to rise, this rise was consistent over the entire 1990–2014 period. As shown in Tables 5.2a and 5.2b, GRD against Muslims increased in twenty-three of the thirty-three countries in this grouping but dropped in Croatia, Estonia, and Spain. Unlike SRD, GRD against Muslims increased substantially in both Western democracies and former-Soviet states, but the increase was more substantial in Western democracies. Of the thirty-five types of GRD included in RASM3, eighteen increased against Muslims, and only limitations on clergy access to hospitals and prisons dropped. Fourteen types were not present at all against Muslims. Restrictions on religious burial remained present but stable.

Switzerland provides a good example of rising GRD against Muslims. This rise is at least partially due to the rise of the anti-immigrant and anti-Muslim Swiss People's Party. Perhaps the most dramatic shift in Switzerland was the 2009 national referendum that banned minarets on mosques, which was a major part of the Swiss People's Party agenda. However, such bans already existed in several of Switzerland's Cantons, and many local governments denied permits to build mosques well before this referendum. While there have been numerous attempts by local governments to ban wearing head coverings in schools, these bans have been consistently struck down by the courts. However, Switzerland's Supreme Court allowed a rule requiring female Muslim students to attend swim classes even if the teacher is male. The court stated the girl could wear a modest bathing suit, but that the need to promote integration, equal education, and socialization justified the minor violation of the freedom of religion (Copley & Bart, 2015; Cumming-Bruce & Erlanger, 2009).

Overall, the patterns of discrimination show disproportionate and rising SRD against Jews and Muslims as well as disproportionate and rising GRD against Muslims and Christian minorities in these countries.

THE MULTIPLE, CROSSCUTTING, AND COMPLEX CAUSES OF DISCRIMINATION IN EWNOCMD STATES

What explains these patterns of discrimination? More specifically, what explains why some minorities in EWNOCMD states experience more discrimination than others? I posit that several factors can explain much of this variance: the securitization of Islam, the SRD-GRD link, anti-Semitism, and several additional cultural factors. That is, these factors

TABLE 5.2A *Levels of SRD and GRD in EWNOCMD states*

		SRD			GRD	
		1990	2014	Avg.	1990	2014
Hostile						
France	Buddhists	0	0	0.00	0	0
	Jehovah's Witnesses	3	6	3.24	13	13
	Jews	15	25	19.68	0	0
	Muslims	7	7	6.28	4	7
	Orthodox Christians	0	0	0.00	0	0
	Protestants	0	0	0.00	2	3
Neutral						
Australia	Buddhists	0	0	0.00	0	0
	Hindus	0	0	0.00	0	0
	Jews	15	17	15.24	0	0
	Muslims	7	10	7.64	1	1
Canada	Buddhists	0	0	0.00	0	0
	Chinese religions	0	0	0.00	0	0
Multiple religions preferred						
Austria	Eastern Orthodox	0	0	0.00	0	0
	Jehovah's Witnesses	0	0	0.04	1	0
	Jews	11	14	13.20	0	0
	Mormons	1	1	1.00	1	1
	Muslims	3	7	4.32	1	3
Belgium	Protestants	0	0	0.00	1	1
	Buddhists	0	0	0.00	1	1
	Jews	2	20	10.76	0	1
	Muslims	8	12	9.16	1	3
	Other Christians	0	0	0.00	0	1
Czech Republic	Jews	15	13	13.92	2	2
Estonia	Muslims	6	9	7.00	7	8
	Jews	1	0	0.57	0	0
	Muslims	0	0	0.00	0	1

(*continued*)

141

TABLE 5.2A (continued)

Country	Religion	SRD 1990	SRD 2014	SRD Avg.	GRD 1990	GRD 2014
	Hindus	0	0	0.12	0	0
	Jews	7	11	9.80	0	0
	Muslims	3	8	5.68	0	0
	Protestants	0	0	0.00	0	0
	Sikhs	0	0	0.04	0	0
Netherlands	Buddhists	0	0	0.00	0	1
	Hindus	1	1	1.00	0	1
	Jews	1	10	6.00	0	1
	Muslims	3	11	6.74	0	4
	Protestants	0	0	0.00	0	1
New Zealand	Buddhists	0	0	0.00	0	0
	Hindus	0	0	0.00	0	0
	Jews	0	3	0.68	0	0
	Muslims	0	1	0.48	0	1
	Sikhs	0	1	0.20	0	0

Country	Religion	SRD 1990	SRD 2014	SRD Avg.	GRD 1990	GRD 2014
Germany	Jews	19	21	20.80	1	1
	Muslims	9	13	11.20	12	17
	Orthodox Christians	0	0	0.00	0	0
	Scientologists	15	15	15.00	11	11
Hungary	Jews	11	12	11.64	0	1
	Muslims	0	0	0.04	0	2
	Orthodox Christian	0	0	0.00	0	2
	Protestants	0	0	0.00	0	7
	Jehovah's Witnesses	0	0	0.00	5	8
Latvia	Jews	0	3	2.08	2	1
	Muslims	0	0	0.00	3	8
Lithuania	Jews	5	5	5.37	2	1
	Muslims	0	0	0.00	1	2
	Orthodox Christians	0	0	0.00	1	1
	Protestants	0	0	0.08	1	1

Country	Religion					
USA	Bahai	0	1	0.08	0	2	2
	Buddhists	0	0	0.00	0	2	2
	Catholics	1	2	1.16	0	2	2
	Hindus	0	2	0.52	0	2	2
	Jews	16	17	16.08	0	1	1
	Mormons	0	0	0.00	0	2	2
	Muslims	2	14	6.36	2	0	0
	Orthodox Christians	0	0	0.00	0	0	0

Country	Religion					
Luxembourg	Jews	0	1	0.28	2	2
	Muslims	0	1	0.08	2	2
	Orthodox Christians	0	0	0.00	2	2
	Protestants	0	0	0.00	2	2
Slovenia	Jews	1	1	1.04	1	1
	Muslims	1	1	1.04	2	2
	Orthodox Christians	0	0	0.00	0	0
	Protestants	0	0	0.00	0	0
Switzerland	Buddhists	0	0	0.00	2	2
	Hindus	0	0	0.00	2	2
	Jews	6	7	6.40	4	4
	Muslims	0	4	2.12	5	12

TABLE 5.2B *Levels of SRD and GRD in EWNOCMD states*

One religion preferred

		SRD			GRD	
		1990	2014	Avg.	1990	2014
Andorra	Hindus	0	0	0.00	0	0
	Jews	0	1	0.04	0	0
	Muslims	0	0	0.04	0	1
	Protestants	0	0	0.00	0	0
Croatia	Jews	9	7	7.66	11	9
	Muslims	11	3	4.50	12	8
	Orthodox Christians	35	19	24.60	11	4
	Other Christians	4	4	4.00	9	8
	Protestants	0	0	0.04	9	8
Ireland	Jews	0	1	0.40	2	2
	Muslims	0	3	0.28	2	2
	Protestants	0	0	0.00	1	1
Italy	Buddhists	0	0	0.00	0	0
	Jews	0	8	2.72	0	0
	Muslims	0	3	2.16	6	9
	Orthodox Christians	0	0	0.00	0	0
	Protestants	0	0	0.00	0	0
Poland	Jews	10	13	11.64	1	2
	Muslims	0	0	0.20	0	1
	Orthodox Christian	0	0	0.16	1	2
	Other Christians	0	0	0.00	2	2
	Protestants (Lutheran)	0	0	0.00	1	2

Active official religion

		SRD			GRD	
		1990	2014	Avg.	1990	2014
Finland	Jews	2	6	4.4	1	2
	Muslims	6	7	6.44	1	2
Iceland	Orthodox	0	0	0	1	1
	Catholics	0	0	0	1	1
	Jews	0	0	0.08	3	3
	Muslims	0	3	0.88	3	3
	Pagans	0	0	0	1	1
Liechtenstein	Jews	0	2	0.72	2	2
	Muslims	0	5	2.04	3	3
	Protestants	0	0	0	2	2
Malta	Jews	0	0	0	0	0
	Muslims	2	4	2.04	1	2
	Other Christians	0	0	0	0	0
Norway	Buddhists	0	0	0	7	8
	Catholics	0	0	0	8	8
	Jews	2	2	2.4	9	9
	Muslims	2	6	2.4	11	12
UK	Buddhists	0	0	0	1	1
	Catholics	3	1	2.56	0	0
	Hindus	0	0	0.04	1	1
	Jews	12	16	13.36	1	1
	Muslims	6	15	10.2	1	5

Portugal	Spiritists	0	0	0.00	1	2
	Buddhists	1	1	1.00	3	3
	Jews	1	1	1.08	3	3
	Muslims	1	1	1	3	3
	Other Christians	0	0	0	3	3
Slovak Republic	Jews	6	6	5.82	1	1
	Muslims	0	0	0.05	12	12
	Orthodox Christians	0	0	0	0	0
	Other Christians	0	0	0.05	7	7
	Protestants	0	0	0	7	7
	Christians (non-Catholic)	0	0	0.04	6	6
Spain	Jews	2	4	3.2	6	3
	Muslims	0	5	2.64	6	4
	Orthodox Christians	0	0	0	0	0
	Sikhs	0	0	0.04	2	2
Official religion: Control						
Denmark	Buddhists	0	0	0	3	3
	Catholics	0	0	0	3	3
	Jews	2	3	2.6	3	5
	Muslims	2	8	5.08	4	8

combine to cause discrimination in conjunction with each other and are not competing explanations.

The Securitization of Islam in EWNOCMD States

Securitization theory posits that when a minority is perceived as a security threat, this can attract discrimination. This phenomenon has the potential to explain the high relative levels of GRD and SRD against Muslims in EWNOCMD states. The theoretical and empirical literature on the topic strongly supports this claim. In fact, much of it was developed specifically to explain why levels of discrimination against Muslims in the West have been so high in seeming contrast to the West's liberal democratic ideals. The central argument is that a process of "securitization" can occur if a group or minority is perceived as an existential threat. This securitization of the group lifts policy toward the group from normal politics to extraordinary politics (Buzan et al., 1998; Mabee, 2007; Wæver, 1995, 2011). "The theory suggests that a state representative can 'securitize' an issue by invoking 'security'. 'Securitized' issues are lifted above normal ordinary politics and moved from normal to emergency politics. They are assigned an urgency that requires extraordinary measures to eliminate the threat" (Fox & Akbaba, 2015: 176). This justifies actions taken against the perceived security threat that under normal circumstances would be illegitimate.

Many argue that Islam has become securitized in the West (Cesari, 2013; Donnelly, 2007; Gearty, 2007; Razack, 2008). For example, Chebel d'Appollonia (2015: 2) argues along these lines that

since the 1990s, the categories of "new comers," "illegal immigrants," "bogus" asylum seekers, and "suspicious minorities" have been increasingly conflated in the media and general public discourse. Western governments have responded to concerns raised by the so-called new immigration (itself a euphemism for "non-European") by linking immigration policy to other high profile issues.

While these issues include job security, drug trafficking, and other types of crime, terrorism and other security issues are particularly important. Muslims are not the only immigrant minority to trigger these perceptions, but they are the minority most closely associated with terrorism, the issue most likely to be securitized. Thus, the reasons for and nature of securitization can be complex, but its presence is difficult to deny. In addition, religious threats are particularly likely to attract securitization in secular societies (Laustsen & Wæver, 2000). While many, like Cesari (2013) and

Chebel d'Appollonia (2015), trace the roots of the securitization of Muslims to the 1990s, their discussions of its impact focus mostly on post-2001 policies.

It is difficult to argue that any of the twenty-seven types of acts included in the SRD variable increase security, but they certainly can be motivated by the fear and prejudice associated with the securitization process. As shown in Figure 5.1, SRD against Muslims was stable from 1990–2001, then jumped in 2002 and continued to rise through 2014. This has some interesting implications. First, whatever was motivating SRD against Muslims until the end of 2001, when the events of 9/11 occurred, whether it was securitization or other factors, these factors were consistent over the 1990–2001 period. The timing of the rise in SRD against Muslims is consistent with what we would expect if 9/11 provoked or increased a securitization-motivated response from the public.

Securitization is also a plausible explanation for GRD. However, 9/11 was not the first attack by Muslim terrorists on the West. That GRD rose steadily throughout the 1990–2014 period, as shown in Figure 5.2, is consistent with a perception among policy-makers that Muslims pose a security threat. Securitization theory at its core focuses on exclusionary immigration policies and extraordinary security procedures and laws. Yet many of the types of GRD present against Muslims in these countries have little connection to security or immigration and, rather, limit religious freedom.

Cesari (2013) argues that when a minority is hypersecuritized, governments can place limitations on it that do not directly relate to security. Some of the limitations placed on Muslims that fit this description include restrictions on Halal slaughter of meat, Muslim women wearing their traditional head coverings, and the building of new mosques. Other policies such as increased surveillance and arrest, detention, and harassment can, in theory, be linked to security but are often applied beyond any justifiable security concern. In fact, these restrictions can arguably undermine security by agitating and radicalizing the targeted minority.

The securitization argument is a top-down argument. It focuses on elite speech acts that justify government policy.[1] While it is possible to argue that these elite speech acts can also motivate societal behavior and prejudice, including those measured by RASM3's SRD variable, the thrust of the literature has focused on government actions. It is, accordingly, an

---

[1] There are exceptions to this in the literature. For example, Cesari (2013) investigates practices of discrimination more than speech acts.

argument designed to explain acts by governments such as GRD. Thus, that GRD is higher against Muslims than against any other minority is consistent with this theory. That SRD is high, but not as high as it is against Jews does not contradict the theory. This is because nothing in the securitization argument precludes other causes of discrimination.

Helbling and Traunmuller (2015: 3–5) argue that state support for religion leads to a more cultural and identity-based trigger for religious discrimination against Muslims:

> These institutional settings are important because when the political, social, and cultural life of a public is defined by strong references to religious tradition, religious minorities pose a direct threat to this collective identity. Their practices are not easily accommodated because this would entail a loss in what is essentially perceived a zero-sum game. Under institutional conditions of state support of religion, accommodating new religious minorities involves the changing of existing rules as well as the loss of long-standing traditions, valuable privileges, and maybe even everyday habits ... Muslim immigrants' religious practices and claims for religious rights are the decisive features of this particular group that trigger the feelings of cultural threat in citizens of the host society.

I posit that the securitization argument is most likely responsible for the lion's share of the rise in both SRD and GRD against Muslims. The timing of the rises in both forms of discrimination is consistent with this argument. The cultural issue also likely plays a role. As immigration increases, the numbers of Muslims in EWNOCMD countries and Muslims become a more "visible" minority, this cultural impetus to discrimination likely increases.

The SRD-GRD Link and Securitization

SRD also has a role to play in explaining the securitization of Islam. As noted in Chapter 3, Grim and Finke (2011) posit that societal attitudes and prejudices are a cause of government restrictions on religious freedom. I argue, also in Chapter 3, that when looking at specific minorities the SRD-GRD link will only be present when a trigger activates it. In Chapter 4, I demonstrate that this dynamic occurs in Muslim-majority states where the SRD-GRD link is activated only for Christian and Bahai minorities.

An examination of the cross-tabulation of SRD and GRD in Table 5.3 reveals that the SRD-GRD link is also present for only some minorities in EWNOCMD states. The SRD measure appears to be correlated with SRD only for Muslim minorities. While this is certainly not a perfect one-to-

TABLE 5.3 *Cross-tabulation of SRD and GRD in 2014 controlling for religious minorities in EWNOMD states*

SRD score \ GRD score	0	1	2	3	4	5	6	7	8	9	10	11	12	13	17
0	CCCC CCCC CCCC CCJJbb bbbb ######	CCCC CCCC MMbb b##	CCCC CCCC MMb# ##		CCCjb			C	CC	CCC CCC Mbb				M	
1	CMJ##	MJ##	MMJ		MJb										
2	C#														
3	J	J	M	M	M	M	J			M	J			M	
4				M	J	M				C	M			M	
5		J			M										
6		J	J	M		J								M	
7					M				M	M	J				
8	M									M					
9															
10		MJ													
11	J					M						M	J		
12		J			M								J		
13				JJ											
14	J		M				M						#		
15							M								M
16		J													
17	JJ														
19						C									
20		J													
21	J														
25	J														

C = Christian, M = Muslim, J = Jewish, b = Buddhist, # = Other.

one correlation, in general higher SRD predicts higher GRD for Muslims. This is not the case or other minorities. For example, seventeen Jewish minorities experience levels of SRD that are 5 or higher. Yet, of these seventeen Jewish minorities, only those in Croatia and Sweden, also experience levels of GRD that are 5 or higher. Thus for Jews, high SRD, in most cases, does not predict high GRD.

This lack of correlation is even stronger for the other minority categories. Only five of the forty-six Christian minorities in these countries experience any SRD at all, but thirty experience GRD. Among the fourteen Buddhist minorities, only one experiences SRD but eight experience GRD. Among the twenty minorities in the "other" category, three experience SRD but no GRD, and five experience GRD but no SRD. Three experience both.

Table 5.4 presents a multivariate analysis predicting GRD and SRD in EWNOCMD states using mostly the same control variables used in Chapter 4 but with some differences due to the differences between the problem sets. I added a control for Catholic-majority states because of posited differences between Catholic and Protestant state religion policies (Anderson, 2007; Martin, 1978; Philpott, 2007; Woodbury & Shaw, 2012). I also did not include the Polity variable because all of these countries are democracies, so there is very little variation on that variable. Finally, I included only the neutral official government religion policy variable because this is the only category that differs from the others in EWNOCMD states.

The results confirm the securitization of Islam argument. All but two of the fourteen minorities that engaged in violent and semiviolent actions (VSVA) between 1990 and 2014 were Muslim. The exceptions are Orthodox Christians in Croatia, who engaged in considerable violence between 1990 and 1994 in the civil war that occurred during the breakup of Yugoslavia and an incident in Switzerland, where Hindu fundamentalists tried to burn Bibles and Korans in front of the Parliament building in Bern. Thus, that VSVA is strongly and significantly correlated with GRD in all models in which it is included indicates that GRD is higher precisely against those Muslim minorities whose members engage in actions that can contribute to a perception that they pose a security threat.

While the evidence is weaker, there are indications that SRD causes GRD for Muslims. The general SRD variable does not significantly predict GRD. Thus, when looking only at a global analysis of minorities in EWNOCMD countries, Grim and Finke's finding of a SRD-GRD

TABLE 5.4 *Multivariate analysis predicting GRD and SRD in EWNOMD states*

	GRD											SRD	
	Model 1		Model 2		Model 3		Model 4		Model 5		Model 6		Model 6	
	Beta	Sig.	Beta	Sig.	Beta	Sig.	Beta	Sig.	Beta	Sig.	Beta	Sig.	Beta	Sig.
Minority percent	0.085	.239	0.144	.062	0.086	.236	0.080	.283	0.072	.324	0.046	.539	−0.070	.398
Regime durability	−0.175	.164	−0.211	.120	−0.171	.178	−0.165	.201	−0.155	.217	−0.145	.265	−0.214	.137
Per capita GDP (log)	0.062	.545	0.108	.319	0.062	.543	0.087	.405	0.062	.542	0.117	.260	0.075	.521
Population (log)	0.071	.404	0.101	.279	0.066	.448	0.075	.397	0.056	.518	−0.047	.572	0.283	.004
Majority Catholic	−0.305	.026	−0.331	.026	−0.300	.031	−0.267	.059	−0.268	.051	0.010	.925	−0.215	.168
Religious support	0.136	.193	0.150	.183	0.138	.189	0.160	.137	0.149	.155	0.347	.000	−0.118	.324
Regulation of the majority religion	−0.084	.374	−0.072	.479	−0.084	.381	−0.067	.488	−0.082	.390	0.064	.464	−0.061	.574
Regime neutral to religion	−0.458	.001	−0.453	.002	−0.455	.001	−0.413	.002	−0.427	.001	−	−	−0.148	.322
Violent and semiviolent minority actions	0.335	.000	−	−	0.331	.000	−	−	0.255	.005	0.243	.010	0.260	.002
SRD	−	−	0.086	.268	0.017	.822	−	−	−	−	−	−	−	−
SRD Christian	−	−	−	−	−	−	0.076	.284	0.045	.523	0.048	.508	−	−
SRD Muslim	−	−	−	−	−	−	0.283	.000	0.129	.154	0.161	.085	−	−
SRD Buddhist	−	−	−	−	−	−	0.037	.603	0.036	.608	0.038	.599	−	−
SRD Jewish	−	−	−	−	−	−	−0.066	.371	−0.064	.374	−0.045	.547	−	−
SRD Other	−	−	−	−	−	−	0.154	.032	0.158	.025	0.176	.015	−	−
DF	145		145		145		145		145		145		145	
Adjusted R^2	.315		.213		.310		.299		.335		.285		.101	

connection is not confirmed.[2] However, in the models with minority-specific SRD variables, SRD is a predictor of GRD for Muslims and "other" minorities but not Christians, Buddhists, and Jews. For Muslims it is significant at the .001 level for model 4 and at the .1 level in model 6. The model in which it is most significant is the one that excludes the VSVA variable, which indicates that while there is a SRD-GRD link for Muslim minorities in these countries, it is overshadowed by VSVA.

Given this, I posit that the SRD-GRD link for Muslims in EWNOCMD countries is triggered by the securitization of Islam, especially in countries where Muslims engaged in violence against the majority religion. This is consistent with similar patterns in other groupings of states where the SRD-GRD relationship is only present for some religious minorities, usually those that pose some form of perceived existential threat to the majority.

For "other" minorities, the SRD-GRD relationship is significant at the .05 level for all three models in which it is included. However, this is largely driven by a single outlier, Scientologists in Germany. Many governments, including Germany's, consider Scientologists a cult. This provides some confirmation for the impact of anticult policies and attitudes on discrimination and that the SRD-GRD dynamic applies in these countries to cults. However, given the small number of such groups in RASM3, this result cannot be considered definitive. I discuss the issue of cults in more detail later.

The only other variable consistently significant in predicting GRD is whether the country has a neutral official religion policy. The regulation of the majority religion, which is relatively low in most of these countries, does not significantly influence GRD. Support for religion is significant only in the model that omits the official religion variable. This confirms that in these countries having a neutral policy toward religion reduces GRD but otherwise the specifics of government religion policy do not significantly influence GRD in EWNOCMD states.

Anti-Semitism

Anti-Semitism is the first of four cultural explanations for GRD in EWNOCMD states that I propose here. Across the entire Christian

---

[2] Barr (2014) similarly fund no correlation between societal and governmental restrictions on religious minorities in Western democracies when examining Grim and Finke's (2011) data.

world, anti-Semitism has historically been a motivation for discrimination against Jews. Both the European Parliament Working Group on Anti-Semitism and the US Department of State rely on the International Holocaust Remembrance Alliance (IHRA) definition of anti-Semitism as "a certain perception of Jews, which may be expressed as hatred toward Jews" (IHRA, 2018). Former UK Chief Rabbi Jonathan Sacks defines anti-Semitism as follows:

Antisemitism means denying the right of Jews to exist collectively as Jews with the same rights as everyone else. It takes different forms in different ages. In the Middle Ages, Jews were hated because of their religion. In the nineteenth and early twentieth century they were hated because of their race. Today they are hated because of their nation state, the state of Israel. It takes different forms but it remains the same thing: the view that Jews have no right to exist as free and equal human beings. (Sacks, 2016)

Sacks argues that whatever is considered the highest authority in a society is used to justify anti-Semitism, and Jews are accused of whatever is considered the most despicable crime one can commit in a society. For example, in a capitalist society, Jews are called Communists but in a Communist country Jews are called capitalists. So, anti-Semitism, like a virus, mutates as its host changes. It began with traditional religious hatred for the religious other. It mutated into the social Darwinism and "racial studies" of the Nazis. "Today the highest source of authority worldwide is human rights. That is why Israel ... is regularly accused of the five cardinal sins against human rights: racism, apartheid, crimes against humanity, ethnic cleansing and attempted genocide" (Sacks, 2016).[3]

Numerous polls show that anti-Jewish attitudes and prejudices are present in Europe and the West.[4] Studies find a correlation between anti-Jewish attitudes and negative attitudes toward Israel (Kaplan & Small, 2006). The presence of these negative attitudes predicts hate crimes against Jews (Brackman, 2012). While this correlation is by no means absolute, both anti-Jewish and anti-Israel attitudes have increased in recent years. This correlation manifests in multiple incidents where European Jews are attacked in reaction to incidents that occur in Israel, essentially blaming all Jews for Israeli actions. "Accusing Jews as a people

[3] For a detailed discussion of how "pathological" fantasies of Judaism are deep-rooted in the Western tradition, see Nirenberg (2013).
[4] See, for example, the ADL Global 100 study at http://global100.adl.org/ and the Simon Wiesenthal Center's reports on anti-Semitism at www.wiesenthal.com/.

of being responsible for real or imagined wrongdoing committed by a single Jewish person or group, or even for acts committed by non-Jews" is one of the examples of anti-Semitism listed by the IHRA (US Department of State, 2016). The Muslim population in Europe and the West is also increasing. Muslims are more likely than Christians to hold negative opinions of Jews. Additionally, anti-immigrant political parties and politicians are becoming increasingly popular and are likely to express anti-Semitic attitudes (Tausch, 2014).

As shown in Figures 5.1 and 5.2, while SRD against Jews is substantially higher in these countries than against any other minority, GRD against Jews is lower than GRD against Muslim and Christian minorities and similar to levels found against Buddhist and "other" minorities. Thus, in EWNOCMD countries, the anti-Semitism explanation for discrimination applies to SRD but not GRD. I posit that the legacy of the Holocaust deters GRD against Jews. Western governments make overt efforts to combat anti-Semitism. While there is no binding international treaty or document specifically banning anti-Semitism (Sabel, 2016), in 2017 the European Parliament approved a resolution calling on EU member states to adopt the working definition of anti-Semitism developed by the IHRA. This resolution also urges EU member states to "protect their Jewish citizens and Jewish institutions from hate crime and hate speech; support law enforcement efforts to identify and prosecute anti-Semitic attacks ... [and] appoint national coordinators on combating antisemitism."

Secular-Religious Clashes

This is not to imply that there is no GRD in Europe and the West against Jews. Some of this GRD is part of a clash between the secular-liberal ideology popular in many Western countries and Jewish theology. This is part of a larger competition between secular and religious values that is occurring worldwide. Across the world, including EWNOCMD countries, secular and religious political actors try to influence government policy in accordance with their values. This dynamic is especially pertinent to Muslim and Jewish minorities in EWNOCMD countries. Some types of GRD against Jews and Muslims can be explained by religious acts that are considered by some to be in contradiction with European and Western secular ideology (Fox, 2015, 2019). I propose that this type of secular-religious clash is a second cultural explanation for GRD in

EWNOCMD states that is present against some religious minorities but not others.

For example, several Western European countries – Denmark, Germany, Iceland, Norway, Sweden, Switzerland, and as of 2019 Belgium – limit ritual slaughter because it is considered cruel to the animals and requires a form of stunning of animals that makes ritual slaughter impossible. Jews and Muslims require ritual slaughter for all meat they eat. This is what makes meat Kosher for Jews and Halal for Muslims. However, many believe that Kosher and Halal slaughter are cruel to animals and should be banned. These beliefs have become law in several countries. All of these countries allow Kosher and Halal meat to be imported. Other countries have similar requirements to stun animals but allow exemptions for religious slaughter. These include Austria, Cyprus, France, Luxembourg, the Netherlands, and Spain.

One interesting example of this trend occurred in Lower Austria, one of Austria's nine states, in July 2018. The Cabinet Minister in charge of animal welfare proposed allowing Kosher meat to be sold only to Orthodox Jews who will require a permit to purchase the meat. Minister Waldhäusl "claimed the proposal was 'from the point of view of animal welfare' and that religious rites slaughter should 'generally be rejected'" (Embury-Dennis, 2018).

While few countries do so, there is also a growing movement to ban circumcision of male children, a ritual central to both Judaism and Islam. In June 2012 this issue rose to the fore when a German court ruled that the Jewish and Muslim practice of circumcision inflicts "grievous bodily harm" on young boys. The judge ruled that "the fundamental right of the child to bodily integrity outweighed the fundamental rights of the parents" to perform the religious ritual of circumcision. This ruling technically was limited to a single jurisdiction and applied only to one Muslim boy whose procedure led to complications. However, the ruling raised fears that circumcision might be banned in the entire country, and doctors and hospitals across Germany suspended the procedure. In December 2012, Germany's Lower House settled the issue by passing a law allowing circumcision (Dempsey, 2010; Eddy, 2012; Kulush, 2012).

Since 2001 Sweden regulates male circumcision. Circumcision of male infants must be performed by a licensed doctor or if someone certified by the National Board of Health and Welfare (NBHW) attends. The NBHW has certified mohels (persons trained to perform the Jewish ritual of circumcision) to perform circumcisions, but they may do so only in the presence of an anesthesiologist or other medical doctor. This places a significant burden on performing the ritual (Deisher, 2013; Ritual Circumcision Ban," 2014; "Sweden Restricts," 2001; US Department of State, 2013). Denmark passed a similar law in 2005 (Dons, 2014) as did Norway in 2014 (JTA, 2014). Advocacy groups and politicians in Denmark, Finland, Norway, Sweden, and Iceland have called for bans on male infant circumcision.

It is likely that those motivated by more classical anti-Semitism and anti-Muslim sentiment use these secular-liberal arguments to advocate banning ritual slaughter and circumcision as a politically correct cover for their less politically correct sentiments (Kortmann, 2018). However, many who support these types of GRD are clearly motivated by belief that they are pursuing a moral agenda. In many ways this is similar to a majority religion that imposes its belief system and laws on religious minorities that do not share their beliefs. One example of this sentiment was expressed by Anne de Greef, director of the Global Action in Interest of Animals, a Belgian animal rights group who disagrees with the insistence of Muslim and Jewish religious authorities that stunning of animals is incompatible with religious slaughter. "They want to keep living in the Middle Ages and continue to slaughter without stunning – a technique that did not exist back then – without answering to the law ... Well I'm sorry, in Belgium the law is above religion, and that will stay like that" (Schreuer, 2019).

For this reason, secular belief systems are a second cultural explanation for discrimination in EWNOCMD countries.

Anticult Policies

The third cultural explanation for GRD in EWNOCMD states considered here is anticult policies. I discussed the definition of the term *cult* in more detail in Chapter 2. Based on RAS3 codings, among the EWNOCMD countries, only Belgium, France, Germany, Latvia, and the Slovak Republic have explicit anticult policies. Belgium and France began monitoring and restricting cults in response to mass suicides by religious groups. Their official lists of cults include

groups more commonly considered cults such as the Church of Scientology, the Unification Church, and Jehovah's Witnesses. Both lists also include groups that are considered more mainstream elsewhere. In France the list includes Mormons, Seventh-Day Adventists, and Pentecostals. In Belgium it includes Seventh-Day Adventists, Zen Buddhists, Mormons, Hassidic Jews, and the YWCA.

(Fox, 2016: 42)

While most religions that are considered cults have too few members in these countries be included in RASM3, the Scientologists in Germany and the Jehovah's Witnesses in France and Latvia are included. GRD against these groups is substantial. In Germany, for example, Scientology is not illegal, but Scientologists are heavily monitored and restricted by the government. A Federal Constitutional Court ruling allows the government to deliver "accurate warnings and information" on cults. Germany's Office for the Protection of the Constitution monitors Scientologist activities and maintains a list of members' names for use in citizenship and employment proceedings because it considers Scientology a cult that threatens democracy. Most major German political parties ban Scientologists from being members. In several German states and cities, multiple government documents include a section where applicants must declare no connection with the Church of Scientology. This includes documents for business permits, government contracts, and applications for public-sector jobs. This type of attitude is also present in German society. The Roman Catholic and Protestant churches in Germany have "sect commissioners" who warn the public of alleged dangers from the Church of Scientology and other cults. There are also multiple reports that employers ask job applicants to confirm are not Scientologists (Baig, 2013; Seiwert, 2004).

Nationalism and Protection of Culture

A fourth potential cultural explanation for the patterns of discrimination in these states that restrict some minorities differently from others is nationalism and protection of culture. This type of argument focuses on hatred of those who belong to a culture other than one's own. This is distinct from discrimination motivated by religious belief. In this case, the key element is culture in general in which certain religions are included and others are considered to not be part of the national culture.

For example, Huntington (1993, 1996), in his "clash of civilizations" theory, argues that most conflict will be between different world cultures largely, though not exclusively, defined by religion. He specifically argues that there will be considerable conflict between the West and Islam. The arguments in the more Western and European-specific literature posit that a combination of religious, demographic, anti-immigrant, and racial prejudices can single out a minority, especially if that minority is perceived as failing to assimilate (Carol et al., 2015; Helbling, 2014). This prejudice divides minorities into those that have a legitimate historical presence in a country and those that do not. Minorities that do not have this type of legitimate historical presence are more likely to be targets of discrimination. For instance, Helbling and Traunmuller (2015: 3) argue that "when the political, social, and cultural life of a public is defined by strong references to religious tradition, religious minorities pose a direct threat to this collective identity. Their practices are not easily accommodated because this would entail a loss in what is essentially perceived a zero-sum game."

While this type of argument can, in theory, apply to any non-Western religious minority, the literature focuses on Muslims. Huntington (1993, 1996) predicts that clashes between the Western and Islamic civilization will be particularly intense. Others, such as Bowen (2010), Kuru (2009), and Fetzer and Soper (2005), make a similar argument but for different reasons. They posit that Western secularism is the source of a bias against Muslims who are perceived as disproportionally nonsecular.

Yet the results presented in this chapter reveal this explanation as problematic. While it is consistent with levels of both SRD and GRD against Muslims, many other religious minorities are not historically part of Western or European culture. Buddhists, for example, experience almost no SRD and levels of GRD that are well below the mean. Minorities in the "other" category, including Hindus, Sikhs, and Bahai, none of which can be considered indigenous to these countries, also experience low levels of both SRD and GRD. On the other hand, Jews are generally considered to be indigenous to these countries but experience high levels of SRD. While none of this rules out that cultural factors might be exacerbating discrimination against Muslims, it does show that it is unlikely that this type of cultural impetus is the primary cause of discrimination in these countries.

The Complexity of Discrimination in EWNOCMD Countries

A recurring theme in this study is that the causes of discrimination are complex and crosscutting. Among EWNOCMD countries, government religion policy, securitization, anti-Semitism, securitization, nationalism, the protection of indigenous culture, anticult policies, violence by religious minorities, and secular-religious clashes all combine to influence both SRD and GRD. SRD is also a cause of GRD if a trigger is present. In this case, the evidence shows that securitization acts as a trigger for Muslims. The exact mix of causes likely differs from country to country and may include other country-specific factors such as local history and the influence of specific political parties and movements. Also, that this grouping of states is uniformly democratic likely plays a role, but as I discuss in the next section, this role is evidently less influential than many would assume.

THE FLAWED ASSUMPTION OF LOW DISCRIMINATION IN THE WEST

The substantial levels of SRD and GRD in EWNOCMD countries run counter to assumptions of religious freedom and secularity in the West. That is, there is a general assumption that religious freedom – which includes a lack of GRD and perhaps also SRD – is an essential trait of Western liberal democracies and to a lesser extent the democracies of the former-Soviet bloc. In addition, as I discuss in more detail in Chapters 7 and 8, Christian-majority states in the developing world, even those that are not democracies, have levels of both SRD and GRD that are lower than that found in EWNOCMD countries. This poses a conundrum of why reality differs from this widely held assumption.

There are several reasons for this assumption. Some of these explanations focus on how specific strands of Christianity inspired increased religious tolerance. Martin (1978: 25–49), for example, argues religious tolerance in the West is due to factors inherent in the rise of Protestantism. Protestantism altered the religion-state relationship because Protestant denominations were less likely to have the symbiotic relationship with the state that had previously been the case when the West was mostly Catholic. Theologically, Protestantism focuses more than Catholicism on individualism. Consequently, Protestants are less likely to put the Church above the state. Similarly, the doctrine of election found in some Protestant theologies evolved into the concept of free grace, which, in turn, led to support for universal rights. The Protestant Reformation also resulted in religious pluralism, which led to increased religious tolerance. Like Martin (1978), Woodbury and Shaw (2012) argue that Protestantism promotes major foundations for democracy, including an independent civil society, pluralism, mass education, economic development, reduced corruption, and religion's independence from the state.

Philpott (2007) and Anderson (2007) focus on evolving Catholic ideology in the twentieth century. They argue that Vatican II (1962–1965) caused basic changes in the Catholic Church. It has become more supportive of democracy, tolerant of religious minorities, more explicitly and actively supportive of human rights and socioeconomic justice, and more tolerant of religious minorities. Also, the Church became less involved in local politics, leaving more room for democracy.

These theories, while intended to explain liberalism and tolerance in the West, in practice focus on Christianity in general. Because of this, they fail to explain why these processes would, in theory, apply more to the West and Europe than to Christian-majority democracies in the developing world. However, they may help to explain why, as I demonstrate in Chapters 7 and 8, developing world Christian-majority countries are among the most tolerant of religious minorities in the world.

Another body of theory emphasizes Western culture and ideals that are posited to support religious freedom, often as a consequence of secularism. These cultural trends, especially secularism, are contrasted to those of the non-West. Usually this contrast is implicit, but it is sometimes explicit. Calhoun (2012: 86), for example, argues that "the tacit understanding of citizenship in the modern West has been secular. This is so despite the existence of state churches, presidents who pray, and a profound role for religious motivations in major public movements." Cesari (2014: 1) similarly argues that "drawing on the historical experience of Western countries, an academic consensus has emerged that modernization, democratization, and secularization are inextricably linked in any process of political development."

Huntington (1993, 1996) is perhaps the most obvious example of the academic consensus noted by Cesari (2014). He explicitly argues that these characteristics are unique to the West. "The separation and recurring clashes between the church and state that typify Western civilization have existed in no other civilization. The division of authority contributed immeasurably to the development of freedom in the West" (Huntington, 1996: 75). There is no shortage of concurring arguments. Appleby (2000: 2) argues that "the core values of secularized Western societies, including freedom of speech and freedom of religion, were elaborated in outraged response to inquisitions, crusades, pogroms, and wars conducted in the name of God." Demerath and Straight (1997: 47) argue that "there is no question that the secular-state secular-politics combination is often associated with Western Europe in particular." Inboden (2013: 164) more directly contrasts the West and non-West. "The post-Enlightenment tradition in the West of treating religion as an exclusively private and personal matter sometimes prevents policymakers from perceiving the public and corporate nature of religion in many non-Western societies."[5]

---

[5] Others focus their arguments on contrasting the West and the Muslim world (e.g., Facchini, 2010; Hefner, 2001: 492–493; Hurd, 2007: 349; Tibi, 2000), but this is not pertinent to differences between Christian-majority democracies.

To a great extent, this assumption also rests on secularization theory – the prediction that modernity will reduce the influence of religion in government and society.[6] While in the past this theory was applied more universally, since the 1990s many have begun to argue that this process of secularization is specific to the West. Berger (1996/1997, 2009), for example, argues that while religion is resurging across the world, Western and Central Europe and certain intellectual circles are an exception. Marquand and Nettler (2000: 2) argue that "Western Europe appears to be an exception . . . Organized religion almost certainly plays a smaller role in politics in 2000 over most of the territory of the European Union than it did in 1950." Haynes (1997: 709) similarly argues that "secularization continues in much of the industrialized West but not in many parts of the Third World."[7]

A final but related body of theory argues that various political and social processes unique to the West have led to increased secularization and religious freedom. Haynes (1997, 1998, 2009) argues that Western governments have co-opted and subordinated religious institutions and instituted equality policies. Crouch (2000) argues that the trauma of past religious wars and increased individualism and liberalism among Europeans has led to a rejection of religion in politics. In addition, European churches have had to adapt to increased liberal ideals by focusing their theologies more on tolerance. Kuhle (2011) argues that this is what occurred in Sweden, Norway, Denmark, Finland, and Iceland but due to government pressure in addition to changing ideals. The governments of these countries forced their national (Lutheran) churches to adopt more liberal policies on a wide variety of issues, including gay marriage and the ordination of women.

Taylor (2007) focuses more on the evolving nature of religious belief and argues that religion no longer legitimizes the state in the West because the West has shifted from "a society where belief in God is unchallenged . . . to one in which it is understood to be one option among others" (Taylor, 2007: 3). Norris and Inglehart (2004) arrive at a similar conclusion but base their arguments on economics. Developed countries, including the West, have what they call existential security. This means

---

[6] For a review and discussion of the theory, see Fox (2015) and Gorski and Altinordu (2008).
[7] See also Bruce (2002, 2009), Halman and Draulan (2006), Kaspersen and Lindvall (2008), and Voicu (2009), among others.

that people no longer need worry about basic issues like food, shelter, and safety. This decreases the need for religion.

The findings presented in this chapter contradict all these assumptions. They call into question either our understanding of essential traits of liberal democracies or whether many countries we consider to be liberal democracies are, in fact, liberal democracies. Whether motivated by anti-Semitism, anticult sentiment, culture, or security concerns, among other motivations, many minorities in these countries experience significant restrictions on their religious freedom.

However, they do get one thing partially correct. States that are neutral on the issue of religion do have lower levels of GRD in EWNOCMD countries. This is also true across the world. What they get wrong is that most of the EWNOCMD countries are not neutral on the issue of religion. In fact, as we will see in Chapters 7 and 8, a higher proportion of Christian-majority states in Asia, Africa, and Latin America are neutral than are EWNOCMD countries, even among nondemocracies.

This finding is part of a growing literature that is falsifying the assumption of secularism and religious freedom in the West. For example, Minkenberg (2017: 2) argues that

for a long time, the so-called Western world has been interpreted as undergoing a long-term process of secularization or decline of religion. However, there is sufficient empirical evidence to demonstrate that religion, even in the Western world, is a power that shows no sign of vanishing and assumes a new significance in an ever more complex and diverse world.

Most of the literature does not address the issue head on but, rather, simply investigates the role of religion in politics in the West and elsewhere.

In Chapter 7, I discuss explanations for why SRD and GRD are less common in non-Western and European democracies than in EWNOCMD countries. In Chapter 8, I discuss why many nondemocracies also have lower levels of GRD and SRD.

As for EWNOCMD countries, I do not dispute that modernity and the political and social forces that advocate secularization are important. Nor do I dispute that democracy has a tendency to support toleration. Rather, I argue that there are two counterbalancing forces. First, religious political actors remain active and compete with the advocates of secularism (Fox, 2015, 2019). Second, the multiple, complex, and crosscutting causes of discrimination that I discuss in this chapter are sufficiently influential to cause discrimination despite the influence of democracy and secular political actors.

6

Orthodox, Buddhist, and Communist States

The causes of discrimination are complex, diverse, and crosscutting. This is further complicated by the fact that the multiple causes of government religious discrimination (GRD) manifest differently in different settings. This chapter examines levels of GRD in an eclectic group of states: Christian-Orthodox-majority states, Buddhist-majority states, and Communist states. While this may seem to be an odd grouping of states, there are at least four commonalities between them. First, each of these groupings contains relatively few states. Second, GRD is distinctly common in these states and high in many of them, though the reasons for this differs across groupings. Third, some form of ideology and government religion policy both play a strong role in causing GRD in these states, but the many other causes of GRD also play an important role. Fourth, as I discuss later, GRD against Christians is particularly high in these countries. Orthodox-majority states focus this GRD on Christian denominations they consider nonindigenous, mostly North American protestant denominations. The Buddhist-majority and Communist states seems more generally hostile to Christians, most of whom they also consider nonindigenous and in some cases a threat to the state.

Like the other groupings of countries I examine in this book, each of these three groupings of countries has clear characteristics that differentiate it from all the other countries in the world. In the case of Orthodox-majority and Buddhist-majority states, it is the majority religion. In the case of Communist states, it is the state's guiding ideology. The states within each of these groupings share additional commonalities and distinct patterns of GRD that differentiate them from all of the other groupings of states I examine in this study.

ORTHODOX-MAJORITY STATES

Orthodox-majority states are characterized by high levels of conformity across countries in government religion policy and high levels of GRD. All but one of the Orthodox-majority states are in the same general geographic region as the European and Western non-Orthodox Christian-majority democracies (EWNOCMD) states discussed in the previous chapter, and many of them are democratic, but patterns of GRD are very different in these states than the patterns in EWNOCMD states. Briefly, as shown in Tables 6.1 and 6.2, GRD is more common and consistently higher. In fact, only three religious minorities in these states – Catholics in Ukraine and Catholics and Jews in Montenegro – experienced no GRD. This is true regardless of factors like world region, level of democracy, and the nature of religion-state bonds. I argue that this is due to a combination of societal religious discrimination (SRD), the desire to protect indigenous culture, and agitation against religious minorities by Orthodox clergy and institutions.

State Religion Bonds, Regime, and GRD

The pattern of state-religion bonds in Orthodox-majority states differs from those in Muslim-majority states and EWNOCMD states in its specifics. However, it follows the general cross-state-grouping pattern where neutral states engage in less GRD than those that support religion or are hostile to it, though there are no states classified as hostile to religion among Orthodox-majority states. Ten of the fourteen Orthodox-majority states fall into the one religion preferred category. Given this relative uniformity of government religion policy and the small number of countries in other categories, any discussion of the impact of state-religion bonds on GRD should not be taken as conclusive. This is not to say that this factor is uninfluential. Rather, there are simply too few cases and too little diversity on religion policy for the assumptions of statistical probabilities to hold.

That being said, the impact appears to be similar to other groupings of states examined in this study, though it manifests uniquely. For these states, the key difference seems to be whether the government prefers one religion, but whether that preference is official or unofficial does not make a large difference. Ethiopia and the Ukraine are neutral on the issue of religion. While all but one minority in these countries experience GRD,

TABLE 6.1 Levels of SRD and GRD in Orthodox-majority states

		SRD 1990	SRD 2014	SRD Avg.	GRD 1990	GRD 2014
Neutral						
Ethiopia (Polity = -3)	Animists	0	0	0.00	5	5
	Catholics	0	0	0.00	4	3
	Muslims	3	3	3.28	2	6
	Other Christians	0	0	0.00	4	3
	Protestants	7	7	7.16	5	4
Georgia (Polity = 7)	Armenian Apos.	7	7	7.16	14	16
	Jehovah's Wit.	22	22	22.08	21	27
	Jews	1	1	1.24	9	14
	Muslims	2	3	2.61	14	20
	Other Christians	10	10	10.37	20	25
Ukraine (Polity = 4)	Catholics	1	1	1.08	0	0
	Jews	4	9	6.56	1	1
	Muslims	0	1	0.64	3	4
	Other Christians	6	7	6.12	2	4
	Protestants	0	0	0.00	2	1
Multiple religions preferred						
Macedonia (Polity = 9)	Catholics	0	0	0.00	3	4
	Jews	0	0	0.08	2	3
	Muslims	1	1	1.46	6	6
	Other Christians	0	0	0.08	9	11
	Protestants	0	0	0.00	8	7
Moldova (Polity = 9)	Jews	8	5	5.50	6	6
	Muslims	2	7	2.96	11	7
	Other Christians	11	13	12.58	12	12
Montenegro (Polity = 9)	Catholics	0	0	0.44	0	0
	Jews	0	0	0.00	0	0
	Muslims	0	0	0.33	2	3
	Other Orthodox	4	4	4.00	3	3
Romania (Polity = 9)	Catholics	9	10	9.72	7	9
	Jews	6	8	7.96	4	5
	Muslims	0	0	0.00	6	6
	Protestants	5	7	6.04	11	12

(continued)

165

TABLE 6.1 (*continued*)

One religion preferred

		SRD			GRD	
		1990	2014	Avg.	1990	2014
Armenia *Polity = 5*	Catholics	1	1	1.00	12	13
	Jews	6	5	5.76	12	13
	Muslims	1	1	1.00	12	13
	Other Christians	17	21	21.20	29	31
	Protestants	11	13	13.16	12	14
	Yedzis	3	4	4.00	12	13
Belarus *Polity = -7*	Catholics	0	0	0.20	21	22
	Jews	10	10	10.75	22	24
	Muslims	1	1	1.04	19	20
	Non-Cath. Chr.	6	6	6.91	34	41
Bulgaria *Polity = 9*	Catholics	0	0	0.00	8	11
	Jews	5	6	5.72	9	11
	Muslims	7	7	6.84	16	21
	Other Christians	16	16	16.24	13	18
Cyprus *Polity = 10*	Jews	2	5	2.64	4	5
	Muslims	0	5	2.48	3	5

		SRD			GRD	
		1990	2014	Avg.	1990	2014
Russia *Polity = 4*	Animists	0	0	0.00	0	21
	Buddhists	0	0	0.00	2	2
	Catholics	4	4	4.00	2	15
	Hindus	0	0	0.04	3	17
	Jews	18	18	18.24	2	4
	Muslims	4	6	4.76	4	12
	Other Christians	17	17	17.60	6	34
Serbia (Yugoslavia) *Polity = 8*	Catholics	1	1	1.00	1	3
	Jews	4	4	4.32	1	3
	Muslims	0	0	0.24	0	2
	Other Christians	5	5	5.16	7	12
	Protestants	0	0	0.04	5	9
Positive state controlled religion						
Greece *Polity = 10*	Jews	13	14	13.76	13	13
	Muslims	13	13	13.12	17	18
	Non-Orth. Chr.	1	1	1.00	12	14

TABLE 6.2 *Mean levels of religious support, religious regulation, SRD, and GRD in Orthodox-majority states in 2014 controlling for official religion*

		Official religion policy		
	Neutral	Multiple religions preferred	One religion preferred	Official religion: Control
Religious support	6.50	8.00	8.87	15.00
SRD 2014	2.80	1.00	5.53	9.33
GRD	3.10	1.50	13.38	15.00
-Democracies	–	1.50	8.08	15.00
-Nondemocracies	3.10	–	18.91	–
No. of countries	2	1	10	1
No. of minorities	10	4	47	3
Comparison to GRD for				
Muslim-majority	0.08	5.72	8.57	14.39
EWNOCMD states	0.38	3.56	3.28	4.75

the levels are low relative to those states that give preference to the Orthodox Church.

In Ethiopia, much of this GRD is by local governments. Local officials often discriminate against Protestants on access to cemeteries and against both Muslims and Protestants when they seek land to build places of worship. Some GRD is at the national level. All religions other than the Orthodox Church, Catholics, and Jews are required to register to be legal. The government does not issue work visas to foreign religious workers unless they are associated with the development arm of a registered religious organization. Since 2011, the government has been harassing and arresting Muslims it considers radical or disruptive (Baptist Mid-Missions, n.d.; Bruguière, 2012).

GRD levels in the Ukraine are also low relative to most Orthodox-majority states. Muslims in Kiev have a cemetery, but it has inadequate burial space. Crimean Tatars have difficulty registering their religious organizations, and there is some government propaganda against them. There are also various forms of harassment against small Christian sects such as the Jehovah's Witnesses.

Montenegro recognizes four religions, which it treats mostly equally – the Montenegrin Orthodox Church, the Roman Catholic Church (since 2011), the Jewish community (since 2012), and the Islamic Community (since 2012). There are some limitations on nonrecognized religious communities, including the Serbian Orthodox Church. The police actively prevent Serbian Orthodox clergy and faithful from entering certain Orthodox churches. The government regularly denies visas and residency permits to Serbian Orthodox clergy. The government restricts and harasses Muslims it considers radical, calling them Wahhabis.

In the ten countries that prefer Orthodox Christianity but do not declare it the official religion, all forty-seven minorities experience GRD. All but thirteen of them experience levels of GRD that are eleven or higher, and only Cyprus lacks a minority that experiences levels of GRD of eleven or higher. GRD in Greece, the only Orthodox-majority country that designates its Orthodox Church as its official religion, engages in levels of GRD consistent with the ten countries that unofficially prefer Orthodox Christianity over other religions.

Interestingly, while democracy plays a role in these findings, its impact seems to be less than that of religion-government bonds. The two neutral states with low levels of GRD – the Ukraine and Ethiopia – are non-democracies. Among the states that prefer Orthodox Christianity, democratic states, on average, engage in less GRD, but all of them engage in substantial levels. In fact, the mean level of GRD in Orthodox-majority democracies that prefer the Orthodox Church is about the same as countries that prefer Islam and considerably higher than in EWNOCMD countries in this category.

Patterns of Discrimination against Specific Minorities

Levels of SRD between 1990 and 2014 in these countries are presented in Figure 6.1. SRD in this grouping of states is far higher than in EWNOCMD countries. As is the case in EWNOCMD countries, SRD is highest against Jews. Interestingly, SRD against Christian minorities is nearly as high as SRD against Jews. As shown in Table 6.1, this finding is driven largely by SRD against denominations seen as nontraditional or nonnative to the region. In most of these countries, SRD against Catholics is relatively low. In Armenia, Bulgaria, Moldova, Russia, and Serbia these groups, classified as "other Christians," all experience higher levels of SRD than other Christian denominations in the same country included in RASM3. In Georgia, "other Christians" and Jehovah's Witnesses experience more SRD than Catholics and Armenian Apostolistic Christians. These findings are likely driven by a combination of anti-Semitism and

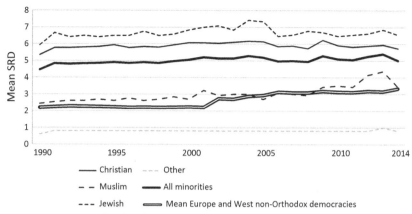

FIGURE 6.1 Mean levels of SRD 1990 to 2014 in Orthodox-majority countries

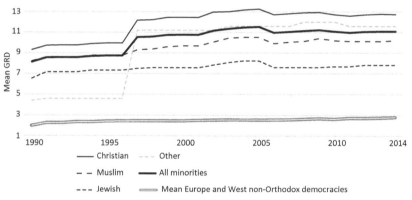

FIGURE 6.2 Mean levels of GRD 1990 to 2014 in Orthodox-majority countries

the desire to protect one's culture from religions perceived as nonindigenous.

As presented in Figure 6.2, patterns of GRD show some similarities and some differences with those for SRD. Like SRD, GRD is considerably higher in these countries in this grouping of states than in EWNOCMD countries. In fact, each minority type in Orthodox-majority states experiences higher mean levels of GRD than the mean level in EWNOCMD countries.

For most of the period, GRD against Jews is lower than against any other minority. Until 1997 it was lowest against "other" minorities.

This changed with a large jump in GRD against Hindus in Russia because of Russia's 1997 Law on Freedom of Conscience and Religious Associations. The law acknowledges Christianity, Islam, Judaism, Buddhism, and other religions as constituting an inseparable part of the country's historical heritage and recognizes the "special contribution" of Orthodoxy to the country. However, it places significant restrictions on all other religions (Immigration and Refugee Board, Canada, 1997).

This type of law that either recognizes certain religions as indigenous and legitimate but allows others to be restricted or requires some minority religions to register with the government but not others is common in Orthodox-majority countries. This type of law or policy is present in Cyprus, Ethiopia, Macedonia, Montenegro, Romania, Russia, and Serbia. Moldova has no such law explicitly but in practice consistently denies registration to groups such as the Pentecostal Church, the Falun Gong, Jehovah's Witnesses, and some Muslim groups. These types of laws and arrangements are particularly, but not exclusively, targeted against nonindigenous Christian denominations, especially North American denominations. This is why Christian minorities experience the highest levels of GRD. Like SRD, GRD tends to be present but lower against Christian groups usually considered indigenous such as Catholics.

Explaining Patterns of GRD in Orthodox-Majority Countries

Anti-Semitism plays a similar role as it does in EWNOCMD countries. SRD is high against Jews in a region where anti-Semitism has been present historically. However, governments seem to avoid GRD against Jews. Likely, they do so for the same reasons as EWNOCMD countries, which I discuss in more detail in Chapter 5.

Table 6.3 presents a cross-tabulation of SRD and GRD. It shows that SRD predicts GRD for some minorities, particularly Christians. While there are too few cases for a multivariate analysis, bivariate correlations confirm this finding. The correlation between SRD and GRD is significant only for Christian minorities (correlation = .633. significance = .000). It is marginally significant for Muslim minorities (correlation = .492, significance = .096).

As will be recalled, I argue that SRD is an influence on GRD only in the presence of a trigger. In this case, I posit that there are two related triggers. The first is a desire to protect indigenous culture. Both SRD and GRD tend to be higher against religious minorities considered new and nonindigenous to these countries. This is especially true of North

TABLE 6.3 *Cross-tabulation of SRD and GRD in 2014 controlling for religious minorities Orthodox Christian-majority countries*

	GRD score														
SRD score	0	1	2	3	4	5	6	7	9	11	12	13	14	15-19	20+
0	CJ	o	M#	CoMJ	C	#	oM	o	o	C				#	C#
1	C			C	M		M	o	o		C	M	J		M
3				o			M								M
4						MJ	J		J			#		C	
5						J						J			
6											o	o			o
7								M		J	M			o	M
8				oo							o				
9													o		
10									C						oJ
13											o				
14					J										
15-19														o	o
20+															oo

C = Catholic, o = Other Christian M = Muslim J = Jewish # = Other.

American Christian denominations, many of which attempt to proselytize actively in these countries. Many government and societal actors simply consider these outside religious influences unwelcome. As noted earlier, many Orthodox-countries have laws or policies designed specifically to restrict or deny benefits to nonindigenous religious.

The second trigger is the Orthodox Church and clergy. While the evidence is anecdotal, there is no shortage of incidents where Orthodox clergy and institutions instigate or participate in both GRD and SRD. To be clear, the examples I present here focus on cases where there is direct evidence that Orthodox clergy or institutions are directly involved in acts of GRD or SRD. In all these countries, there are additional instances where the Orthodox Church and clergy likely influence discrimination, but clear evidence of a direct link is lacking. Also, while these incidents tend to focus on nonindigenous Christian denominations, other religious minorities are targeted by Orthodox institutions and clergy.

In Greece, there are multiple reports of Greek Orthodox clergy verbally and physically harassing proselytizers, often Mormons. Local Orthodox bishops often spread messages of religious intolerance, such as issuing a list of minority religious groups and practices that they consider "sacrilegious" and harmful to Orthodox worshipers ("Church Responsible for Bias," 2009). Clergy often ask Orthodox parishioners to shun members of these groups, which include Jehovah's Witnesses, Mormons, Evangelical Protestants, and the Bahai. The Church actively opposes issuing permits to non-Orthodox groups to open houses of prayer. Often Orthodox priests sit on the committees that issue these permits. The government closes houses of prayer operating without a permit and sometimes arrests and prosecutes those running them. Senior Greek Orthodox clergy expressed anti-Semitic attitudes such as that Jews control the banks. In 2010 the Greek Orthodox Church's Bishop of Piraeus made anti-Semitic statements on national television. The Greek Orthodox Church's Holy Week liturgy includes anti-Semitic passages. Orthodox Church officials have actively encouraged both SRD and GRD. They publically oppose initiatives to allow the cremation of the dead, despite this being central to burial rituals for several religions. As a result, there are no cremation facilities in Greece. The Orthodox Church in Cyprus similarly blocks cremation facilities ("Cyprus Considered the Law," 2013; Hazou, 2013).

In Bulgaria in 2009, an Orthodox bishop led a protest march and presented a petition to the mayor of Gabrovo signed by 5,000 city residents opposing the construction of a Jehovah's Witnesses prayer house that had been approved by local authorities. Authorities rescinded the approval after the protest. Also in 2009, the Orthodox Church organized a march protesting an international congress of Jehovah's Witnesses. The Bulgarian Orthodox Church has publicly accused the Jehovah's Witnesses of being dangerous and anti-Bulgarian (Novnite-Sofia News Agency, 2009).

In Macedonia, there is a dispute between the Macedonian Orthodox Church and the Serbian Orthodox Church. The government has taken the side of the Macedonian Orthodox Church. No Orthodox groups, other than the Macedonian Orthodox Church, have been able to register because they are prohibited from using the word "Orthodox" in their name. The Serbian Orthodox Church unsuccessfully challenged this in court. Inter-Orthodox disputes of this nature also exist in Moldova with the Romanian Orthodox Church and in Montenegro with the Serbian Orthodox Church. The 2019 split of the Ukrainian Orthodox Church from the Russian Orthodox Church is likely to also follow this pattern.

In Moldova, local authorities are reluctant to allot land to minority religious groups in local cemeteries, which are usually under the administration of local Orthodox churches. Governments in rural areas sometimes permit Orthodox priests to veto public religious activities of other faiths. The Orthodox Church successfully quashed an antidiscrimination law passed in 2012 that would have protected LGBTQ individuals from discrimination. There are multiple reports of Orthodox clergy attempting to shut out other religions, speaking out against Islam and other "imported" religions, and inciting individuals and local authorities into acts of discrimination and hostility against minority religious groups. For example, in 2009 a group of demonstrators led by an Orthodox priest vandalized and disassembled a menorah erected to celebrate the Jewish holiday of Hanukkah that had been authorized by the city government. The group erected a cross in the menorah's place, laid the pieces of the menorah upside down at the feet of a statue of Stefan the Great, a Moldovan Orthodox Church saint, and chanted anti-Semitic slogans. Also in 2009, an Orthodox priest shoved a Jehovah's Witness to the ground, grabbed her hair, and dragged her around. He then doused her with water and insulted her with obscene language. There are multiple reports of Orthodox priests and followers publically demanding that Jehovah's Witnesses leave their villages. In 2013, a local Orthodox priest summoned a crowd and pressured the mayor to revoke a permit for a

Baptist children's summer camp. The Orthodox group then sent a letter to the mayor calling on the local administration to restrict the initiatives and activities of the Baptist church. In 2011, the Moldovan Alliance of Orthodox Organizations organized the first of several anti-Islamic protests that incited followers to hatred and violence against Muslims (Gillet, 2013; Ticudean, 2013).

In Romania, Orthodox priests often successfully pressure local authorities to deny minorities permits to construct places of worship. Orthodox priests on multiple occasions opposed the enforcement of court orders to return religious property seized in the Communist era to the Greek Catholic Church. In addition, the Orthodox Church regularly demolishes Greek Catholic churches, with the tacit approval of local authorities, or finds other ways of sabotaging the restitution process. Members of minority religious groups report that some local officials were subject to threats and intimidation by Orthodox clergy, and therefore officials did not take sufficient action to stop or prevent attacks by Orthodox clergy on members of minority religious groups. There are multiple reports of Orthodox priests in coordination with local authorities blocking religious activities by minority groups, especially in rural areas or small localities. Orthodox priests also deny access by minority religions, especially Greek Catholics, to cemeteries unless Orthodox rituals are used for the burial. There are multiple reports of Orthodox priests either instigating or engaging in physical and verbal conflict with minority religions.

In addition to all of this, Orthodox clergy in many of these countries regularly hold local government posts such as mayor and members of planning boards responsible for giving building permits and, in the case of Greece, house of prayer permits. Thus, they can have considerable impact on GRD against religious minorities through these offices.

In sum, the patterns of discrimination in Orthodox-majority countries are influenced by a range of complex and cross-cutting phenomena. Government religion policy plays a role, but due to the relative uniformity of this policy among these states, it does not differentiate between different countries as much as in other groupings of states. Democracy also plays a role but a limited one. The various Orthodox churches and clergy play a central role in causing broth GRD and SRD, and many of their actions are in and of themselves SRD. This, combined with the tendency of government and society to protect indigenous culture from "foreign" religions, is likely the dominant explanation for levels of GRD and to some extent SRD among these countries.

COMMUNIST COUNTRIES

Five countries currently have governments who self-identify as Communist: China, Cuba, Laos, the People's Democratic Republic of Korea (North Korea), and Vietnam. While it is disputable whether the ideology these countries presently follow is truly Communist, it is clear that the secular antireligious elements of Communism are influential in these countries. These countries are among the most hostile in the world to religion in general. The RAS3 dataset classifies all of them as states hostile to religion. Also, as shown in Figure 6.3, these five governments regulate religion more strongly than do the other ten states in the world that the RAS3 dataset classifies as hostile to religion.

This finding is not surprising as Communist ideology is hostile to religion. It classifies religion as a "false consciousness," which distracts the proletariat from their true interests. This is what Karl Marx meant when he called religion the opiate of the masses. He considered religion similar to a drug used to pacify the masses. Religion alleviated their suffering in this world at the hands of their rulers because of promised rewards in the next world. This allowed governments that served the elite to remain in power. For this reason, among others, Communists have historically been hostile to organized religion. The levels of regulation of the majority and all religions in the world's remaining five Communist countries attest to the continuation of this historic legacy.

Yet, as also shown in Figure 6.3 and Table 6.4, levels of GRD in these countries are high. In fact, the mean levels of GRD in these countries are

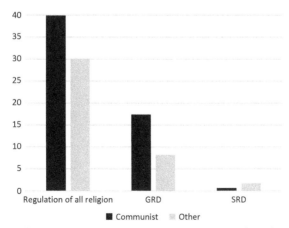

FIGURE 6.3 Religious regulation, GRD, and SRD in states hostile to religion

TABLE 6.4 *Levels of SRD and GRD in Communist states*

		SRD			GRD	
		1990	2014	Avg.	1990	2014
China	Animists	0	0	0	9	10
	Buddhists	1	1	1.00	19	25
	Christian	1	1	1.00	21	24
	Falun Gong	4	4	4.04	25	30
	Muslims	1	1	1.04	21	25
	Other Chinese Religions	0	0	0.00	12	18
	Taoist	0	0	0.00	6	8
Cuba	Catholics	0	0	0.00	17	19
	Hindu	0	0	0.00	16	18
	Protestants	0	0	0.08	17	19
	Spiritists	0	0	0.12	16	18
Laos	Animists	0	2	0.20	12	12
	Christians	2	2	2.00	38	47
	Muslims	0	0	0.00	13	13
North Korea	Animist	0	0	0.00	3	3
	Buddhist	0	0	0.00	11	11
	Chondokyists/Chinese religions	0	0	0.00	3	3
	Christian	0	0	0.00	18	18
Vietnam	Animists (including Cao Dao)	0	0	0.00	11	11
	Bahai	0	0	0.00	0	0
	Catholics	0	0	0.00	25	26
	Chinese religions	0	0	0.00	19	21
	Hoa Hoa	0	0	0.00	16	16
	Muslims	0	0	0.00	6	6
	Protestants	4	4	4.28	29	31

higher than in the other ten countries that are classified as hostile to religion. This poses a conundrum. If Communist countries are hostile to all religion, why are they restricting religious minorities in a manner in which they are not restricting the majority religion? Ideologically their hostility to religion should be uniform rather than selective. As this category of country includes only five countries with twenty-five religious minorities, it is difficult to get at the answer to this question through statistical analysis.

In Chapter 4 I argued that GRD is present in states hostile to religion for many of the same reasons as it is present in other states. Once GRD is activated by these motivations, the general hostility to religion magnifies the levels of GRD. Next, I discuss each of these countries briefly on order to examine what are the proximate causes of GRD in Communist countries. As will be seen, their policies include many similarities across countries. Yet the likely motivations for these policies include some substantial differences.

China

China's motivation for GRD is largely based on two related issues, control and opposition. China seeks to control all religious activity in the country. There is likely an ideological motivation to limit religion, as the spread of religion might undermine the legitimacy of the government's atheist ideology, which, in turn, would undermine the government's legitimacy. This motivation manifests largely in the form of control. This control is linked to the second issue. Religious organizations are capable of developing the civil society necessary to form a coherent opposition movement (Fox, 2018; Sarkissian, 2015). The government tightly controls all legal religious organizations in the country to prevent this from happening. Also, the government severely represses any manifestation of religion that it perceives as an element of opposition.

China established five "patriotic" religious organizations for Catholicism, Protestantism, Islam, Taoism, and Buddhism. Religious activities are legal if they occur under the auspices of these government-supported religious organizations. The organizations' leaders are closely affiliated with the state, are sometimes paid by the state, and are required to support the Communist party. The China State Administration of Religious Affairs (SARA) oversees and closely monitors these organizations (International Center for Law and Religion Studies, 2012). The government sometimes tolerates small-scale religious activities that take place outside the auspices of this framework. However, in most cases, the government pressures unaffiliated groups to join one of the five existing religious organizations and represses those that do not. The primary purpose of this arrangement is to ensure that religion cannot be the basis for political opposition.

This framework itself causes significant GRD. Only the five religions with SARA-administered organizations may register. Only registered religions may own property, collect donations, teach their religion, and hold public religious services. All other religions as well as religious organizations from these five religions that refuse to join the appropriate patriotic religious organization are illegal.

While local authorities sometimes do not enforce this, many of these religious groups are the victims of coercive and punitive measures. Many Catholic organizations that object to China's appointment of Chinese bishops and are loyal to the Vatican refuse to register. This often attracts harsh repression. The government designates several groups as "evil religions." This designation applies mostly to certain Christian groups and the Falun Gong because of perceived oppositional activity and results in severe repression. For example, members of the Falun Gong are often sent to China's high-security psychiatric hospitals for the criminally insane. The Falun Gong reported that detained practitioners were repeatedly subjected to various methods of physical and psychological coercion in attempts to force them to deny their belief in Falun Gong. On a more general level, arrests, imprisonment, and disappearances, most likely to reeducation camps, of clergy and followers of unregistered religions are common.

As the opposition movement in Tibet is associated with Buddhism, there is significant repression of Buddhist clergy, institutions, and activists perceived to be part of this opposition. This results in the close monitoring and often harassment of Buddhist clergy and institutions in Tibet. The government regularly engages in "patriotic education" campaigns in monasteries and restricts the travel of Buddhist monks and nuns. Travel is a significant part of Buddhist training and teaching.

While there are Muslims in every region of China, most repression of Muslims is against the Uighur in the Xinjiang region. The Uighur are a Muslim ethnic group. Uighur nationalists have an active independence movement. This has caused significant repression, including against religious institutions and clergy seen as supporting this independence movement. Recently this has evolved into a massive repressive effort. For example, there are reports of large numbers of Uighurs, likely over one million, being sent to internment camps (Nebehay, 2018).

Thus, GRD in China is directed against two types of religion the government sees as existential threats: religions that are not under its direct control and supervision and religious groups perceived as actively opposing the government's rule.

Laos

While Laos is a Communist state and the Communist Lao People's Revolutionary Party is the only legal political party, the majority of the population is Buddhist. The government both finances and substantially controls the country's Buddhist institutions. This includes control over the appointment and training of clergy. The government uses the Ministry of Propaganda and Culture and the Central Committee of the Lao Front for National Construction (LFNC) to control most aspects of religion in Laos under the guidance of the 2001 *Decree on Management and Protection of Religious Activities in the Lao People's Democratic Republic* (LFNC, 2001). This includes most aspects of religious practices and institutions, including the appointment of monks and clergy, preaching or religious education outside of places of worship, publishing and importing religious materials, repair and maintenance of sacred sites, building new religious structures, and communication and contact with foreign religious organizations. These restrictions are enforced more rigorously on non-Buddhist religious organizations and clergy.

The government recognizes four religions: Buddhism, Christianity, Islam, and Bahai. All religious groups must register under one of these four categories. Christian groups must affiliate with one of three recognized churches: Roman Catholic, Lao Evangelical, or Seventh-Day Adventist. Since a 2004 order of the LFNC, no other Protestant groups have been permitted to register. The government generally permits religious activities within the context of these organizations. Religious leaders are expected to maintain close contact with the government. Thus, like China, Laos has a policy of keeping religion under its direct control.

Other than banning unregistered religions, GRD in Laos occurs mostly at the hands of local governments and focuses primarily on Christians, especially those denominations that seek converts. Proselytizing is illegal in Laos. Government officials particularly harass those who have converted away from Buddhism to Christianity with the intent of forcing them to renounce their conversion. On a more general level, this harassment of Christians includes arrests for proselytizing or holding religious services in private homes. Many provinces make it difficult to obtain permits to build Christian places of worship, and some ban all Christian religious activities (Bos, 2012; "Christians Arrested," 2015; "Lao Christians Evicted," 2014; "Laotian Christians Evicted," 2014; "Pastors Released," 2013; "Persecution Continues," 2014; "Seven Christians Arrested," 2014).

This pattern of hostility to religion in general, but antipathy toward Buddhists who convert to Christianity indicates a complicated relationship with the majority religion. It is difficult to argue that a Communist government has a religious motivation to prevent conversion away from

Buddhism. Yet, in practice, many local governments behave in this manner. There are two likely explanations for this incongruity. First, officials of at least some local governments are paying lip service to Communism yet still adhere at least to some extent to Buddhism. Second, Buddhism is seen as part of the national culture, and Christianity is seen as foreign. In fact, government policy is to see that all religious activities serve the national interest. Thus, nationalism is likely a significant influence on this behavior. Likely, the explanation is a combination of nationalism and ideology.

Vietnam

In Vietnam, the Committee for Religious Affairs (CRA) oversees government religion policy. Religious organizations must obtain government permission for nearly all aspects of their activities. For example, the state bans all religious, cultural, and traditional activities – even when conducted in private homes – that are not registered or approved by the local or national governments. This ban includes any mass gathering; building, repairing, or renovating places of worship; engaging in charitable activities; operating religious schools; publishing religious literature; and appointing, training, ordaining, promoting, or transferring clergy. The government expects religious leaders to actively support the Communist Party and the state. Officially, recognized organizations must consult with the government about their religious and administrative operations, including leadership selection, although not about their religious tenets of faith. All recognized religious groups must operate under government-formed and controlled umbrella bodies. The government requires all Buddhist monks, including those who practice in a different tradition, to gain approval from and work under the government-sponsored and approved Buddhist organization (Feuerberg, 2014; Lodge, 2015; Nguyen, 2008; Vandenbrink, 2012).

The primary method for restricting minority religions in Vietnam is denial of registration, which effectively makes all religious activities illegal and gives the government a pretext to engage in any type of GRD that it sees fit. This is a common method for restricting religious organizations and activities in autocratic regimes (Sarkissian, 2015). This includes demolishing religious structures as well as general harassment and arrest of clergy and worshipers. Many of these arrests are for opposing the government, though it is unclear whether any oppositional activity other than unauthorized religious activities occurred. The government claims ownership of the property on which many religious buildings stand and has demolished many of these structures, especially Catholic structures. Many local governments discourage small Christian congregations and require them to unify into a single congregation, despite them belonging to different denominations with different religious practices, ethnicities, and sometimes languages. Unregistered religious groups are subject to surveillance and severe harassment. Montgard Christians are increasingly targeted by the state. Montgards are a group of hill tribe minorities that are traditionally animist but have been widely converted to Protestant Christianity. They have been subject to intense efforts to renounce their conversion, including fines, threats of expulsion, and denial of social services (Benge, 2012; Brummitt, 2013; Cairnduff, 2011; Feuerberg, 2014; Human Rights Watch, 2011; Murdoch, 2015; Reimer, 2015).

Overall, Vietnam's religion policy is guided by a combination of nationalism, Communist ideology, and a desire to control all organized activity in the country. The persecution of Christians combines all three, as the religion is relatively new to the country and is less under state control.

North Korea

North Korea is among either the most antireligious states or the most religious states in the world, depending on one's perspective. RAS3 classifies it as a secular Communist state due to its official Communist ideology and overt declaration of separation of religion and state. From another perspective, it can be considered religious because its state ideology can be seen as a form of leader worship. Based on the former perspective, it is among the most repressive of religion in the world, but most of this repression is directed at all religions so it does not qualify as GRD.

The government forcefully promotes an ultranationalist ideology known as *Juche* (often defined as "self-reliance") based on the cult personalities of Kim Il Sung, Kim Jong Il, and Kim Jung Un. All citizens are required to adhere to this belief system or face onerous fines and penalties. Juche is a type of Marxism, but its pseudo-religious features distinguish it from all other types of Marxism. It considers the leader to be a messianic-like "eternal head of state," North Korea a chosen nation, and North Koreans a chosen people whose mission is to liberate the world (Juche, 2018). The government considers all religions a challenge to the national ideology and the government.

Like the other Asian Communist governments, North Korea has government-supported "religious federations" for Buddhists, Chondokyos (a belief system based on Confucianism, which also incorporates elements of Taoism, Shamanism, Buddhism, and Catholicism), Protestants, and Catholics. However, it is unclear whether any worship activity takes place within these organizations or they are simply used as propaganda tools to bolster claims of religious freedom to the international community. While most Buddhist temples are treated as cultural relics, many are maintained by Buddhist monks.

That being said, most North Koreans are unaware of the religious facilities in the country. The government considers the spread of Christianity to be a direct threat and all religious individuals enemies of the state. Ownership of Bibles and other Christian religious materials as well as worship outside of the state-supported religious organizations is illegal and leads to imprisonment, torture, or even execution (United Nations Human Rights Office of the High Commissioner, 2014). While North Korea is likely the most antireligious and religiously repressive state in the world, RAS3 classifies GRD as lower in North Korea than in other Communist states. This is not because of a lack of repression, but because most of this repression is uniform against all religions. As GRD is defined as discrimination placed on minority religions that are not placed on the majority religion, repression that is placed equally on all religions does not qualify as GRD. In this respect North Korea is more ideologically consistent than the other Communist states.

Cuba

Cuba is currently the only non-Asian Communist state. The government requires religious organizations to register in order to be legal. In practice, the government does not interfere with many unregistered places of worship, though members of unregistered groups like the Jehovah's Witnesses and Mormons may be subject to higher levels of harassment than other religious organizations. The Office of Religious Affairs of the Central Committee of the Cuban Communist Party monitors all religious activity in the country. While the government does not establish official religious organizations, it does require religious organizations to report their activities to the government. Also, Protestants have established an umbrella organization, the Cuban Council of Churches, to represent its interests to the government.

The government rarely allows new places of worship to be built but sometimes allows the repair and maintenance of existing facilities. The government severely restricts printing equipment, which effectively makes printing religious materials difficult, and the government supervises the importation of religious materials. Most harassment of worshipers and religious figures appears to be tied to oppositional activities. Even if these oppositional activities do not take place in the context of a religious organization, individuals who criticize the government are often barred from attending religious services (Human Rights Watch, 2015).

General Patterns

These five countries show distinct patterns of discrimination in several respects. First, as shown in Table 6.4, SRD is extremely low. Only seven of the twenty-five minorities experienced any SRD between 1990 and 2014. This is likely because these authoritarian governments discourage civil disorder. Also, it is possible that when the government heavily represses a minority, societal actors feel less of a need to do it themselves. Despite the small number of cases, GRD in 2014 correlates with SRD in 2014 (.595 significance = .002) and the average SRD between 1990 and 2014 (.645, significance = .000). Thus, even among autocratic, antireligious states, SRD can predict GRD.

Second, as shown in Figure 6.4, mean levels of GRD are higher than in any other grouping of states examined thus far in this study. Both Orthodox-majority and Muslim-majority countries have considerably lower levels of GRD than do Communist states. Third, GRD is

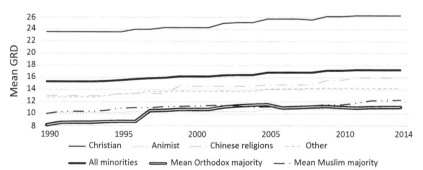

FIGURE 6.4 Mean levels of GRD 1990 to 2014 in Communist countries Difference (*t*-test) between mean for 1990 <.05 for 1994–2004, .01 for 2005–2008, .001 for 2009–2014

increasing in these countries. Fourth, Figure 6.4 confirms the comparative analysis's finding that Christian minorities are singled out in many of these states for higher levels of GRD. However, the reasons for this vary. In Laos it is likely due to a combination of nationalism and residual affinity by local officials toward Buddhism. In Vietnam, it is likely motivated by a combination of nationalism, Communist ideology, and a desire to control all organized activity in the country. North Korea sees the spread of Christianity as a direct threat to the dominant state ideology. In Cuba and China, GRD against Christians is not substantially higher than that against at least some other religious minorities.

This raises the question of the motivation for GRD. As I noted earlier, the antireligious ideologies of these states explains why all religions would be restricted uniformly but not why these governments would engage in GRD, an extra dose of repression against minorities only. I posit that the common denominator is threat perception. Each of these regimes sees a threat in these religious minorities, and GRD is a response to this threat. What differs across the countries is the nature and source of this perceived threat as well as whether the threat combines as a trigger with SRD.

In China and Cuba, GRD is focused against minorities seen as engaging in oppositional activity. In North Korea it focuses on religions seen as the greatest threat to the national ideology. In Laos and Vietnam it is based on a more complicated combination of nationalism, protection of the national culture, Communist ideology, and the desire to keep all religious activity under state control.

BUDDHIST-MAJORITY STATES

The Buddhist-majority states in this section are those that do not have Communist governments. GRD in Buddhist-majority states is common. As shown in Table 6.5, of the twenty-five minorities in these six states, only the Christians in Thailand experienced no GRD. While GRD is high in these countries compared to the EWMOCD states, it is lower than in Orthodox-majority, Muslim-majority, and Communist states. It is higher against Christian and Muslim minorities than other minorities. In fact, Christian and Muslim minorities experience more GRD in each of these countries except in Thailand, where Christian minorities experience no GRD, and Cambodia, where Muslims experience the same levels of GRD as all other non-Christian minorities.

TABLE 6.5 *Levels of SRD and GRD in Buddhist-majority states*

		SRD			GRD		Regulation of maj. rel.
		1990	2014	Avg.	1990	2014	
One religion preferred							
Mongolia	Animist	0	0	0.04	2	2	2
	Chinese religions	0	0	0.00	2	2	
	Christians	1	5	1.40	5	9	
	Muslims	0	0	0.00	3	4	
Myanmar (Burma)	Animist	0	0	0.00	6	6	39
	Chinese religions	0	0	0.00	6	6	
	Christians	1	3	1.44	35	37	
	Hindus	0	0	0.00	7	7	
	Muslims	3	30	23.08	37	36	
Sri Lanka	Bahai	1	0	0.84	0	2	1
	Christians	14	26	19.12	1	4	
	Hindus	1	0	0.48	1	3	
	Muslims	1	2	0.96	1	4	
Thailand	Animists	0	0	0.16	2	2	
	Chinese religions	0	0	0.00	3	3	17
	Christians	1	0	0.48	0	0	
	Muslims	1	4	1.92	3	6	
Active official religion							
Bhutan	Animists	2	2	2.00	5	5	11
	Christians	2	2	2.00	16	17	
	Hindus	2	2	2.00	10	10	
	Muslims	2	2	2.00	12	12	
Cambodia	Animists	0	0	0.00	1	1	12
	Chinese religions	0	0	0.00	1	1	
	Christians	0	0	0.16	1	4	
	Muslims	0	0	0.00	1	1	

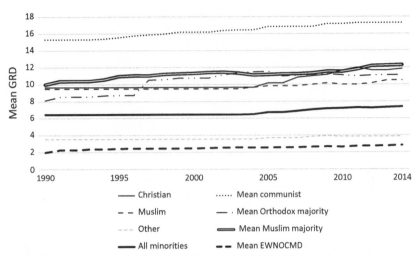

FIGURE 6.5 Mean levels of GRD 1990 to 2014 in Buddhist-majority countries Difference (*t*-test) between mean for 1990 <.05 for 2004–2007, .01 for 2008–2014

Yet levels of GRD vary widely across these countries. Myanmar engages in levels of GRD against Christians and Muslims that are far higher than in any of the other Buddhist-majority countries. Bhutan has levels against all minorities that are higher than that found in the other Buddhist-majority states other than Myanmar.

Yet there is no global factor that explains this finding. There is little variation in official government policy. All these states either prefer Buddhism without declaring it the official religion or have active official religions. Regime is not a factor. Only Mongolia can be considered democratic, and levels of GRD in Mongolia are neither the highest nor lowest among these states. There is also no apparent link between the regulation of the majority religion and GRD. Thus, the factors that help to explain levels of GRD across states for other groupings of states are not helpful in understanding Buddhist-majority states.

However, SRD does help to explain which minorities are most likely to experience GRD. GRD in 2014 is significantly correlated with SRD in 2014 (correlation = .503, significance = .010) and average SRD between 1990 and 2014 (correlation = .495, sig = .012). That being said, the explanations for levels of GRD in these countries become apparent in a case-by-case analysis. In this section I focus on three countries where GRD is particularly high against at least some minorities – Mongolia, Myanmar, and Bhutan, which show some similar patterns. These include support for Buddhism but a desire to keep religion out of politics combined with maintaining the indigenousness of the state culture. Religions seen as foreign are more likely to experience GRD. However, there are also motivations that are more specific to each of these states.

Mongolia

While Mongolia's constitution guarantees separation of religion and state, it also states that "the State shall respect the dominance of the Buddhist religion in Mongolia, in order to uphold the solidarity and cultural and civilization heritage of the people of Mongolia. This will not hinder a citizen to practice another religion" (US Department of State, 2014). Yet there is a series of national laws and local policies that limits minority religions, particularly Christians.

The law requires that 95 percent of employees of religious organizations be citizens. This proves difficult for religions, such as Christianity, which depend upon foreign clergy. Local governments often deny registration to minority religions, especially Christians and Muslims, and use this to prevent them from building places of worship. In other cases, local officials denied churches the right to open social services such as schools or nurseries because they feared these services would be used to attract converts. Some local governments restrict children under the age of sixteen from participating in church services.

Spreading religious views by "force, pressure, material incentives, deception, or means which harm health or morals or are psychologically damaging" is illegal. Proselytizing may not occur on the premises of public schools or institutions or by groups providing child care, child welfare, or child protection services. While foreigners may legally proselytize, those who do so are often harassed or expelled from the country (Religlaw International Centre for Law and Religion Studies, 2013).

Thus, in the case of Mongolia, much of the GRD is likely motivated by a combination of a desire to protect the national culture and Buddhism as well as resentment against proselytizing. This is a common motivation for both SRD and GRD. As SRD is also present against Christian minorities, the link between SRD and GRD is likely triggered by these factors.

Myanmar

GRD in Myanmar is extremely high against Muslims and Christians. It is apparently motivated by a combination of the government's preference for Buddhism and retaliation against opposition movements. The government supports Buddhism but also strongly regulates it. The Ministry of Religious Affairs includes the Department for the Promotion and Propagation of Buddhism. Its tasks include promoting Buddhism, encouraging conversion to Buddhism, and supporting Buddhist schools, community centers, meditation centers, pagodas, and monasteries, among many other activities (Department for the Promotion and Propagation of Sasana, 2005). However, the government recognizes only nine Buddhist monastic orders that are controlled by the State Monk Coordination Committee and bans all other Buddhist orders. Most of this regulation is directed at preventing Buddhist monks from becoming involved in politics.

A significant portion of the GRD against Christians is directed at those who proselytize or those who are seen by the government as converts to Christianity (Chin Human Rights Organization, 2014; Kellner, 2015). The government strongly discourages proselytizing. The 2015 "Religious Conversion Law" requires official government permission to convert from one religion to another. There are also sporadic reports of government attempts to force Christians to convert to Buddhism (Chin Human Rights Organization, 2013; "Myanmar Christians Forced to Convert," 2012). Other forms of GRD against Christians focus mostly in the Kachin and Chin regions, where the Kachin Independence Army has been fighting the government. During the fighting the army destroyed over sixty-five churches, attacked and harassed religious leaders, and burned Bibles. The government often denies permits to build new churches to replace the destroyed ones but funds the building of Buddhist temples in Christian areas (Arora, 2015; "Christian Preachers Closely Monitored," 2010).

There are also significant restrictions against Muslims. As is the case with Christians, the government discourages proselytizing and often denies permits to build or repair mosques. In addition, the government monitors Islamic ceremonies and festivals and censors Islamic sermons. Islamic events require prior written permission. GRD against the country's Rohingya ethnic group, who are Muslims, is particularly high. The government does not consider them citizens. This leads to multiple restrictions beyond simply restricting their religious institutions and practices. Violence between the government and Rohingya militant organizations escalated in 2017 to a government "clearance operation," which can be described as ethnic cleansing and perhaps genocidal.

There is also considerable SRD against Muslims but not Christians in Myanmar. The radical Buddhist-nationalist 969 Movement engages in anti-Muslim rhetoric online, in pamphlets, and on graffiti. They advocate boycotting Muslim-owned businesses. There are reports of Buddhist monks encouraging people not to employ Muslims. Some Buddhists refuse to sell property to Muslims (Marshall, 2013; Pitman & Peack, 2013; Schatz, 2015; Ten Veen, 2005). Since 2011, sectarian violence between Buddhists and Muslims has increased. This violence has led to hundreds of deaths and significant property damage (Campbell, 2014; Shibani, 2014; Strathern, 2013; "Why Is There Communal Violence," 2014).

Bhutan

Bhutan's constitution declares that religion should be "separate" from and "above" the state. It also declares that "Buddhism is the spiritual heritage of Bhutan." The government is strongly associated with Buddhism. Ten seats in the 150-seat National Assembly and 2 seats on the 11-member Royal Advisory Council are reserved for Buddhist monks. The basis for Bhutan's family law is Buddhism, and monks preside over such issues. Hindus may follow Hindu family law (Aid to the Church in Need International, 2008). The government provides financial support to Buddhist monks and nuns and funds the construction of Buddhist temples and shrines. Accordingly, the RAS project considers Buddhism to be the official religion of Bhutan. However, the government restricts the role of religion in politics. Clergy of any religion may not engage in any political activity.

Nonregistered religions may not engage in most activities. These include owning property, organizing publicly, most financial activities, importing literature, opening places of worship, and holding religious ceremonies including worship and burial rituals. As the only non-Buddhist organization allowed to register is a Hindu umbrella organization, this results in significant restrictions on all other minority religions.

The apparent motivation for this GRD is a combination of culture and religion. Hindus are about 11 percent of the population and have a long history in the country, particularly in Southern Bhutan. Others, including Christians and Muslims, are present in much smaller numbers and considered more recent to the country and therefore less legitimate.

CONCLUSIONS

This chapter examined three very different groupings of states that nevertheless have at least three commonalities beyond the small number of states in each grouping. The first is that in all of these states very few minorities escape GRD. In fact, of the ninety-seven religious minorities included in this chapter, only five experienced no GRD between 1990 and 2014. While there are many reasons for this, which I discussed in this chapter, the one common to all of them is ideology. The secular-communist regimes dislike religion, while the Orthodox-majority and (non-Communist) Buddhist-majority states support their majority religions for reasons that are at least in part ideological. This ideological impetus to discriminate is the second commonality between these states.

Third, the mean level of GRD in these three groups is highest against Christians Again, while motivations for focusing GRD on Christians vary, the most common themes are religious ideology, nationalism, and protection of national culture. In the Orthodox-majority countries, this discrimination against Christians focuses largely on denominations perceived as nonindigenous, especially North American Protestant denominations. All the other countries, other than Cuba, are not Christian-majority and in many cases Christians are considered nonindigenous and a threat to the national culture.

While this general commonality of GRD especially against Christians might be expected of the Communist states, many would likely be surprised to find that this is also the case for Orthodox-majority and especially Buddhist-majority states. The evidence shows that Orthodox Christians are often intolerant of other Christian denominations and that Buddhists, who are often perceived as pacifist and tolerant, in many cases are neither. In fact, several Buddhist-majority states evidently consider the spread of Christianity within their borders to be a significant threat. This demonstrates that few world religions are immune to the motivations that can precipitate GRD.

SRD is a cause of GRD in all three of these groupings. The lack of a sufficient number of cases prevents a more thorough quantitative analysis of the triggers that activate this relationship. However, anecdotal evidence suggests that it is the activities of Orthodox clergy and institutions in Orthodox-majority states. It is also likely that other factors like nationalism, ideology, protection of culture, and perceived security threats are triggers in all the countries discussed on this chapter.

7

The Rest 1

Democracies

The previous chapters covered the West, the former-Soviet Bloc (except Bosnia),[1] as well as all Muslim-majority, Orthodox-majority, Buddhist-majority, and Communist states around the world. This and the following chapter focus on "the rest," that is, all states that do not fit into these categories. This chapter focuses on the democratic states in this category and refers to them as "the rest-democracies" (TRD). These 32 countries and 166 minorities are found primarily in Latin America, Asia, and sub-Saharan Africa, and the majority of them, but by no means all of them, are Christian-majority. As I did in Chapter 5, for operational purposes I define democracy here as any state that scores 8 or higher on the Polity index, which measures countries on a scale of −10 (most autocratic) to 10 (most democratic) (The Polity Project, 2018). Countries with no polity score were included if they were determined to be "free" by the Freedom House democracy index (Abramowitz, 2018).

These TRD states engage in the lowest levels of government-based religious discrimination (GRD) of any grouping of states examined thus far in this study, including the non-Orthodox democracies of the West and former-Soviet bloc (EWNOCMD). As is the case for other groupings of states, government religion policy and societal religious discrimination (SRD) help to explain both variation in GRD within the TRD states and the differences between TRD and EWNOCMD states. That is, both government support for religion and SRD are lower in TRD states, and this helps explain why GRD is lower. In addition, economic development

---

[1] Bosnia has no religious majority and is not democratic based on the criteria used on this study of a Polity score of 8 or higher.

also explains some of the difference between TRD and EWNOCMD states. Specifically, I argue in this chapter that discrimination is costly in resources, and wealthier states simply have more resources to afford more GRD.

That being said, in absolute terms the TRD states are more secular in that their government religion policies have them less intertwined with religion and that they have more religious freedom than Western democracies as well as the democracies of the former-Soviet bloc. This is particularly interesting given that these states tend to have populations that are more religious than the EWNOCMD states (Norris & Inglehart, 2004). This finding that GRD is lower in TRD states than in EWNOCMD states further calls into question major assumptions about religious freedom and secularity in Western liberal democracies, which I discussed in more detail in Chapter 5. I argue in this chapter that three factors help to explain the lower levels of GRD in TRD states. First, economically developed states discriminate more. Second, TRD states are more likely to be neutral on the issue of religion, making them less prone to engage in GRD. Third, SRD, an important cause of GRD, is higher in EWNOCMD states.

Also, largely, the findings in this chapter provide a basis for a "North-South" democracy comparison. More specifically, outside of the former-Soviet bloc and Western democracies, only Turkey, Indonesia, Comoros, and Mongolia meet this study's criteria for democracy and are not included in the TRD states discussed in this chapter. In addition, all of the former-Soviet bloc states outside the EWNOCMD states that are democracies are Orthodox-majority (Bulgaria, Macedonia, Moldova, Montenegro, Romania, and Serbia) or Muslim-majority states (Albania, and Kosovo) and are, accordingly, not TRD states. In addition these Orthodox-majority and Muslim-majority states tend to engage in levels of GRD even higher than those in EWNOCMD states. All of this adds to the evidence presented in this study, which calls into question basic assumptions on the link between liberal democracy, particularly Western liberal democracies, secularity, and religious freedom.

PATTERNS AND TRENDS IN TRD STATES

GRD is less common in TRD states as compared to not only EWNOCMD states but also all of the groupings of states thus far examined in this study. SRD is less common in TRD states than in all groupings of states

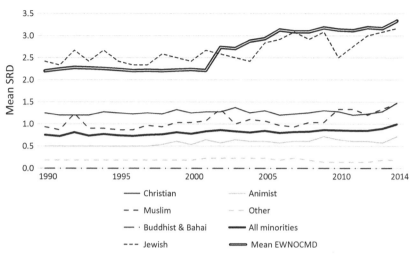

FIGURE 7.1 SRD in TRD states

Significance of change between 1990 and marked year for all minorities <.05 in 2003, 2007–2009, 2012, 2013, <.01 in 2001, 2005, 2014

Significance of change between 1990 and marked year for Muslims <.05 in 2012, 2014

Significance of difference between Buddhists and all other groups <.001 in 1990–2014

Significance of difference between Bahai and all other groups <.001 in 1990–2014

Significance of difference between Jews and all other groups <.05 in 1990–2004, <.01 in 2005–2014

examined here other than Communist states. This is an extremely significant finding because as I discussed in Chapter 5 and will later in this chapter, there is an assumption that religious freedom is strongest both as a value and in practice in Western liberal democracies. This finding directly contradicts this assumption.

As presented in Figure 7.1, the mean level of SRD is considerably lower in TRD states as compared to EWNOCMD states. In 2014, for example, levels of SRD in TRD countries were 29.8 percent of those in EWNOCMD states, which makes levels in EWNOCMD states well over three times higher than in TRD states. In fact, as shown in Table 7.1, 109 of the 166 (65.7 percent) of the minorities in TRD states experienced no SRD at all between 1990 and 2014 as compared to 62 of 146 (42.5 percent) in EWNOCMD states. Also, with the exception of Jewish minorities in 1990–2001, each minority in TRD states experienced levels of SRD lower than the overall mean for EWNOCMD states.

TABLE 7.1A *Levels of SRD and GRD in TRD states*

		SRD			GRD	
		1990	2014	Avg.	1990	2014
Hostile						
Mexico	Animists	0	0	0.00	1	2
	Jehovah's Witnesses	4	4	4.08	3	3
	Jews	0	0	0.16	0	0
	Muslims	0	0	0.04	0	0
	Protestants	13	12	13.04	9	11
Uruguay	Bahai	0	0	0.00	0	0
	Jews	1	5	1.52	0	0
	Muslims	0	0	0.00	0	0
	Orthodox Christians	0	0	0.00	0	0
	Protestants	0	0	0.00	0	0
	Spiritists	0	0	0.00	0	0
Neutral						
Barbados	Bahai	0	0	0.00	0	0
	Catholics	0	0	0.00	0	0
	Hindus	0	0	0.00	0	0
	Jews	0	0	0.00	0	0
	Muslims	0	1	0.04	0	0
	Other Christians	0	0	0.00	0	0
	Rastafarians	1	1	1.00	0	0

		SRD			GRD	
		1990	2014	Avg.	1990	2014
South Africa	Animists	4	4	4.04	0	0
	Bahai	0	0	0.00	0	0
	Buddhists	0	0	0.00	0	0
	Hindus	0	0	0.04	0	0
	Jews	5	6	5.52	0	1
	Muslims	0	2	0.76	0	0
South Korea	Animist	0	0	0.00	0	0
	Buddhist	0	0	0.00	0	0
	Christian	0	1	0.04	0	0
	Confucian	0	0	0.00	0	0
Taiwan	Muslim	1	3	1.68	0	0
	Animists	0	1	0.56	0	0
	Chinese religions	0	1	0.56	0	0
	Christian	1	1	1.00	0	0
	Muslims	0	0	0.00	0	0
Trinidad & Tobago	Bahai	0	0	0.00	0	0
	Buddhists	0	0	0.00	0	0
	Chinese religions	0	0	0.00	0	0
	Hindus	0	0	0.04	0	0
	Muslims	0	0	0.00	0	0
	Spiritists	0	0	0.00	0	0

Country	Religion					
Botswana	Animists	0	0	0.00	0	0
	Bahai	0	0	0.00	0	0
	Muslims	0	0	0.12	0	0
Brazil	Afro-Animists/Spiritists	6	10	7.04	3	3
	Buddhists	0	0	0.00	2	2
	Jews	8	8	8.12	2	2
	Muslims	1	1	1.04	1	1
	Protestants	0	0	0.04	1	1
Ghana	Animists	0	0	0.16	2	1
	Christian, sects	0	0	0.00	2	2
	Muslims	0	1	0.28	3	2
Jamaica	Animists	0	0	0.00	0	0
	Catholics	0	0	0.00	0	0
	Hindus	0	0	0.00	0	0
	Jehovah's Witnesses	0	0	0.00	0	0
	Muslims	0	0	0.00	0	0
	Other Christians	0	0	0.00	0	0
	Rastafarians	3	1	2.40	2	1
Japan	Chinese religions	0	0	0.00	0	0
	Christians	0	0	0.04	0	0
	Muslims	0	0	0.04	0	0
	Animists	0	0	0.00	0	0
	Bahai	0	0	0.00	0	0

Multiple religions preferred

Country	Religion					
Kenya	Animist	1	1	1.00	4	6
	Bahai	0	0	0.00	0	0
	Hindus	0	0	0.00	0	0
	Muslim	3	5	3.20	1	4
Mauritius	Animists	0	0	0.00	0	0
	Bahai	0	0	0.00	0	0
	Buddhist	0	0	0.00	0	0
	Chinese religions	0	0	0.00	0	0
	Christians	0	0	0.08	0	0
	Muslims	0	0	0.08	0	0
	Sikh	0	0	0.00	0	0
Philippines	Animists	0	0	0.00	0	0
	Buddhists	0	0	0.00	0	0
	Muslims	3	3	3.48	3	0
	Prot.(Domestic denom)	0	2	0.08	2	0
	Protestants (Intl. denom)	0	0	0.00	0	0
Solomon Islands	Animists	0	0	0.00	0	0
	Bahai	0	0	0.00	0	0
	Buddhists	0	0	0.00	0	0
	Catholics	0	0	0.16	0	0
	Muslims	0	0	0.00	0	0

TABLE 7.1B *Levels of SRD and GRD in TRD states*

		SRD			GRD	
		1990	2014	Avg.	1990	2014
Multiple religions preferred (continued)						
Vanuatu	Animists	0	0	0.00	0	0
	Bahai	0	0	0.00	0	0
	Catholics	0	0	0.00	0	0
One religion preferred						
Argentina	Indigenous Religions	0	0	0.00	4	4
	Jews	12	13	13.08	4	5
	Muslims	1	1	1.12	4	4
	Orthodox Christians	0	0	0.00	4	4
	Protestants	0	6	0.40	4	6
Bahamas	Bahai	0	0	0.00	0	1
	Catholic	0	0	0.00	0	0
	Jews	0	0	0.00	0	1
	Muslims	0	0	0.00	0	1
	Other Christian	0	0	0.00	0	0
	Spiritist	0	0	0.00	0	4
Belize	Bahai	0	0	0.00	0	1
	Buddhists	0	0	0.00	0	1
	Hindus	0	0	0.00	0	1
	Jews	0	0	0.00	0	1

		SRD			GRD	
		1990	2014	Avg.	1990	2014
India (continued)	Jains	0	0	0.00	7	7
	Muslims	11	17	12.76	8	10
	Parsis (Zoroastrians)	0	0	0.00	2	2
	Sikhs	0	1	0.04	6	4
Nicaragua	Animists	0	0	0.00	0	2
	Bahai	0	0	0.00	0	2
	Muslims	0	0	0.04	0	2
	Protestants	0	0	0.00	0	1
Panama	Bahai	0	0	0.00	0	0
	Buddhists	0	0	0.00	0	0
	Jews	0	0	0.00	0	0
	Muslims	1	1	1.00	0	1
	Protestants	0	0	0.00	0	0
Paraguay	Spiritists	0	0	0.00	0	0
	Animists	0	0	0.00	8	3
	Bahai	0	0	0.00	8	3
	Buddhists	0	0	0.00	8	3
	Jews	0	0	0.20	8	3
Peru	Protestants	0	0	0.00	8	1
	Animists	0	0	0.00	4	6
	Bahai	0	0	0.00	4	6

	Religion					
	Muslims	0	0	0.00	0	1
	Protestants	0	0	0.00	0	0
	Animists	0	0	0.00	0	1
Cape Verde	Bahai	0	0	0.00	0	1
	Muslims	0	0	0.00	0	1
	Non-Catholic Christians	0	0	0.00	0	1
	Official religion					
Chile	Bahai	0	0	0.00	9	6
	Jehovah's Witnesses	0	0	0.00	9	6
	Jews	2	5	2.76	9	6
	Muslims	0	0	0.08	9	6
	Protestants	0	0	0.00	9	4
El Salvador	Animists	0	0	0.00	2	2
	Bahai	0	0	0.00	2	2
	Jehovah's Witnesses	0	0	0.00	2	2
	Mormons	0	0	0.00	2	2
	Muslims	0	0	0.00	2	2
	Protestants	0	0	0.04	2	2
Guatemala	Animists	2	2	2.24	3	2
	Muslims	0	0	0.00	2	3
	Protestants	1	0	0.32	2	2
India	Animists	0	0	0.00	3	3
	Buddhists	0	0	0.00	6	6
	Christians	19	19	19.00	9	11

	Religion					
	Buddhists	0	0	0.00	4	6
	Jews	1	1	0.60	4	6
	Muslims	0	0	0.00	4	6
	Protestants	0	0	0.00	4	6
	Official religion					
Costa Rica	Bahai	0	0	0.00	5	3
	Chinese Religions	0	0	0.00	5	3
	Jehovah's Witnesses	0	0	0.00	5	3
	Jews	1	0	0.08	5	3
	Other Christians	0	0	0.00	5	3
	Protestants	0	0	0.00	6	5
Dominican Republic	Animists	1	1	1.00	3	3
	Jehovah's Witnesses	1	1	1.00	3	3
	Muslims	1	1	1.00	3	3
	Other Christian	1	1	1.00	3	3
Israel	Bahai	0	0	0.00	1	1
	Buddhist	0	0	0.00	2	1
	Chinese religions	0	0	0.00	1	1
	Christian	10	12	10.12	3	4
	Druze	0	0	0.00	0	0
	Muslim	6	8	5.32	2	2

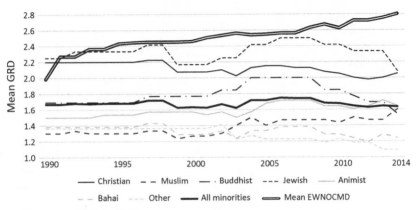

FIGURE 7.2 GRD in TRD states

As is the case for every grouping of states in which Jewish minorities are present, other than Muslim-majority states, Jewish minorities experience the highest levels of SRD. In fact, these levels are over double the levels of Christian minorities who experience the second-highest levels of SRD in TRD states. However, it is important to note that in absolute terms, levels of SRD against Jews in TRD states are considerably lower than in other groupings of states. For example, Jews in EWNOCMD states experienced levels of SRD nearly four times higher than Jews in TRD states in 2014. Muslims experience levels slightly lower than Christians do in most years. All other minorities experience low levels of SRD or no SRD.

As presented in Figure 7.2, GRD is also lower and less common in TRD states as compared to EWNOCMD states. In 2014, for example, levels of GRD in TRD countries were 58.3 percent of those in EWNOCMD states. Just under half – 81 of 166 (48.8 percent) of minorities in TRD states experienced GRD as compared to 103 of 146 (60.5 percent) in EWNOCMD states. This contrast is highlighted by the fact that while in 2014 among EWNOCMD states only Canada engaged in no GRD against any minority, 11 TRD states engaged in no GRD against any minority. This includes Barbados, Botswana, Japan, Mauritius, the Philippines, the Solomon Islands, South Korea, Taiwan, Trinidad and Tobago, Uruguay, and Vanuatu. When one compiles a list of the most religiously free states in the world, arguably, these are not the countries that usually first come to mind. This demonstrates a considerable rift between perception and reality.

Another manifestation of this contrast is that with the exception of Jewish minorities in 1990 and 1992, all minorities in TRD states experienced levels of GRD lower than the overall mean for EWNOCMD states. Thus, while there is variation across minorities in SRD and GRD within TRD states, the overall levels are considerably lower than in all other groupings of states examined thus far.

TRD states also differ from other groupings in that the proportionally higher levels of SRD against Jews are matched by proportionally high levels of GRD against them. For the entire 1990–2014 period, Jews experienced the highest levels of both SRD and GRD in this grouping. Also, Christian minorities experience the second-highest levels of both SRD in most years and GRD for the entire period. However, Buddhists, who experience no SRD, experience the third-highest levels of GRD. In contrast, the Bahai, who also experience no SRD in TRD states, experience among the lowest levels of GRD.

That being said, many of these findings seem to be driven by location. That is, some countries engage in more GRD than others, and if a minority happens to be present disproportionally in either high GRD or low GRD countries, this can influence the results. Especially in a grouping where GRD is low, as is the case in TRD states, small variations caused by this factor can have a measurable impact in proportional levels of GRD. For example, as shown in Table 7.1, both Buddhists and Bahai tend to experience levels of GRD similar to other minorities in the states in which they are present. In eight of the nine TRD states with both minorities, Buddhists and Bahai experienced the same levels of SRD. In Israel, Buddhists experience slightly higher levels. Yet, due to being present in more states with relatively high levels of GRD, Buddhists in TRD states experience higher mean levels of GRD than the Bahai. Similarly, Jews experience the highest mean levels of GRD in this grouping, yet in eleven of the twelve countries in which they are present, at least one minority experiences GRD at the same or higher levels as Jews. Given this, it is difficult to draw conclusions on relative GRD across minorities in this grouping of states.

This is not the case for SRD. Jews experience higher levels of SRD because half of the twelve Jewish minorities in TRD states experience SRD. Of all other minorities in this grouping, 21.4 percent experience SRD. This makes Jews well over twice as likely to experience SRD in this grouping of states. Thus, the finding that Jews experience the highest levels of SRD in TRD states is a valid finding.

As is the case with other groupings of states, the nature of state-religion bonds influences GRD. Table 7.2 shows levels of GRD controlling for the

TABLE 7.2 *GRD and support for religion in TRD and EWNOCMD states controlling for government religion policy*

	GRD		Support for religion	
Official religion policy	TRD states	EWNOCMD states	TRD states	EWNOCMD states
Hostile	1.46	3.83	3.00	6.00
Neutral	0.31	0.41	4.90	6.40
Multiple religions preferred	0.42	3.56	7.50	9.67
One religion preferred	2.96	3.29	8.30	10.25
Official religion	2.63	3.18	13.33	11.86
All cases	1.63	2.81	7.17	9.67

	Regulation of the majority religion		% of states in official religion policy category	
Official religion policy	TRD states	EWNOCMD states	TRD states	EWNOCMD states
Hostile	10.50	11.00	6.9	3.0
Neutral	2.50	1.60	34.5	15.2
Multiple religions preferred	3.00	5.42	13.8	36.4
One religion preferred	6.30	3.00	34.5	24.2
Official religion	7.67	6.42	10.3	21.2
All cases	4.97	4.64		

state-religion relationship. As is the case for the other groupings of states, TRD states that are neutral toward religion engage in the lowest mean levels of GRD. The TRD states that support multiple religions also engage in very low levels of GRD. Those that are hostile to religion and those that support a single religion, either officially or unofficially as a preferred religion, engage in more GRD.

The multivariate analysis presented in Table 7.3 confirms the trends within TRD states using the same models that I used in Chapter 5. Government religion policy influences GRD in the same manner as it does in the bivariate analysis. State support for religion increases levels of GRD, and states that are neutral toward religion engage in less SRD. Catholic-majority states engage in higher levels of GRD. Minorities that engage in violent and semiviolent actions against the majority experience higher SRD and GRD. All of this is similar to the findings for other groupings of states

TABLE 7.3 *Multivariate analysis predicting GRD and SRD in TRD states*

| | GRD | | | | | | | | | | | | SRD | |
| | Model 1 | | Model 2 | | Model 3 | | Model 4 | | Model 5 | | Model 6 | | Model 7 | |
	Beta	Sig.	Beta	Sig.	Beta	Sig.	Beta	Sig.	Beta	Sig.	Beta	Sig.	Beta	Sig.
Minority percent	-0.012	.857	-0.054	.331	-0.003	.953	-0.062	.270	-0.010	.860	-0.015	.795	0.006	.944
Regime durability	-0.001	.987	0.014	.809	0.015	.789	0.017	.766	0.016	.767	0.024	.661	-0.036	.626
Per capita GDP (log)	-0.036	.589	-0.055	.351	-0.054	.351	-0.053	.361	-0.044	.440	-0.076	.180	0.066	.390
Population (log)	0.383	.000	0.262	.000	0.266	.000	0.280	.000	0.275	.000	0.220	.001	0.312	.000
Majority Catholic	0.156	.054	0.179	.013	0.182	.011	0.219	.003	0.237	.001	0.351	.000	-0.059	.530
Religious support	0.211	.012	0.166	.023	0.199	.007	0.174	.017	0.213	.003	0.285	.000	0.064	.508
Regulation of the majority religion	0.008	.918	-0.026	.716	-0.033	.639	-0.085	.246	-0.094	.187	-0.080	.270	0.047	.605
Regime neutral to religion	-0.250	.004	-0.232	.003	-0.235	.002	-0.208	.008	-0.200	.009	–	–	-0.050	.616
Violent and semiviolent minority actions	-0.067	.334	–	–	-0.141	.023	–	–	-0.222	.003	-0.229	.002	0.214	.009
SRD	–	–	0.385	.000	0.409	.000	–	–	–	–	–	–	–	–
SRD Christian	–	–	–	–	–	–	0.378	.000	0.374	.000	0.388	.000	–	–
SRD Muslim	–	–	–	–	–	–	0.194	.001	0.319	.000	0.335	.000	–	–
SRD Jewish	–	–	–	–	–	–	0.073	.198	0.071	.193	0.065	.249	–	–
SRD Animist	–	–	–	–	–	–	0.041	.463	0.039	.472	0.021	.709	–	–
SRD Other	–	–	–	–	–	–	0.047	.390	0.044	.408	0.024	.652	–	–
DF	165		165		165		165		165		165		165	
Adjusted R²	.381		.510		.523		.521		.546		.528		.164	

SRD against Buddhist and Bahai minorities are not included in this analysis because SRD is 0 for all such minorities.

SRD and GRD are linked in a manner similar to other groupings of states in general, though the specifics differ slightly. As will be recalled, in most groupings SRD in general is associated with GRD, but when controlling for SRD against specific minorities, this link is present only for some minorities. I argue that this SRD-GRD relationship exists only where there is a trigger present that catalyzes this relationship.

The findings here are consistent with this trend. In models 2 and 3 the general SRD variable significantly influences GRD. Models 4, 5, and 6, which look at SRD against specific minorities, reveal that SRD influences GRD only for Muslim minorities and Christian minorities. These results are not due to a few outliers. As shown in Table 7.1, in 2014 ten of the forty Christian minorities in TRD states experience SRD, and nine of these also experience GRD. Similarly, in 2014 seven of the thirty Muslim minorities in this grouping experienced SRD, and six of these minorities also experienced GRD.

Given this, what are the triggers in these cases? For Muslims it is likely securitization. That is, Islam is being securitized in these countries in a manner similar to the securitization in the EWNOCMD states. I discussed this in more detail in Chapter 5. However, the securitization in this grouping of states is less common and at a lower level.

Kenya, a Christian-majority country, provides a good example of this dynamic. SRD is present against Muslims. Muslims in Kenya complain about general societal attitudes toward them and assert that the business community deliberately impedes development in predominantly Muslim areas. There are also multiple reports of harassment of Somalis, a predominantly-Muslim ethnic group. There is also a history of societal violence by Muslims against Christians that can account for the securitization of Islam in Kenya. Converts from Islam to Christianity are often threatened by their families and Muslim religious leaders. There are multiple violent attacks on Christians and churches. Al-Shabaab, a Muslim terrorist organization, claims responsibility for many of these attacks, and most of them are believed to have been perpetrated by Muslims. There have also been several riots by Muslims that include violence and arson against Christians. This is countered by moderate Muslim leaders, who repeatedly denounce the violence and call upon the Muslim community to protect churches. Likely as a result of this increasing violence by Muslims, societal violence against Muslim escalated in 2014 with the killing of two moderate Muslim clerics (Christian

Solidarity Worldwide, 2014; "Kenya Cleric," 2014; Mutiga, 2014; "Pro-Government Cleric," 2014; Straziuso & Odula, 2013).

Much of the GRD against Muslims in Kenya can be linked to security. Authorities regularly profile Muslims and scrutinize their identity documents. They sometimes demand additional documentation, including proof of their parents' and grandparents' citizenship. Muslims claim that the government uses the 2012 Prevention of Terrorism Act and the war against terror as a pretext to harass and deport Muslims. There are multiple incidents of security officials raiding and banning meetings in Muslim places of worship. In 2014, security officials briefly closed four mosques in Mombasa on the grounds that they were linked to extremism and incitement to violence. These officials threatened to close other mosques and madrassahs on similar grounds (Jackson, 2014; Somerville Sustainable Conservation, 2014).

The trigger for Christian minorities in the TRD states is not securitization. Rather, I posit that it is the presence Christian denominations considered nontraditional to these countries who are seen as encroaching on the dominant denomination. Thus, in this case the trigger is ideological and perhaps cultural. In Mexico, for example, there is considerable discrimination against Protestants, mostly US-based denominations. Most of this discrimination is not by the central government. Rather, it occurs in rural villages and townships, often with indigenous populations, and straddles the line between SRD and GRD, as the perpetrators of the discrimination can be seen as both societal and government actors.

Members of Mexico's indigenous communities do not pay taxes. Rather, they pay fees to community leaders, who arrange directly with the state for the provision of services, such as electricity, water, and access to federal food assistance programs. These local leaders are often church leaders who frequently require Protestant families to pay for communal Catholic events or to conform to Catholic practices. Refusal can result in ostracism and denial of these services. This denial of services also occurs to families who refuse to convert to Catholicism. There are multiple cases where Protestants were attacked, beaten, stoned, and banished from their villages. This violence also involves arson of Protestant homes and churches, sometimes with the direct involvement of community leaders. In a particularly extreme incident in 2009, local authorities in Oaxaca burned down an evangelical church then threatened to lynch seventy evangelical Christians, including children. Threats of violence to those who refuse to renounce their faith are more common. The central government rarely intervenes in these matters (Chiaramonte, 2016; Friedman, 2014; "Head of Town," 2013; Lee, 2015; Thomas, 2014).

All of this being said, it is important to reiterate that both SRD and GRD are less common in TRD states than in any of the grouping of states thus far examined in this book, with the exception of Communists states and SRD. Thus, these triggers explain the influence of SRD on GRD in cases where they are present. However, the majority of Christian and Muslim minorities among these states experience no SRD, and only slightly more than half of Christian (52.5 percent) and Muslim (53.3 percent) minorities experience GRD. Thus, these dynamics, while similar to those found in other groupings of states, are weaker and less common.

THE WEST VERSUS THE REST

In Chapter 5, I discussed the inaccurate assumption of religious freedom in the West. Both GRD and SRD are quite common in EWNOCMD states, as well as in the two Western Orthodox-majority states of Greece and Cyprus. This undermines assumptions that the West is secular and maintains religious freedom.

The findings presented here place another nail in the coffin of these assumptions. Not only do all EWNOCMD states other than Canada engage in GRD, but also the average level of GRD in EWNOCMD states is substantially higher than in TRD states. As shown in Table 7.2, this is a consistent finding. The mean level of GRD is lower in TRD states not only in general, but also for states that engage in each type of official government religion policy.

This is part of a larger pattern where TRD states are less connected to religion than EWNOCMD states. A larger proportion of TRD states are neutral on the issue of religion than EWNOCMD states. TRD states also support religion at lower levels, though those with official religions do so at slightly higher levels than EWNOCMD states with official religions. Finally, TRD states restrict the majority religion at slightly higher levels than EWNOCMD states, which indicates a higher level of hostility toward religion. All of this adds up to show that TRD states have religion policies that are more secular than those of EWNOCMD states.

Though no state in the world is completely separate from religion (Fox, 2015), Taiwan and Uruguay, for example, are more separated from religion than any of the EWNOCMD states beyond the fact that they engage in no GRD. Taiwan treats all religions equally, despite having a majority that is Buddhist and Taoist. Its only significant general restriction on religion is that while religious organizations may operate private schools, they cannot gain accreditation if they teach religion during their normal curriculum, though religious education is allowed after school hours if it is not compulsory. In contrast, all Western democracies other than the United States and France have religious education in at least some public schools. While registration is not required in Taiwan, religious organizations may voluntarily register with the government to receive tax subsidies. Taiwan does not fund religious organizations except that religious organizations can gain subsidies for welfare and religious tolerance programs. Most Western countries engage in considerably higher levels of funding for religion (Fox, 2015).

The only restriction Uruguay places on Catholicism, its majority religion, is that it denied the Catholic Church a license to open a radio station because "giving in to the wishes of the Catholic Church would be against the traditions of the Uruguayan people" (Fox, 2008: 310). While abortion was restricted until 2012, since then even abortion on demand became legal. In order to gain tax exemptions, religious organizations must register with the Ministry of Education and Culture and be given status as a religion.

In contrast, Canada, the only EWNOCMD state that engages in no GRD, is more closely connected to religion, mostly through its support of religious education. While it varies by province, many religious schools receive government funding. In some cases, fully funded religious schools are considered public schools. This means that religious education is present is some public schools in Canada and that there is some segregation in public education by religion. Also, clergy receive a tax deduction for housing. While Canada does not generally restrict religion, it does ban hate speech even if that speech is a form of religious speech. Some of Canada's municipalities and provinces prohibit or restrict hunting on Sundays (New Brunswick Department of Energy and Resource Development, 2014; Nova Scotia Department of Lands and Forestry, 2014; Ontario Federation of Anglers and Hunters, n.d.; Saskatchewan Human Rights Commission, 2010; Supreme Court of Canada, 2013; "Top Court Upholds," 2013).

This lower level of connection between religion and state in TRD states is an important finding because, as I discussed in more detail in Chapter 5, the assumption that the West is the most religiously free region in the world is based to a great extent on the assumption that the West is the most secular region of the world. There is no shortage of evidence that scholarship specifically assumes the West is secular or secularizing but religion remains strong elsewhere. For example, Beger (2009: 69) argues that "a consensus now exists that secularization theory can no longer explain the worldwide persistence and spread of modern religious movements, with the exception of western and central Europe as well as intellectuals in general." Haynes (2009: 293) argues that past views of religion's decline have "undergone revision, with some seeing a near-global religious resurgence, with only Western Europe not conforming to the trend." Tezcur et al. (2006: 218) state that "the steady decline in religious beliefs and the privatization of religion that has occurred in Western Europe has been an exception to the trends of vibrant religiosity and participation in most other parts of the world." Marqand and Nettler (2000: 2) similarly notes that "organized religion almost certainly plays a smaller role in politics in 2000 over most of the territory of the European union than it did in 1950."

Bruce (2009: 145–147) is likely among the strongest advocates of this view:

Since at least the middle of the nineteenth century the religion that once dominated European societies and most of their colonial offshoots has been in decline. The liberal democracies of the west are now markedly less religious than they were in 1900 or at any point in the previous ten centuries ... The details of the decline in the power, popularity and prestige of religion vary from society to society but that decline has been general and unrelenting ... Not only is the decline general, it is also regular. None of the great upheavals of the nineteenth or twentieth centuries produced significant religious revivals ... the fact that, despite great difference in church–state relations, the trajectory of change in Christianity across Europe has been similar, suggests that secularization is to be explained by general social processes rather than by idiosyncratic features of particular settings.

Thus, for Bruce, the West has become secular. This trend is deep, it is consistent, and it driven by societal processes common to all Western states,

Yet the patterns of both SRD and GRD in TRD states, as well as patterns of support for religion, falsify these assumptions that the West is the most religiously free and secular world region. On average, the non-Western democracies discussed in this chapter have measurably lower levels of SRD, GRD, and support for religion. The only aspect of religion policy where TRD states score slightly higher than EWNOCMD states is regulation of the majority religion, a form of policy that is consistent with secular governments.

This assumption of the secular West is coming under increasing scrutiny. A growing literature acknowledges that religion is integral to

Western politics. Rather than dealing with the larger questions of whether the West is secular, most of these studies tend to assume religion is relevant and focuses on more specific topics. This literature discusses the role of religious political parties in Europe (Mantilla, 2016; Minkenberg, 2009), how religious organizations act as interest groups (Grzymala-Busse, 2015a, 2016b; Minkenberg, 2012; Pfaff & Gill, 2006; Warner, 2000), the role of religion in European integration and the European Union (Nelsen & Guth, 2015), and the registration of religious communities in Europe (Flere, 2010). Polling data shows an influence in the West of religion on attitudes toward immigration (Bohman & Hjerm, 2013; Grotsch & Schnabel, 2012, 2013), European integration and the European Union (Boomgaarden & Woost, 2009; Hagevi, 2002; Minkenberg, 2009; Nelsen et al., 2001), democracy (Vlas & Gherghina, 2010), party choice (van der Brug et al., 2009) and identity in Europe (Schnabel & Hjerm, 2014; Verkutyten et al. 2014). There is also a significant amount of study of Western attitudes toward Muslims as well as comparisons between Muslim and Christian political attitudes in the West (Brekke, 2018; Fetzer & Soper, 2003; Helbling, 2014; Helbling & Traunmuller, 2015).

Not all of these studies focus on narrow topics; some make broader arguments relating to the nonsecularity of the West in general and Europe in particular. Branas-Garza and Solano (2010) find that in Europe "the proportion of clearly religious-averse citizens is very small and never larger than 6 percent. That is, almost all individuals are somewhat concerned about societal secularization. Therefore, in electoral terms, the potential cost of pro-religion policies is very low." Helbling and Traunmuller (2015: 2) note that "European democracies are far from secular ... Institutions of state support of religion are not only widespread in Western Europe but also are a significant and tangible element of the public life and collective identities of its citizens." Madeley and Enyadi (2003: 2) similarly argue that "it is probably no exaggeration to say that almost nowhere in Europe's 50-odd sovereign territories are significant issues of the relationship between religious organizations, society, and the state completely absent from the political agenda." While many argue that this nonsecularization of Europe has always been the case, others like Thomas (2010: 17) argue that it is due to demographic trends: "religion is coming back into European politics. Europe has become a mission field for devout Muslims and evangelical Christians from the global South."

Why Would We Expect Less GRD in the Non-West?

That being said, the finding that any aspect of religion, much less religious discrimination, is less common in non-Western democracies than in the West would likely be surprising to many of these authors. Few studies directly compare the West and the non-West, and it is difficult to find studies that posit that any religious factor is stronger in the West than the non-West. This begs the question of why would religious freedom and secularism be stronger in TRD states as opposed to EWNOCMD states? More specifically why is GRD less common in the TRD than in EWNOCMD states? This finding that GRD is lower in parts of the non-West is not a new finding, but there is little theorizing on why this may be the case.

Perhaps one reason for this lack of theorizing is that this study demonstrates this result more thoroughly and directly than previous studies. For example, in Fox (2008, 2016), I found that among Christian-majority countries, GRD is lower in developing countries than in democracies in the West and the former-Soviet bloc. However, my previous work does not focus on this issue, and the finding emerges in an analysis of other questions. Nor do these previous studies systematically examine why this is the case, in part because the tools to do so were not available at that time. Also, these studies examine this issue as part of a larger focus on GRD worldwide and devoted limited attention to trends and comparisons in different parts of the Christian world. In addition, they examine the Christian world in its entirety and do not focus on democracies.

The TRD states examined in this chapter are a slightly different set of cases than Christian-majority democracies in the developing world because they include a number of democracies that are not Christian-majority, including India, Israel, Japan, Mauritius, South Korea, and Taiwan in addition to the twenty-six Christian-majority states in this grouping. Also, it is difficult to call Israel, Taiwan, South Korea, and Japan developing countries. However, here too, GRD among the TRD states is lower than in the EWNOCMD states.

I identify three testable factors that may help account for why GRD is lower in TRD states as compared to EWNOCMD states. The first is economic development. In previous studies, I found consistently that more developed countries, as measured by per capita GDP, engage in higher levels of GRD (Fox, 2008, 2015, 2016). One potential explanation for this finding is that GRD requires resources, and resources are more limited in less developed countries. Gill (2008) includes this argument as an integral part of his explanation of the causes of religious liberty. While his focus is not on this particular issue, it is a central argument in his more general rational choice explanation for why politicians choose to support religious freedom policies. He argues that politicians support a religious monopoly in return for the legitimacy that a religion can grant to a government. This support has costs that often include the material costs of repressing minority religions. In fact, repressing minority religions is considered by most theorists to be necessary in order to achieve a true religious monopoly (Casanova, 2009; Froese, 2004: 36; Gill, 2008: 45; Grim & Finke, 2011: 70; Stark & Finke, 2000: 199).

All repression is costly in material resources. It requires police or similar institutions, jails, and perhaps courts. As most of the TRD countries have fewer resources than do the EWNOCMD states, we would expect them to engage in less GRD.

Interestingly Finke (2013) argues that the influence of economic development on SRD is the opposite. Defending religious minorities from negative actions by societal actors can cost resources. In fact, the resources to prevent SRD are similar to those needed to engage in GRD. They include police or similar forces to protect the minorities and catch offenders who may be prosecuted in courts and incarcerated in prisons. Finke (2013: 301–302) argues that "like other freedoms, protecting religious freedoms can be both inconvenient and costly. Even when the state lacks explicit motives for restricting religious freedoms, the state often allows restrictions to arise because it lacks either the motive or the ability to protect such freedoms." This is because "when the state is weak … the tyranny of the majority and the actions of religious, political, and social movements can quickly deny the religious freedoms of others" (Finke, 2013: 303).

The second explanation is government religion policy. Previous studies show that, on average, developing Christian-majority countries engage in less support for religion. This is also true of TRD states as compared to EWNOCMD states. As shown in Table 7.2, support for religion is lower in TRD states both in general and at each level of government religion policy other than one. TRD states with official religions support that religion slightly more than EWNOCMD states with an official religion. In addition, TRD states are shown to be more secular in general. The patterns in official religion policy show that more TRD states are neutral toward religion than EWNOCMD states. As I discussed in more detail in

Chapter 2, there are multiple reasons why states that are more closely linked to a religion are more likely to engage in GRD.

Finally, as discussed in Chapters 2 and 4, states that regulate the majority religion are more likely to engage in GRD. As shown in Table 7.2, overall this regulation is slightly higher in TRD states. Thus, while this factor may not explain the differences between the two groupings of states, it is still a potential influence on GRD. In sum, states that more strongly support religion and more strongly regulate religion will engage in more GRD while states that have neutral religion policies will engage in less GRD.

The third explanation is that, as shown in Figure 7.1, SRD is lower on TRD states as compared to EWNOCMD states. Given this, differing levels of SRD may explain the lower GRD in TRD states.

There is a fourth potential explanation, though it is not currently testable directly. Most studies show that outside the West, people tend to be more religious (e.g., Norris & Inglehart, 2004). In contrast, as I discuss in more detail in Chapters 5 and 9, policies restrictions on infant circumcision, religious clothing, and ritual slaughter are limited mostly to Western democracies, indicating the relative popularity of secular ideologies in these countries. Thus the lower GRD in the TRD states may be a combination of the influence of secular ideologies in the West combined with a religious population in the TRD states that have a more tolerant view of minority religions or at least an understanding of the importance of religious practices and institutions. However, as reliable religiosity data is not available in many TRD states and data on the popularity of secular ideologies is even scarcer, this is not currently a testable proposition.

That being said, if the three testable factors account for the differences between EWNOCMD and TRD states, controlling for them should account for the differences between these two groupings.

Testing the Causes of GRD

Table 7.4 presents a multivariate analysis of the causes of GRD an SRD in EWNOCMD and TRD states. It uses the same models as in Table 7.3 but adds several variables. First, as there are more minorities in the analysis, there is a sufficient number of minorities to add Hindus and Bahai to the minorities analyzed specifically. Second, I added a control variable for EWNOCMD states.

TABLE 7.4 *Multivariate analysis predicting GRD and SRD in TRD and EWNOCMD states*

| | GRD | | | | | | | | | | | | SRD | |
| | Model 1 | | Model 2 | | Model 3 | | Model 4 | | Model 5 | | Model 6 | | Model 7 | |
	Beta	Sig.	Beta	Sig.	Beta	Sig.	Beta	Sig.	Beta	Sig.	Beta	Sig.	Beta	Sig.
EWNOCMD state	-0.023	.793	-0.057	.508	-0.054	.533	-0.065	.431	-0.081	.327	-0.031	.715	0.227	.016
Minority percent	0.027	.595	0.020	.696	0.012	.824	-0.022	.647	0.003	.950	-0.018	.727	-0.031	.599
Regime durability	-0.124	.087	-0.099	.170	-0.099	.171	-0.087	.201	-0.087	.202	-0.043	.542	-0.110	.173
Per capita GDP (log)	0.152	.070	0.144	.082	0.143	.086	0.148	.059	0.153	.051	0.083	.300	0.103	.243
Population (log)	0.273	.000	0.220	.000	0.218	.000	0.210	.000	0.212	.000	0.096	.086	0.257	.000
Majority Catholic	0.184	.081	0.187	.072	0.185	.075	0.224	.023	0.233	.018	0.347	.001	0.004	.972
Majority non-Catholic Christian	0.337	.002	0.309	.003	0.308	.004	0.320	.002	0.324	.001	0.236	.022	0.091	.417
Religious support	0.199	.003	0.201	.002	0.196	.003	0.192	.002	0.209	.001	0.324	.000	-0.006	.947
Regulation of the majority religion	0.033	.582	0.029	.620	0.029	.620	-0.001	.988	-0.001	.982	0.076	.175	0.046	.451
Regime neutral to religion	-0.380	.000	-0.357	.000	-0.357	.000	-0.341	.000	-0.339	.000	–	–	-0.003	.972
Violent and semiviolent minority actions	-0.041	.419	–	–	0.021	.697	–	–	-0.087	.120	-0.091	.115	0.187	.001
SRD	–	–	0.161	.002	0.158	.003	–	–	–	–	–	–	–	–
SRD Christian	–	–	–	–	–	–	0.180	.000	0.181	.000	0.178	.000	–	–
SRD Muslim	–	–	–	–	–	–	0.268	.000	0.305	.000	0.328	.000	–	–
SRD Jewish	–	–	–	–	–	–	-0.053	.270	-0.051	.294	-0.037	.463	–	–
SRD Hindu	–	–	–	–	–	–	-0.012	.798	-0.010	.825	-0.029	.546	–	–
SRD Animist	–	–	–	–	–	–	0.043	.353	0.042	.369	0.026	.588	–	–
SRD Bahai	–	–	–	–	–	–	-0.018	.690	-0.017	.716	-0.023	.638	–	–
SRD Other	–	–	–	–	–	–	0.129	.005	0.129	.005	0.144	.003	–	–
DF	311		311		311		311		311		311		311	
Adjusted R^2	.259		.281		.279		.361		.364		.315		.155	

SRD against Buddhist minorities are not included in this analysis because SRD is 0 for all such minorities.

These results confirm three of the hypotheses. States that support religion engage consistently in more GRD and those neutral to religion engage in less. The results for states that regulate the majority religion are not significant. SRD is related to GRD in a similar manner as in the previous analyses in this study. Specifically, the general SRD variable is significantly related to higher GRD. When looking at specific minorities, the SRD-GRD link was only present for some minorities. As was the case for both TRD and EWNOCMD states, it was present for Muslim minorities. It was also present for Christian minorities, as was the case in TRD but not EWNOCMD states. As was the case for EWNOCMD but not TRD states, it was present for "other" minorities.

The triggers discussed earlier explain these results for SRD. Securitization explains the SRD-GRD link for Muslims. The protection of national cultures from religions perceived as nonindigenous explains it for Christian and "other" minorities.

The link between economic development, as measured by per capita GDP and GRD is present but weak. The results are significant at the 0.1 level of significance in four of the models. However, this indicates that while there might be a relationship, it is difficult to be confident of this relationship.

However, when looking at all Christian-majority democracies, thus including Orthodox-majority democracies and excluding states that are not majority Christian, the results are stronger. As shown in Table 7.5, for this set of states with a total of 311 minorities, all of the preceding explanations for the different levels of GRD between "northern" and "southern" Christian-majority democracies are confirmed. All three aspects of government religion policy influence GRD as predicted. Economic development results in higher GRD. Also the results for SRD as a cause of GRD are the same as in Table 7.4. In addition, Orthodox-majority states engage in higher levels of GRD as do states with larger populations.

The combined results of Tables 7.4 and 7.5 demonstrate that the difference between EWNOCMD states and other democracies (not including those with Muslim or Buddhist majorities) is explained by the combined influence of economic development, government religion policy, and SRD. In Table 7.4 these variables neutralize the EWNOCMD control variable. The results in Table 7.5 are a bit more intriguing. For models 1 through 3 the EWNOCMD is not significant, but in models 4 and 5 it is significant at the 0.1 level, which shows some borderline

TABLE 7.5 *Multivariate analysis predicting GRD and SRD in Christian-majority democracies*

| | GRD | | | | | | | | | | | | SRD | |
| | Model 1 | | Model 2 | | Model 3 | | Model 4 | | Model 5 | | Model 6 | | Model 7 | |
	Beta	Sig.	Beta	Sig.	Beta	Sig.	Beta	Sig.	Beta	Sig.	Beta	Sig.	Beta	Sig.
EWNOCMD state	-0.100	.228	-0.132	.106	-0.131	.110	-0.136	.076	-0.138	.073	-0.186	.015	0.146	.128
Minority percent	-0.033	.477	-0.012	.786	-0.025	.589	-0.049	.241	-0.044	.298	-0.049	.261	-0.039	.482
Regime durability	-0.158	.027	-0.126	.071	-0.128	.068	-0.108	.099	-0.107	.103	-0.050	.437	-0.142	.078
Per capita GDP (log)	0.257	.002	0.226	.005	0.229	.004	0.208	.005	0.206	.006	0.204	.008	0.209	.029
Population (log)	0.157	.004	0.115	.036	0.110	.045	0.106	.043	0.108	.039	0.035	.465	0.281	.000
Majority Catholic	-0.054	.398	-0.034	.589	-0.035	.579	-0.012	.846	-0.010	.867	0.086	.098	-0.133	.101
Majority Orthodox	0.321	.000	0.280	.000	0.284	.000	0.276	.000	0.274	.000	0.316	.000	0.180	.010
Religious support	0.197	.002	0.200	.002	0.195	.002	0.197	.001	0.199	.001	0.307	.000	-0.027	.687
Regulation of the majority religion	0.172	.001	0.166	.001	0.165	.001	0.139	.003	0.139	.003	0.159	.001	0.002	.974
Regime neutral to religion	0.203	.002	0.197	.002	0.201	.001	0.184	.002	0.181	.002			-0.066	.400
Violent and semiviolent minority actions	0.078	.090	–	–	0.058	.200	–	–	-0.028	.529	-0.039	.386	0.124	.022
SRD	–	–	0.193	.000	0.186	.000	–	–	–	–	–	–	–	–
SRD Christian	–	–	–	–	–	–	0.203	.000	0.204	.000	0.199	.000	–	–
SRD Muslim	–	–	–	–	–	–	0.285	.000	0.296	.000	0.309	.000	–	–
SRD Jewish	–	–	–	–	–	–	-0.012	.780	-0.012	.779	-0.012	.782	–	–
SRD Hindu	–	–	–	–	–	–	-0.008	.854	-0.008	.852	-0.011	.796	–	–
SRD Animist	–	–	–	–	–	–	0.029	.483	0.028	.497	0.033	.434	–	–
SRD Bahai	–	–	–	–	–	–	-0.003	.933	-0.004	.930	-0.002	.958	–	–
SRD Other	–	–	–	–	–	–	0.112	.006	0.112	.006	0.109	.008	–	–
DF	310		310		310		310		310		310		310	
Adjusted R^2	.397		.423		.425		.501		.500		.485		.164	

SRD against Buddhist minorities are not included in this analysis because SRD is 0 for all such minorities.

significance. But, in model 6 it has a significance of .015, which is considered significant. All these significant results show EWNOCMD states, when controlling for other factors, have lower levels of GRD than the non-EWNOCMD states.

This has at least two interesting implications. First, predictions of religious freedom in EWNOCMD states can be seen as both accurate and inaccurate depending on one's perspective. In absolute terms, GRD is higher in EWNOCMD states. On the other hand, when controlling for a number of variables the predicted association exists, especially if one looks only at Christian-majority democracies. That being said, many of these control factors themselves undermine the assumptions of religious freedom and separation of religion and state in the West. The stronger support for religion in EWNOCMD states and that fewer of them are neutral toward religion undermines assumptions of separation of religion and state. The higher levels of SRD in EWNOCMD states undermines assumptions that all their citizens share the value of religious freedom and tolerance of religious minorities. Finally, the finding that the wealth of EWNOCMD states facilitates the ability of its governments to engage in GRD is certainly inconsistent with assumptions of religious freedom in these states. Given this, we need to question either whether religious freedom is truly an integral element of liberal democracy or whether those countries we consider liberal democracies are truly liberal democracies.

A second implication is a confirmation of this study's strategy of placing states into different groupings based on their regime-type, majority religion, and national ideology in the case of Communist states. Simply comparing democracies worldwide to nondemocracies would have produced very different results.

CONCLUSIONS

The findings in this chapter have some important implications. First, and perhaps foremost, they further demonstrate that the world is not as many believe it to be. Among democracies, the democracies outside the West, Europe, and Buddhist- and Muslim-majority states have the lowest levels of GRD and have governments that are, on average, the most separated from religion. More specifically, GRD is nonexistent in countries like Barbados, Botswana, Japan, Mauritius, the Philippines, the Solomon Islands, South Korea, Taiwan, Trinidad and Tobago, Uruguay, and Vanuatu but is present in Western democracies such as the United States, Denmark, Norway, France, and the Netherlands. Yet when one thinks of those states with liberal traditions supporting religious freedom, the latter are the ones that come to mind rather than the former.

In this chapter, I show that liberal ideology is commonly trumped by structural factors. Wealthy countries have the resources to restrict religious minorities, while poorer countries are less likely to be able or willing to afford GRD. Wealthy countries are also more likely to support religion while poorer countries are more likely to be neutral on the issue of religion. Both supporting religion and engaging in GRD are costly for governments. This is likely part of a larger pattern where wealthier states have the ability to regulate many aspects of life more completely than less developed countries.

Alternatively, Norris and Inglehart (2004) argue that in wealthy stable states, the lack of fear for one's financial and physical well-being causes an existential security that, in turn, reduces religiosity. Continuing this reasoning, it may also increase belief in secular ideologies that are intolerant of religion in general or of religious practices that are contrary to the beliefs of these secular ideologies.

Be that as it may, these results show that financial means may influence religion policy more than liberal democratic ideology. This study has consistently shown that no matter the grouping of states examined, those that are more strongly connected to religion, another structural factor, are more likely to engage in GRD. Finally, SRD is also lower in TRD states. Thus, these states have a culture of religious tolerance that is stronger than that found in the world's allegedly most liberal democracies, and this also had an impact on GRD.

In the next chapter, I examine GRD in the nondemocracies among those states in "the rest" category. These states also have low levels of GRD, which further undermines many of the assumptions regarding liberal democracy that I discussed in this chapter.

8

The Rest 2

Nondemocracies

This chapter examines discrimination in nondemocracies that are not Western or European democracies, communist, Muslim-majority, Buddhist-majority, or Orthodox-majority. I designate these thirty-eight countries "The Rest Nondemocracies" (TRND). Other than Bosnia,[1] they are found in Asia, sub-Saharan Africa, and Latin America and contain 148 religious minorities that are included in the RASM dataset.

Overall, government-based religious discrimination (GRD) in these countries is approximately as low as in "The Rest Democracies" (TRD) states, which I discussed in Chapter 7. This is part of two related phenomena. First, non-Orthodox Christian-majority states, regardless of whether they are democratic or not, engage in less GRD than all other groupings of states based on majority religion or ideology. Second, "the rest" states in general engage in less GRD than all other groupings of states, including European and Western non-Orthodox Christian-majority Democracies (EWNOCMD). They are also far more likely to have neutral religion policies than EWNOCMD states. As I discuss in more detail in the body of this chapter, this calls into question many of our assumptions regarding the influence of democracy on religious discrimination and secularity, the nature of liberal democracy, and which states are liberal democracies.

Accordingly, this chapter presents the findings for TRND states. It then compares these findings to those for TRD states. Then it addresses the

---

[1] As Bosnia has no religious majority and is not democratic, it does not fit into any of the categories that are covered in the previous chapters.

more general findings of this study regarding GRD in democracies in general and the implications of these findings.

The mean levels of societal religious discrimination (SRD) in TRND and TRD states is approximately the same. As shown in Figure 8.1, until 1995, the first year Bosnia is included in RASM3, SRD was lower in TRND states. From 1995 onward, mean levels between the two groupings of states are approximately the same in any given year. Thus, among "the rest" states, democracy does not seem to have a large impact on mean levels of SRD. Also, SRD is much lower in TRND states than in EWNOCMD states.

However, the distribution of SRD across TRND states differs from that in TRD states. Findings show that 108 of 148 (73.0 percent) minorities in TRND states experienced no SRD as opposed to 109 of the 166 (65.7 percent) of the minorities in TRD states. As shown in Table 8.1, Bosnia heavily influences the SRD mean scores in TRND states because Catholic, Orthodox, and Muslim minorities experience heavy levels of SRD to a great extent due to the legacy of the civil war in that country in the early 1990s. If Bosnia is excluded from the problem set, SRD is considerably lower in TRND states than in TRD states.

As shown in Figure 8.2, levels of GRD in TRND states were lower than those in TRD states in 1990 but increased over time. By 2014 they were slightly higher in TRND states. Yet, these results still show that GRD in TRND states is substantially lower than those in EWNOCMD states.

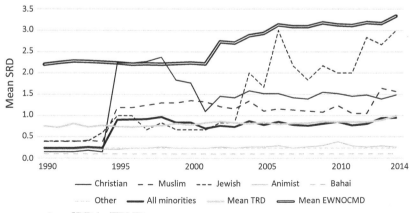

FIGURE 8.1 SRD in TRND states

TABLE 8.1A *Levels of SRD and GRD in TRND states*

		SRD 1990	SRD 2014	SRD Avg.	GRD 1990	GRD 2014
Hostile						
Eritrea	Animists	0	0	0.00	0	15
	Catholics	0	0	0.00	0	4
	Muslims	0	0	0.00	0	3
	Other Christians	1	1	1.00	3	24
Rwanda	Animists	0	0	0.00	0	0
	Muslims	0	0	0.00	0	0
	Other Christians	0	0	0.00	1	5
	Protestants	0	0	0.00	0	3
Neutral						
Benin	Animists	0	1	0.32	0	0
	Christians	0	0	0.12	0	0
Burundi	Muslims	0	0	0.04	0	0
	Animists	0	0	0.00	0	0
	Muslims	0	0	0.08	0	0
Cameroon	Animists	0	0	0.00	0	0
	Bahai	0	0	0.00	0	0
	Muslims	0	0	0.04	0	0
Central African Republic	Animists	0	0	0.00	0	0
	Bahai	0	0	0.00	0	0
	Muslims	3	18	4.20	1	2
Liberia	Animists	0	0	0.00	0	2
	Bahai	0	0	0.00	0	0
	Muslims	0	1	1.16	0	0
Madagascar	Animists	0	0	0.00	0	0
	Christians	0	0	0.00	0	10
Mozambique	Muslims	2	2	2.00	1	2
	Animists	0	0	0.00	0	0
	Hindu	0	0	0.00	0	0
Namibia	Muslims	0	0	0.00	4	2
	Animists	0	0	0.04	0	0
	Bahai	0	0	0.00	0	0
	Muslims	0	0	0.00	0	0
	Non-Lutheran Christians	0	0	0.00	0	0
Singapore	Christians	0	0	0.04	0	0
	Hindus	0	0	0.00	0	0
	Jews	0	0	0.00	0	0
	Muslims	0	0	0.04	0	5
	Sikhs	0	0	0.00	0	0
South Sudan	Animists	0	0	0.00	0	0
	Muslims	1	1	1.25	1	1
Suriname	Bahai	0	0	0.00	0	0
	Buddhists	0	0	0.00	0	0

Country	Religion					
Congo-Brazzaville	Animists	0	0	0.00	0	0
	Bahai	0	0	0.00	0	0
	Muslims	0	0	0.00	0	0
	Christians (non-Methodist)	1	1	1.00	0	0
Fiji	Hindus	2	2	2.00	0	0
	Muslims	1	1	1.00	0	0
	Sikhs	0	0	0.00	0	0
Gabon	Animists	0	0	0.00	2	2
	Muslims	0	0	0.00	1	1
	Other Christians	0	0	0.00	1	1
Guinea-Bissau	Animists	0	0	0.00	0	0
	Christians	0	0	0.00	0	0
Guyana	Muslims	0	0	0.00	0	0
	Animists	0	0	0.00	1	1
	Bahai	0	0	0.00	1	1
	Buddhists	0	0	0.00	1	1
	Chinese Religions	0	0	0.00	1	1
	Hindus	0	0	0.00	1	1
	Muslims	0	0	0.00	1	1

Country	Religion					
	Chinese Religions	0	0	0.00	0	0
	Hindus	0	0	0.00	0	0
	Jews	0	0	0.04	0	0
	Muslims	0	0	0.00	0	0
Uganda	Other Indigenous Spiritists	0	0	0.00	0	0
	Animists	1	1	1.08	1	10
	Bahai	0	0	0.00	1	1
	Hindus	0	0	0.00	1	1
	Muslims	1	0	0.08	0	6
Zaire (Dem. Rep. of Congo)	Animists	0	0	0.04	0	0
	Bahai	0	0	0.00	0	0
Zimbabwe	Muslims	0	0	0.12	0	1
	Animists	1	1	1.00	1	1
	Bahai	0	0	0.00	1	1
	Catholics	1	1	1.00	0	0
	Muslims	1	1	1.00	2	2

TABLE 8.1B *Levels of SRD and GRD in TRND states*

Multiple religions preferred

Country	Religion	SRD 1990	SRD 2014	SRD Avg.	GRD 1990	GRD 2014
Bosnia	Catholics	32	14	18.70	5	9
	Jews	4	3	2.45	8	11
	Muslims	32	21	24.60	7	11
	Orthodox	31	13	17.80	8	12
	Protestants	0	2	0.15	5	11
Malawi	Animists	0	0	0.00	8	7
	Catholics	0	0	0.00	0	0
	Muslims	0	0	0.24	1	0
	Rastafarians	0	0	0.00	2	1
Nepal	Animists	0	0	0.00	2	2
	Buddhists	0	0	0.00	3	4
	Christians	1	2	1.68	5	5
	Muslims	1	3	1.48	2	2
Papua New Guinea	Anglicans	0	0	0.00	0	0
	Animists	0	0	0.00	0	1
	Catholics	0	0	0.00	0	0
	Muslims	1	0	0.72	0	1
Swaziland	Animists	1	1	1.00	1	2
	Bahai	1	1	1.00	1	2
	Hindus	1	1	1.00	1	2
	Muslims	1	2	1.20	1	2
Colombia	Animists	0	0	0	1	1
	Bahai	0	0	0	1	1
	Jews	2	4	2.48	1	1
	Muslims	1	1	1.04	1	1
	Protestants	0	0	0	1	1
Ecuador	Animists	0	0	0.44	0	0
	Jehovah's Witnesses	0	0	0	0	0
	Muslims	0	3	1.08	0	0
	Other Christians	0	0	0	0	0
	Protestants	0	0	0.16	0	0
Equatorial Guinea	Animists	0	0	0	0	1
	Bahai	0	0	0	0	1
	Muslims	0	0	0	0	1
Haiti	Animists	4	4	4.12	1	1
	Bahai	0	0	0	2	2
	Muslims	0	0	0	1	1
	Protestants	0	0	0	1	1
Honduras	Animists	0	0	0	2	2
	Bahai	0	0	0.28	2	2
	Muslims	0	1	0.12	2	2
	Protestants	0	0	0.12	2	2
Ivory Coast	Animists	0	0	0	1	0

Tanzania	Bahai	1	1	1.00	0	0
	Hindus	1	1	1.00	0	0
	Muslims	1	1	1.08	0	1
Timor	Muslims	2	0	0.77	1	1
	Protestants	12	11	12.31	7	8
Togo	Animists	0	0	0.00	1	2
	Bahai	0	0	0.00	1	1
	Muslims	0	0	0.00	0	0

One religion preferred

Angola	Animists	0	1	0.44	1	5
	Muslims	0	2	0.76	1	9
Bolivia	Animists	0	0	0	2	3
	Bahai	0	0	0	2	3
	Jews	0	2	0.16	2	4
	Muslims	0	0	0.04	2	3
	Protestants	0	0	0	5	3

Venezuela	Christians	0	0	0.2	1	0
	Harris	0	0	0	1	0
	Muslims	2	2	2.24	2	0
	Bahai	0	0	0	4	4
	Jews	0	9	3.6	5	6
	Muslims	0	0	0	4	4
	Other Christians	0	0	0.12	4	5
	Protestants	0	0	0	4	6
	Spiritists	0	0	0	3	3

Official religion

Zambia	Animists	0	0	0	0	1
	Bahai	0	0	0	0	1
	Catholics	0	0	0	0	1
	Muslims	0	1	0.08	1	3

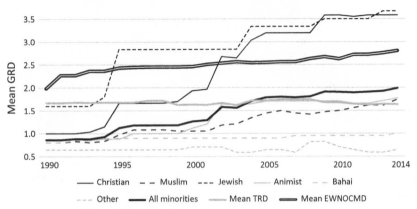

FIGURE 8.2 GRD in TRND states

This similarity in levels of both types of discrimination in the democratic TRD states and the nondemocratic TRND states has important implications for the link between democracy and discrimination that I discuss later in this chapter.

The overall trends in SRD, as shown in Figure 8.1, are different from other groupings of states. Until 1995, levels were extremely low against all minorities. In 1995, they began increasing against Christians, Muslims, and Jews. This is because Bosnia was in a full state of civil war until December 1995, when the RAS dataset began coding the country. The RAS project does not code countries when there is effectively no government. Despite the end of the war and official hostilities, SRD between ethnic groups that coincide with religious groups in Bosnia is extremely high. Bosnia has two governments that control different territories within the country. The Republika Srpska is controlled by Serbs, who are Serbian Orthodox, and the Federation of Bosnia and Herzegovina is controlled by Croats, who are Catholic, and Bosniaks, who are Muslims. Thus, all these religious groups are minorities in parts of the country.

Immediately after the end of the conflict SRD was extremely high. The levels marked as 1990 in Table 8.1 represent 1995 for Bosnia, which was the first year coded. By 2000, levels dropped to only slightly above the levels reported in 2014. Even in 2014, multiple types of SRD were present. This includes antiminority statements by politicians, bullying of religious minorities in schools, attacks against and vandalism of religious property and burial sites, public protests against the restoration of religious property destroyed in the civil war, and sporadic physical attacks. Incidents against Christian and Muslims are similar. Levels of SRD against Jews are lower and involve mostly graffiti and vandalism (Inter-religious Council in Bosnia-Herzegovina, 2015; OSCE, 2012, 2013; Sito-Sucic, 2009; UNICEF, n.d.).

In contrast, GRD has increased steadily in Bosnia. Minorities are often denied permits by local governments to build or reconstruct places of worship while a regions' majority group may often do so even without a permit. This occurs in violation of national laws. Local governments fail to protect religious minorities from societal violence. This often results in a restricted ability to engage in congregational prayer and ceremonies, even in private.

Returning to relative levels of SRD across religious minorities. Levels of SRD against Jews were about the same as other low-scoring religious minorities until 2004, when they began increasing relative to other minorities. There are only six Jewish minorities coded in TRND states, those in Bolivia, Bosnia, Colombia, Namibia, Suriname, and Venezuela. While in most cases this would be too few for a separate category, I did so here for purposes of comparison and the importance of Jewish minorities in other groupings of states.

SRD against Jews increased in Bolivia, Colombia, and Venezuela. The largest increase was in Venezuela and occurred between 2004 and 2006. In 2004, government-affiliated media outlets began producing anti-Semitic content, including anti-Jewish caricatures and political cartoons. For example, the hosts of La Hojilla, a talk show on official government television, made recurring anti-Semitic slurs. This incited similar speech acts in society, the distribution of anti-Semitic leaflets, as well as vandalism and graffiti of Jewish property. On occasion, usually in conjunction with events in the Middle East, violent protests occurred outside synagogues. In one such protest in 2012, approximately fifty protestors chanted anti-Semitic slogans and tossed fireworks inside the synagogue (Sokol, 2015). In Bolivia the incidents began in 2013 and include graffiti on synagogues and one case where a stick of dynamite was thrown into a synagogue (AJC, 2014). In Colombia, there have been sporadic incidents of vandalism and graffiti on synagogues since 2004. While there have been a number of kidnappings, these appear to be financially motivated and also target non-Jews.

Other than Jews, for most of the 1990–2014 period the Christian minorities experienced the highest levels of SRD. This is largely driven by Bosnia, which has two Christian minorities with high levels of

SRD – Catholics and Orthodox Christians. SRD is also high against Protestants in Timor. Timor is a Catholic-majority state that became independent from Indonesia in 2002. In rural areas, there is significant SRD against Protestants, including harassment, threats of violence, and violent attacks against missionaries and Protestants in general. There have also been several attacks against churches and property owned by Protestants. For example, in one local community in October 2013, a Catholic stoned a Protestant church and physically assaulted one of that church's members. Others in the same community threatened church property and church members.

Until 2009, Jews experienced the highest levels of GRD in TRND states. From 2009, Jews and Christians experienced approximately the same levels. The highest levels against Jews are in Bosnia, which I discussed earlier. They are also high in Venezuela, where in addition to the government incitement against Jews, which I discussed earlier, the government often restricts visas for foreign Jewish religious leaders and access of Jewish chaplains to prisons and the military.

Much of the increase in GRD against Christians is attributable to Eritrea. In 2002 Eritrea cancelled the registrations of all religious groups other than Orthodox Christians, Sunni Muslims, Roman Catholics, and members of the Evangelical Lutheran Church of Eritrea and required them to reregister. Many Protestant denominations that were not allowed to reregister effectively became illegal, resulting in multiple types of restrictions and severe government harassment. In addition, in Madagascar GRD increased significantly against the Church of Jesus Christ in Madagascar (FJKM), which is associated with the former government of Marc Ravalomanana. This increase began after Ravalomanana's ouster in a military coup in 2009.

Given the overall low levels of SRD and GRD in the TRND states, large changes in a small number of countries are driving many of the changes in this grouping of states. In addition, high levels of SRD and GRD against a small proportion of religious minorities drive many of the differences between minorities. Thus, while the trends depicted in Table 8.1 and Figures 8.1 and 8.2 are important, this element of their underlying causes should be kept in mind.

In a bivariate analysis, the link between SRD and GRD is present but weak. Of the sixty minorities that experienced SRD at some point between 1990 and 2014, thirty-seven (61.7 percent) also experienced GRD. Of the eighty-five minorities that experienced GRD in 2014, forty-eight (56.5 percent) did not experience any SRD between

1990 and 2014. Thus, SRD does not lead to GRD in over a third of cases in TRND states, and in a majority of cases of GRD, SRD is not present. Nevertheless, there is a significant correlation between SRD from 1990–2014 and GRD in 2014 (.418, significance = .000).

The country-level factors that predict GRD are similarly present but weaker than in other groupings of states. Table 8.2 compares GRD, support for religion, regulation of the majority religion, and the percent of states in each of the official religion categories across TRND, TRD, and EWNOCMD states. Perhaps the most striking trend is that nearly half of TRND states are neutral toward religion. This means that democracies are clearly more involved in religion than the TRND nondemocracies. This is especially true of EWNOCMD states, which include all those Western democracies that are generally considered liberal and secular. Proportionally, over three times as many TRND states are neutral toward religion compared to EWNOCMD states.

As is the case for other groupings of states, religiously neutral TRND states engage in the lowest levels of GRD. However, the mean levels are a bit higher than in the TRD and EWNOCMD states, as shown in Table 8.2. This finding is driven by two outliers. The first is Christians in Madagascar, which, as I discussed earlier, is driven more by politics than religion. The second is Animists in Uganda. This discrimination is largely targeted at groups that the government considers dangerous cults. It involves surveillance and often arrest and harassment when cult members refuse for religious reasons to participate in government programs such as the national census.

While there are differences across official religion categories on support for religion, they are smaller than in the other groupings of states measured in Table 8.2. Levels of support for religion do not differ greatly between states that have official religions, prefer one religion, and prefer multiple religions. Also, like other groupings of states, those that are hostile to religion and those that support one religion, either officially or unofficially, engage in more regulation of the majority religion.

While none of these states are fully democratic, that is, they score 7 or lower on the Polity scale, which ranges from −10 (the most autocratic states) to 10 (the most democratic), there is a wide range between the least democratic and most democratic within these states. As shown in Figure 8.3, levels of GRD are similar across different types of regime. This figure includes both TRND and TRD states for purposes of comparison. Other than the high scores for Eritrea, which I discussed earlier, the distribution of GRD scores is similar across the Polity scale. In addition, a correlational analysis shows perhaps a weak relationship

TABLE 8.2 *GRD and support for religion in TRD, TRND, and EWNOCMD states controlling for government religion policy*

	GRD			Support for Religion		
Official Religion Policy	**TRND states**	**TRD states**	**EWNOCMD states**	**TRND states**	**TRD states**	**EWNOCMD states**
Hostile	6.75	1.46	3.83	4.00	3.00	6.00
Neutral	0.83	0.31	0.41	5.16	4.90	6.40
Multiple religions preferred	3.38	0.42	3.56	7.90	7.50	9.67
One religion preferred	2.08	2.96	3.29	7.42	8.30	10.25
Official religion	1.50	2.63	3.18	7.00	13.33	11.86
All cases	1.99	1.63	2.81	6.26	7.17	9.67

	Regulation of the majority religion			% of states in official religion policy category		
Official religion policy	**TRND states**	**TRD states**	**EWNOCMD states**	**TRND states**	**TRD states**	**EWNOCMD states**
Hostile	17.50	10.50	11.00	5.3	6.9	3.0
Neutral	4.96	2.50	1.60	50.0	34.5	15.2
Multiple religions preferred	4.21	3.00	5.42	21.1	13.8	36.4
One religion preferred	7.47	6.30	3.00	23.7	34.5	24.2
Official religion	8.00	7.67	6.42	2.6	10.3	21.2
All cases	6.21	4.97	4.64			21.2

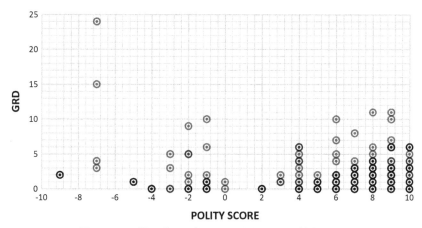

FIGURE 8.3 GRD controlling for polity score in TRD and TRND states in 2014

between GRD and Polity (Correlation = –.113, significance = .057). Thus, when looking at these states on a bivariate level, there is at most a weak connection between democracy and GRD.

Table 8.3 examines the causes of GRD and SRD within TRND states. The results for SRD are similar to other groupings in that violence and semiviolent actions by minority religions predict SRD but is unlike previous results in two ways. First, the population size of these countries does not influence levels of SRD. Second, support for the majority religion increases levels of SRD.

With regard to the causes of GRD, unlike the bivariate analysis, this analysis shows that those states that are less autocratic (as none of the TRND states are fully democratic on the Polity index) engage in less GRD when controlling for other factors. Interestingly, the influence of government religion policy on GRD is different from other groupings of states. Unlike other groupings, support for religion and whether a state is neutral toward religion have no significant impact on GRD. However, TRND states that regulate the majority religion engage in more GRD. These weak results may be attributable to overall low levels of GRD and low variation on the GRD variable with a few outliers.

As is the case with other groupings of states, in TRND states SRD influences GRD. In models 2 and 3 the general SRD variable increases levels of GRD. In Models 4, 5, and 6 the SRD variables for Christians, Muslims, and Jews are significant. As discussed earlier, there are only six Jewish minorities included in TRND countries, so while this result is statistically significant, it is difficult to draw general conclusions from it.

TABLE 8.3 *Multivariate analysis predicting GRD and SRD in TNRD states in 2014*

| | GRD | | | | | | | | | | | | SRD | |
| | Model 1 | | Model 2 | | Model 3 | | Model 4 | | Model 5 | | Model 6 | | Model 7 | |
	Beta	Sig.	Beta	Sig.	Beta	Sig.	Beta	Sig.	Beta	Sig.	Beta	Sig.	Beta	Sig.
Minority percent	-0.044	.602	-0.088	.268	-0.093	.242	-0.069	.384	-0.072	.372	-0.082	.312	0.118	.157
Polity	-0.132	.106	-0.145	.059	-0.140	.069	-0.187	.018	-0.185	.021	-0.190	.017	-0.026	.747
Regime durability	-0.139	.158	-0.125	.175	-0.132	.153	-0.099	.282	-0.102	.275	-0.132	.144	-0.029	.766
Per capita GDP (log)	0.001	.995	-0.004	.969	0.002	.981	-0.059	.534	-0.057	.550	-0.042	.661	-0.007	.942
Population (log)	-0.047	.588	0.039	.639	0.030	.719	0.015	.855	0.011	.893	0.041	.622	-0.138	.115
Majority Christian	-0.074	.388	-0.032	.690	-0.033	.683	0.007	.930	0.006	.942	0.022	.784	-0.064	.450
Religious support	0.137	.135	0.030	.735	0.024	.792	0.078	.397	0.075	.422	0.110	.217	0.234	.011
Regulation of the majority religion	0.184	.030	0.221	.006	0.224	.006	0.216	.008	0.217	.008	0.245	.002	-0.124	.141
Regime neutral to religion	-0.177	.062	-0.127	.156	-0.127	.155	-0.116	.192	-0.117	.192	–	–	-0.108	.249
Violent and semiviolent minority actions	0.194	.017	–	–	0.064	.433	–	–	0.022	.813	0.018	.844	0.267	.001
SRD	–	–	0.416	.000	0.390	.000	–	–	–	–	–	–	–	–
SRD Christian	–	–	–	–	–	–	0.349	.000	0.336	.000	0.352	.000	–	–
SRD Muslim	–	–	–	–	–	–	0.215	.005	0.215	.005	0.222	.004	–	–
SRD Jewish	–	–	–	–	–	–	0.172	.020	0.172	.020	0.178	.017	–	–
SRD Bahai	–	–	–	–	–	–	-0.087	.243	-0.086	.254	-0.079	.293	–	–
SRD Animist	–	–	–	–	–	–	-0.018	.804	-0.017	.816	-0.020	.784	–	–
SRD Other	–	–	–	–	–	–	-0.072	.322	-0.071	.329	-0.075	.304	–	–
DF	147		147		147		147		147		147		147	
Adjusted R²	.175		.275		.273		.290		.285		.281		.189	

The results for Christians are mostly focused on Christian minorities that are considered nonindigenous, as is the case in the TRD states that I discussed in Chapter 7. GRD against Protestants in Catholic-majority Timor, which I discussed in more detail earlier in this chapter, are one example. Another example is the GRD described earlier in Eritrea against Christian denominations that are not among the four that the government recognizes as traditional to the country. That being said, these results may be driven by two outliers – Bosnia and Timor. Bosnia has three Christian minorities that experience among the highest levels of SRD among TRND states, and Timor has one such minority. There are no other Christian minorities in this grouping that experience levels of SRD higher than 2.

The results for Muslims are likely triggered by the securitization of Islam in TRND states. GRD against Muslims began increasing in 2002, just after the September 11, 2001, attacks in the United States and by 2014 were 65.4 percent higher than they were in 2001. Of the thirty-nine Muslim minorities in TRND states, eleven experienced more GRD in 2014 than they did in 1990, but three experienced less. For example, in 2002 Tanzania passed the Prevention of Terrorism Act. The law does not mention Muslims specifically but was clearly aimed at them.

In Uganda, harassment of Muslims by the government dates back to 1996 after a group of Muslims associated with the Tablighi Jamaat movement joined the Allied Democratic Force (ADF) rebels. This GRD includes arrests, detentions, torture, and the destruction of Mosques and Islamic schools. While these government activities subsided along with the fortunes of the ADF, they did not disappear. For example, in 2013 the government closed ten Islamic schools for failing to meet national educational standards and on suspicion that they were being used to recruit for terrorist groups. In the same year, the government arrested eleven Muslim community leaders but did not press any charges. The threat of Islamic terror remains real as the terror group Al-Shabab remains active in the country (Candia, 2013; Miller, 2014; Press TV, 2015). This coincides with low-level SRD against Muslims in Uganda. Muslims experience discrimination in the job market, and many workplaces and universities do not allow women to wear head coverings.

Comparing TRND and TRD States

Perhaps the most striking trend when comparing democracies and non-democracies of "the rest" states – those states that are not Muslim-majority, Orthodox-majority, Buddhist-majority, Communist, Western

democracies, or other European democracies – is that there is little difference in mean levels of both SRD and GRD between the democratic TRD
states and the nondemocratic TRND states. However, as shown in
Table 8.4, when taking other factors into account, democratic states
engage in less GRD. The other causes of GRD in these combined groupings are similar to those presented for each of these groupings individually
earlier in this chapter and the previous chapter other than that regulation
of the majority religion is significant in some of the models.

As shown in Table 8.2, the other differences between the democracies
(TRD) and nondemocracies (TRND) are small but present. Nondemocracies engage in slightly less support for religion and are more likely to be
neutral toward religion. Both of these factors make GRD less likely. They
also engage in more regulation of the majority religion. These small
differences in government religion policy are likely part of the reason
the Polity variable is statistically significant. Specifically, each of these
factors make the TRND states more secular, which, based on the evidence, counterbalances their lack of democracy. Put differently, the levels
of GRD are similarly low in TRD and TRND states, but the exact mix of
causes for this result differs between the two categories of state with the
TRD states being influenced by democracy and the TRND states being
more influenced by their secularity.

Despite the statistical significance of democracy as a cause of GRD in
multivariate analysis, that in absolute terms levels of GRD are similar in
TRD and TRND states is important. That this can be explained by factors
such as SRD, government religion policy, and different levels of secularity
is nontrivial. Nevertheless, in my assessment these similarities in absolute
levels of GRD between any set of democracies and nondemocracies is the
more important finding.

In Chapters 5 and 7, I demonstrated that assumptions that Western
democracies are the strongest supporters of secularism and religious
freedom are not supported by the evidence. The results in this chapter
bolster this finding in that they demonstrate that even a major subset of
nondemocracies – those that are not Muslim-majority, Buddhist-majority, Orthodox-majority, or Communist – also engage in lower levels of
GRD than Western democracies. These exclusions are not insignificant,
but if one wants to argue that Western democracies engage in less GRD
than non-Western countries and nondemocracies, this should apply to all
subsets of democracy and nondemocracy. To find otherwise means, at the
very least, that other factors are in play that can overshadow the assumed
influence of liberal democracy on religious freedom and tolerance.

TABLE 8.4 *Multivariate analysis predicting GRD and SRD in TRD and TNRD states in 2014*

| | GRD | | | | | | | | | | | | SRD | |
| | Model 1 | | Model 2 | | Model 3 | | Model 4 | | Model 5 | | Model 6 | | Model 7 | |
	Beta	Sig.	Beta	Sig.	Beta	Sig.	Beta	Sig.	Beta	Sig.	Beta	Sig.	Beta	Sig.
Minority percent	0.005	.929	−0.047	.354	−0.038	.470	−0.043	.404	−0.032	.548	−0.055	.307	0.095	.111
Polity	−0.135	.020	−0.133	.011	−0.135	.010	−0.175	.001	−0.177	.001	−0.151	.007	−0.025	.681
Regime durability	−0.005	.936	0.001	.988	0.003	.960	0.009	.866	0.011	.830	0.004	.937	−0.020	.729
Per capita GDP (log)	−0.014	.817	−0.035	.516	−0.035	.523	−0.030	.578	−0.029	.597	−0.037	.508	0.064	.305
Population (log)	0.183	.002	0.139	.008	0.142	.007	0.157	.004	0.162	.003	0.155	.005	0.159	.008
Majority Christian	0.019	.741	0.046	.384	0.048	.366	0.067	.207	0.071	.183	0.112	.040	−0.037	.544
Religious support	0.140	.026	0.066	.240	0.076	.186	0.084	.136	0.097	.094	0.163	.005	0.161	.014
Regulation of the majority religion	0.106	.075	0.127	.019	0.125	.021	0.101	.067	0.097	.078	0.138	.013	−0.061	.325
Regime neutral to religion	−0.249	.000	−0.224	.000	−0.225	.000	−0.224	.000	−0.224	.000	—	—	−0.042	.477
Violent and semiviolent minority actions	0.047	.386	—	—	−0.044	.386	—	—	−0.057	.264	−0.056	.285	0.221	.000
SRD	—	—	0.401	.000	0.410	.000	—	—	—	—	—	—	—	—
SRD Christian	—	—	—	—	—	—	0.347	.000	0.357	.000	0.371	.000	—	—
SRD Muslim	—	—	—	—	—	—	0.205	.000	0.216	.000	0.227	.000	—	—
SRD Jewish	—	—	—	—	—	—	0.103	.030	0.101	.032	0.104	.033	—	—
SRD Hindu	—	—	—	—	—	—	−0.052	.265	−0.054	.248	−0.059	.222	—	—
SRD Bahai	—	—	—	—	—	—	−0.077	.104	−0.079	.098	−0.066	.175	—	—
SRD Animist	—	—	—	—	—	—	0.033	.477	0.032	.497	0.019	.697	—	—
SRD Other	—	—	—	—	—	—	0.024	.603	0.024	.606	0.003	.944	—	—
DF	313		313		313		313		313		313		313	
Adjusted R^2	.201		.344		.344		.348		.349		.310		.138	

TABLE 8.5 *Mean GRD in 2014 for democracies and nondemocracies*

	Democracies		Nondemocracies	
	N	Mean	N	Mean
EWNOCMD	146	2.81	–	–
Muslim-majority	23	9.65	174	12.60
Buddhist-majority	4	4.25	3	11.29
Orthodox-majority	33	7.90[a]	31	14.12[a]
Communist	–	–	27	17.28
"The rest"	148	1.63	166	1.98
Combined West and former Soviet ("North")	186	3.66[b]	57	14.63[b]
Combined West and former Soviet ("North") Christian	177	3.70[b]	28	15.89[b]
Combined non-West non-former Soviet ("South")	184	2.64[b]	344	7.90[b]
Combined non-West non-former Soviet ("South") Christian	137	1.84	117	1.93
All minorities	370	3.15	401	8.86

[a] = Significance of mean between democracies and nondemocracies in marked categories <.01.
[b] = Significance of mean between democracies and nondemocracies in marked categories <.001.

Table 8.5 examines this dynamic further by comparing mean levels of GRD across all democracies and nondemocracies. It shows that this finding that democracy is not necessarily related to lower GRD is limited to a subset of democracies. If one looks only at the "north" (the West and the former-Soviet bloc), democracies engage in less GRD. This remains true even if one limits the analysis to Christian-majority countries. However, this difference in the Christian-majority countries is driven by Orthodox-majority countries as no "northern" Christian-majority state that is not Orthodox-majority is a nondemocracy, which in and of itself is an interesting finding. The two Muslim-majority democracies in the former-Soviet bloc, Albania and Kosovo, engage in a mean level of GRD of 2.77 against the nine minorities in these countries, which is comparable to levels in EWNOCMD states and is much lower than the 13.96 mean for the Muslim-majority states of the region that are not democratic.

However, if one looks at Christian-majority countries in the "south," there is little difference in levels of GRD between democracies and nondemocracies. This subset of states largely coincides with those defined here as "the rest." That being said, when looking only at Christian-majority states, as shown in Table 8.6, democracy remains an important

TABLE 8.6 *Multivariate analysis predicting GRD and SRD in Christian-majority states in 2014*

| | GRD | | | | | | | | | | | | SRD | |
| | Model 1 | | Model 2 | | Model 3 | | Model 4 | | Model 5 | | Model 6 | | Model 7 | |
	Beta	Sig.	Beta	Sig.	Beta	Sig.	Beta	Sig.	Beta	Sig.	Beta	Sig.	Beta	Sig.
Minority percent	0.001	.970	0.006	.860	0.010	.771	-0.014	.672	-0.003	.933	-0.008	.807	-0.025	.589
Polity	-0.161	.000	-0.165	.000	-0.165	.000	-0.197	.000	-0.200	.000	-0.200	.000	-0.002	.970
Regime durability	-0.025	.636	-0.008	.878	-0.008	.881	-0.005	.909	-0.005	.914	0.000	.993	-0.039	.545
Per capita GDP (log)	0.113	.031	0.062	.210	0.062	.216	0.101	.028	0.097	.034	0.103	.029	0.227	.000
Population (log)	0.074	.078	0.017	.672	0.020	.623	0.043	.239	0.051	.164	-0.004	.921	0.219	.000
Majority Catholic	-0.091	.083	-0.061	.221	-0.061	.217	-0.073	.111	-0.073	.108	0.045	.260	-0.103	.108
Majority Orthodox	0.428	.000	0.357	.000	0.356	.000	0.296	.000	0.293	.000	0.325	.000	0.241	.000
Religious support	0.124	.004	0.109	.008	0.111	.007	0.113	.003	0.116	.002	0.194	.000	0.031	.562
Regulation of the majority religion	0.105	.019	0.114	.007	0.113	.008	0.113	.004	0.111	.005	0.163	.000	-0.048	.386
Regime neutral to religion	-0.236	.000	-0.212	.000	-0.213	.000	-0.208	.000	-0.209	.000	—	—	-0.079	.185
Violent and semiviolent minority actions	0.002	.965	—	—	-0.019	.588	—	—	-0.057	.089	-0.055	.108	0.096	.033
SRD	—	—	0.266	.000	0.268	.000	—	—	—	—	—	—	—	—
SRD Christian	—	—	—	—	—	—	0.372	.000	0.373	.000	0.383	.000	—	—
SRD Muslim	—	—	—	—	—	—	0.153	.000	0.171	.000	0.178	.000	—	—
SRD Jewish	—	—	—	—	—	—	-0.014	.665	-0.015	.650	-0.009	.791	—	—
SRD Hindu	—	—	—	—	—	—	-0.037	.232	-0.039	.210	-0.043	.175	—	—
SRD Bahai	—	—	—	—	—	—	-0.063	.047	-0.064	.043	-0.050	.120	—	—
SRD Animist	—	—	—	—	—	—	0.029	.350	0.027	.378	0.019	.543	—	—
SRD Other	—	—	—	—	—	—	0.065	.035	0.065	.035	0.071	.023	—	—
DF	458		458		458		458		458		458		458	
Adjusted R²	.436		.496		.495		.578		.580		.558		.158	

predictor of GRD. The other results are largely the same except there is no SRD-GRD link for Jews and in several of the models there is a SRD-GRD link for Bahai, but SRD makes GRD less common. This is a statistical artifact as only two of the thirty-eight Bahai minorities in these countries experienced any SRD between 1990 and 2014.

SOME IMPLICATIONS AND EXPLANATIONS

This chapter is the last of three – Chapters 5, 7, and 8 – that provide the bulk of the evidence that calls into question many assumptions regarding religious freedom and tolerance in Western democracies, as well as democracies in general as compared to nondemocracies. Accordingly, it is useful at this point to discuss these combined findings and their implications. In this section I discuss some of the more direct implications for the findings presented in these three chapters and compare them to those in Chapters 4 and 6. In Chapter 9, I discuss the wider practical and theoretical implications of the entire study.

We have five related findings. First, if one looks at states with any majority religion other than Christianity, democracies engage in less GRD than nondemocracies. Second, among Orthodox Christian-majority states, democracies engage in less GRD. Third, among "the rest" and "southern" Christian-majority states, categories that overlap considerably, democracies and nondemocracies have essentially the same mean level of GRD. Fourth, EWNOCMD states and Western democracies are less secular on measures of government religion policy including GRD than "the rest" states. Fifth, among Christian-majority states multivariate analysis shows that democracy does lower levels of GRD, but this is matched by other crosscutting influences, including that non-Orthodox Christian-majority nondemocracies are less likely to support religion and are more likely to have neutral religion policies.

Regime and GRD

What does all of this mean? I argue that it has several important implications. The first set of implications relates to the relationship between democracy and GRD. The results show that this is a complex relationship. Overall, the relationship holds – that is, when controlling for other factors democracy is correlated with less GRD. That being said, other cultural, religious, political, and economic factors can overshadow the impact of democracy on GRD, and such cases are not rare. Among

Western and European Christian-majority democracies (including Orthodox-majority democracies), this overshadowing of democracy by other crosscutting factors is the rule rather than the exception.

Put differently, not all democracies engage in low levels of GRD. Among democracies, low levels of GRD are found most often in TRD states, especially those with a Christian majority. As I discussed in Chapter 5, EWNOCMD states tend to have significant levels of GRD. Thus, among non-Orthodox Christian-majority countries, the "northern" EWNOMCD countries, on average, engage in more GRD than the "southern" countries.

There are nineteen democracies that are not non-Orthodox Christian-majority countries, eight of which are Orthodox-majority. There is considerable variation across these countries on GRD. Four of them, Japan, Mauritius, South Korea, and Taiwan, engage in no GRD. The others all engage in levels of at least 3 against at least one minority.

Similarly, not all nondemocracies engage in high levels of GRD. As shown in Table 8.5, the TRND states as well as the overlapping category of "southern" Christian-majority nondemocracies engage in low mean levels of GRD, lower than found in EWNOCMD states. All other categories of nondemocracy engage in higher mean levels, both compared to TRND states and "southern" Christian-majority states as well as to democracies within their own categories.

This complex relationship between regime and GRD demonstrates that the contention that democracies discriminate less is simplistic and not always correct. Based on the multivariate analyses, democracy likely has this influence. However, this influence is often weaker than other factors. That is, not only can the influence of democracy on GRD be eclipsed by other political, cultural, and economic forces, but also this overshadowing of democracy is a common occurrence. This finding undermines assumptions of the extent to which democracy promotes tolerance.

Government Religion Policy

Perhaps the most important factor that predicts levels of GRD is government religion policy. Those states that are neutral on the issue of religion in matters other than GRD are far less likely to engage in GRD. As shown in Table 8.7, neutral states engage in low mean levels of GRD regardless of in which grouping they are found and regardless of whether they are democratic or not. This factor, along with support for the majority

TABLE 8.7 *Mean levels of GRD controlling for official government religion policy*

				Official religion policy			
	N	Hostile	Neutral	Multiple religions preferred	One religion preferred	Official religion	All cases
Democracies	370	2.29	0.35	2.43	4.96	4.20	3.15
EWNOCMD states	146	3.83	0.41	3.56	3.29	3.18	2.81
Orthodox-majority	31	–	–	1.50	–	15.00	7.90
Muslim-majority	23	–	–	2.13	14.25	11.33	9.65
Buddhist-majority	4	–	–	–	4.25	–	4.25
"The rest"	166	1.46	0.31	0.42	2.96	2.63	1.63
"South" non-Orthodox Christian	137	1.46	0.40	0.59	2.57	5.08	1.84
Nondemocracies	401	14.50	0.97	4.94	7.77	15.08	10.65
Orthodox-majority	33	–	3.10	–	18.91	–	14.12
Muslim-majority	174	14.10	0.77	7.09	4.31	16.25	12.60
Buddhist-majority	21	–	–	–	8.92	6.38	7.95
"The rest"	148	6.75	0.83	3.38	2.08	1.50	1.98
"South" non-Orthodox Christian	112	6.75	1.09	1.65	2.33	1.50	1.83
Communist	25	17.28	–	–	–	–	17.28
All cases	771	11.49	0.68	3.37	6.07	11.82	6.12

religion and, to a lesser extent, restrictions placed on the majority religion combine to have a large influence on levels of GRD.

Yet, this influence is also complex. One aspect of this complexity is that groupings of states matter. For example, the proportion of states that are neutral varies across groupings of states. As shown in Table 8.2, among the thirty-two EWNOCMD states, only five have neutral religion policies as compared to ten of the thirty-four TRD states. In contrast, half of the TRND states are neutral toward religion. Thus, while official religion policy influences GRD in a similar manner across groupings of states, different groupings of states based on majority religion, ideology, location, regime, and culture have dramatically different patterns of official religion policy.

That being said, just because states across different groupings have a similar government religion policy does not always mean that GRD will be at similar levels. Like regime, government religion policy does not influence GRD in a vacuum. Factors like ideology, culture, regime, and location also influence GRD directly and through their influence on other aspects of government religion policy. For example, among states that support a single religion, non-Orthodox Christian-majority states engage in lower mean levels of GRD. These states have a mean level of GRD that ranges from 1.50–5.08, depending on the category of state and whether the support for religion is through an official religion or through a general preference. All other groupings range from 4.25–16.25. This demonstrates different behavior among states that support a single religion more than all others between non-Orthodox Christian-majority states and all other states.

Far fewer states are overtly hostile to religion, so results focusing on these states are less reliable. That being said, the pattern is similar. Non-Orthodox Christian-majority states that are hostile to religion engage in less GRD than other states that are hostile to religion.

This set of findings has at least two potential implications. First, it is possible that religious non-Orthodox Christians and their governments are more tolerant than religious people and their governments from other religious traditions. As I discussed in Chapter 5, many argue that Western Christianity, particularly elements within the Protestant and Catholic traditions, are the source of current Western support for religious tolerance and religious freedom. These arguments are just as applicable to Christianity outside the West. Thus, these findings may be a result of these processes within Protestant and Catholic Christianity. Also, as I discussed in Chapter 6, much of the GRD in Orthodox-majority states can be attributed to Orthodox institutions and clergy actively lobbying the government to restrict religious minorities. This demonstrates that attitudes toward religious minorities by clergy and religious institutions can be an important factor in explaining levels of GRD. As Orthodox Christianity is not explicitly included in the arguments for Christian religious tolerance and Orthodox-majority countries are found to engage in more GRD, this indicates that whatever the influence of modern Christian traditions on tolerance, its strength varies across Christian traditions.

Second, the nature of government-religion relations may be different across groupings. That is, supporting an official religion may be different for Muslims and Christians, for example. The RAS data shows that there is some truth to this contention. For example, as I discussed in more detail in Chapter 4, there are forms of official religion policy currently only seen in Muslim-majority states. The RAS dataset includes three types of official religions. One is active official religions where the state designates an official religion and actively supports it but the religious institutions remain relatively independent compared to the other two types of official religion. Also, the government makes few or no aspects of the official religion mandatory. All non-Muslim-majority countries with official religions other than Denmark and Greece fit into this category.

Positive controlled religions, the second category of official religion, are characterized by their higher level of control of the institutions of the official religion. They also tend to support the majority religion and enforce aspects of the majority religion's doctrine more than countries in the active support category, but the key aspect of this definition is the control of the region's institutions. Denmark and Greece are in this category. All other states in this category are Muslim-majority.

The final category is states with mandatory religions. While these states tend to support the majority religion and control its institutions, often more strongly than those in the previous category, the defining characteristic of this category is that they make a significant portion, if not all, of the majority religion mandatory. In Saudi Arabia and the Maldives, this is applied to all residents regardless of their religion. In most other states in this category, it is applied primarily to Muslims, but aspects of Islamic law are also applied to non-Muslims.

As I showed in Chapter 4 (Table 4.1), these categorizations have a profound impact on GRD, as well as other aspects of government religion policy. For example, Muslim-majority states with active official religions – the category that includes all but two non-Muslim-majority states with an official religion – have a mean level of GRD of 5.47. This is within the range of where other groupings of states with official religions fall. Thus, it is the presence of a different type of official religion in Muslim-majority states that accounts for the high levels of GRD in these countries.

The RAS dataset similarly has four categories for states hostile to religion. As in 2014 only fifteen countries fell into all of these categories combined, the discussion thus far in this book combined all these categories into a single category. Yet, these categories influence levels of GRD. The mildest of these categories is states that are separationist. These states maintain separation of religion and state but have a hostile attitude toward religion in general. France's *laicite* policy of maintaining a secular public space is an example of such a state (Fox, 2008, 2015). All three democracies coded as hostile to religion – France, Mexico, and Uruguay – fall into this category. The mean level of GRD in these countries is 4.66.

Only Cuba falls into the nonspecific hostility category. This category represents states that seek to control or limit any institution that can be the basis for organizing against the government. They therefore seek to control and limit religion not because it is a religion but because it has this potential. While mean levels of GRD in a single state are difficult to use to represent an entire category (in 1990 there were four states in this category), the mean 2014 level of GRD in Cuba was 18.50.

Negative state-controlled religions are states such as China where the government does not declare an official religion and is hostile to the idea of religion but seeks to limit religion's influence in society and politics through controlling its religious institutions. These states typically set up an official set of religious institutions that the state monitors and controls, while at the same time declaring separation of religion and state or that the state is secular. Religious activity, usually with limits upon it, is legal within the context of these institutions but is harshly repressed if it occurs outside the context of these state-controlled institutions. The seven countries in this category had a mean level of GRD in 2014 of 17.16.

The final hostile category is specific hostility. These states have a national ideology that is opposed to religion in principle and actively repress all religion in the country. Currently only North Korea fits into this category but during the Cold War era, it is likely that many Communist states fell into this category. In 2014 the mean level of GRD in North Korea was 8.75. This lower level is because most repression in North Korea is against all religions. This is not considered GRD, which requires differential treatment. Thus, the nature of the hostility toward religion can account for the different results across different groupings of states that are hostile to religion.

All the states that fall into the categories of hostility stronger than the separationist states are former Communist Muslim-majority (Kyrgyzstan Tajikistan, Turkmenistan, and Uzbekistan) or current Communist states (Cuba, North Korea, China, Laos, and Vietnam). Thus, secular ideology clearly plays a role in creating religion policies that are hostile to religion.

SRD, Economics, and GRD

As I discussed in Chapter 7, there are other reasons that GRD is higher in the "northern" EWNOCMD states as opposed to the "southern" TRD states. Levels of SRD are lower in TRD states, which can explain lower levels of GRD in those states. Also, GRD is costly in resources. The poorer "southern" states may engage in less GRD simply because they lack the resources do so as effectively as the wealthier states of the "north."

Culture, Religious Tradition, and GRD

A second, but related, set of implications, is that different cultures relate to religion differently, and this has implications for all aspects of government religion policy, including GRD. That is, looking at the same information from a different perspective, it is possible that much of the variations across different groupings of state are cultural. Bernard Lewis (1988: 3), for example, classically argued that for Muslims "the very notion of a secular jurisdiction and authority is seen as an impiety, indeed as the ultimate betrayal of Islam." In essence, for Muslims religion is inherently political. Cesari (2014) argues that modern Muslim-majority states have been politicizing Islam since their establishment after the breakup of the Ottoman Empire and decolonialization. She contrasts this to the West.

The modernization of Muslim societies, unlike Western ones, did not lead to the privatization of religion but to the opposite, that is, the politicization of Islam in a way unprecedented in premodern Muslim societies. This is not because Islam does not separate religion and politics (which is by the way historically false) but because the Islamic tradition was integrated into the nation state-building that took place at the end of the Ottoman Empire.

(Cesari, 2014: xiii)

Thus, Cesari, like many others who compares Islam and the West, argues that different cultures relate to the politicization of religion differently (Hefner, 2001: 492–493; Tezcur, 2006: 218; Tibi, 2000).

Survey-based studies also show that members of different religions often have different attitudes toward political issues. This includes support for violence (Canetti et al., 2010), the salience of religion in national identity (Kunovich, 2006) and politics (Norris & Inglehart, 2002, 2004), and interest in politics (Manglos, 2013). However, other factors are involved. For example Kim (2008) found that Muslims living in Western countries are more likely to be supportive of democracies than Muslims living in Muslim-majority countries. Given this, it is reasonable to argue that religious tradition may influence attitudes toward minorities.

Interestingly both Fetzer and Soper (2003) and Helberg (2014) found that religious Europeans are more tolerant of Muslims on issues such as wearing head coverings in public. This is attributed to their being able to understand the need to observe religious practices better than secular Europeans. On the other hand, studies also show that religiosity can lead to intolerance of immigrants (Karpov, 2002). Milligan et al. (2014: 249) find that "people living in Muslim-majority countries tend to be less tolerant than are those living in Western countries." Thus, the relationship between religiosity and tolerance for religious minorities can be complex. All of this assumes that this relationship works in one direction and that attitudes influence policy. Helbling and Traunmuller (2015: 3), among others, argue that policy can influence attitudes.

Returning to the issue of tolerance, the results from this study show that on average non-Orthodox Christian-majority countries are in practice more tolerant of religious minorities than any other grouping of countries. GRD in these countries is on average lower, which, in effect, is more tolerance by governments. SRD is also lower in these countries than most groupings. However, non-Communist Buddhist-majority states have slightly lower levels of SRD than EWNOCMD states but higher than in the "southern" non-Orthodox Christian-majority states. Communist states have the lowest levels of SRD of all states, though this is likely due to repression of this type of activity rather than tolerance among the population.

Thus, the empirical evidence from this study has non-Orthodox Christians and their governments the most tolerant of religious minorities worldwide, though there is wide variation within this grouping of states, and this toleration is found more in the non-West than in the West. While these are macro-level indicators, they likely shed some insight on which religions show more tolerance in today's political and religious environment.

CONCLUSIONS

The results presented in this chapter confound many of our assumptions about how the world works. The liberal democracies of the West are not the most religiously tolerant countries in the world. Even more confounding is that "the rest" states – those states that are not from the West, Orthodox-majority, Muslim-majority, Buddhist-majority, or Communist – engage in less GRD than EWNOCMD states, and this is true whether or not they are democracies. Thus, a large grouping of nondemocracies, the TRND states discussed in this chapter, are, in practice, more religiously tolerant than the liberal democracies of the West.

Also, that SRD is lower in TRND states than in Western democracies indicates higher societal tolerance of minorities in these nondemocracies. That is, Western democracies embrace religious freedom as a value and teach it in their schools, yet have higher levels of both GRD and SRD than a large grouping of nondemocracies. As I discuss in more detail in the following chapter, this lower tolerance both in society and by governments in EWNOCMD states may be due to the higher influence of secular ideologies in these countries.

The findings on GRD can be explained by various aspects of government religion policy, variation in economic resources available to fund discrimination, violent actions by minority groups, and SRD. However, the simple fact of large pockets of religious tolerance among nondemocracies that are stronger than the assumed religious tolerance found in Western democracies overshadows these explanations. That is, the ability to explain this lack of religious tolerance in the West as well as why other groupings of states are more tolerant does not make the relative religious intolerance of the West disappear.

9

Conclusions

Despite the obvious complexity of the world we live in, there is a desire for simple easy-to-understand principles to help us comprehend it. This is one of the roles of theories and models, to take a complex reality and simplify it sufficiently so we can better understand it. Of course, we acknowledge that reality is more complex, but some of this complexity is sacrificed to achieve better understanding. Because of this, it is popular in academic literature when addressing a topic to form a basic parsimonious theory that "explains" the topic at hand.

This study strays quite a bit from this well-worn path. The causes of religious discrimination by governments against religious minorities (GRD) are numerous, multifaceted, and complicated. Furthermore, while it is possible to create a list of major influences on GRD, and this study provides such a list in Chapter 2, these influences play out differently in different groupings of countries. Thus, while theory plays a central role in this study and likely simplifies reality to some extent in order to better understand the causes of GRD, the use and application of theory in this study simplifies reality less than the norm for this type of study.

This complexity rises from a number of factors inherent in GRD. The first is that explaining GRD involves two basic questions. First, why do governments discriminate in general? When looking only at the state-level of analysis this question is sufficient. But the RASM3 dataset uses the religious minority in a state as the level of analysis and includes 771 minorities in 183 states. Furthermore, in most of these countries, there are multiple minorities. As I discussed in more detail in Chapter 2, 150 of these countries treat at least 1 minority different from the others. Excluding the fifteen countries that do not discriminate at all and the five countries with only one minority (which makes differential discrimination impossible), this means that 92 percent of countries that discriminate, discriminate unequally. Furthermore, the remaining 8 percent engage in low levels of GRD, so all countries that discriminate on substantial levels, discriminate unequally.

Because of this, we must ask a second question to understand the causes of GRD. Given that certain countries are more likely to discriminate than other countries, why do countries single out some religious minorities for more GRD? Or perhaps, we should ask why are some religious minorities more likely to be tolerated than others?

The second element of complexity is that the answers to these two questions are different for different groupings of countries. More specifically, the principles that can explain GRD tend to apply in most settings, but the manifestation of these influences differs across groupings of states. The third element of complexity is that the causes of GRD are numerous and crosscutting. In many countries the causes are at cross-purposes, with some pushing for more GRD and others for less, and the question often becomes which set of causes is more influential in a particular setting?

The fourth aspect of this complexity is that the findings of this study are in part counterintuitive. That is, they provide considerable evidence that many long-standing assumptions are inaccurate. This is particularly true of assumptions regarding levels of tolerance, secularity, and religious freedom in democracies in general and liberal democracies in particular. This interacts with the second form of complexity because these counterintuitive findings play out differently across different groupings of states, thereby creating a multiplying effect. In addition, the third form of complexity, crosscutting and competing influences, is at least a partial explanation for this finding.

That being said, in this chapter I attempt to make sense of the complex reality revealed by the findings of this study. It is possible to take a step back and look at all the moving parts at once. Essentially, I provide an overview of the results of this study and their implications, as I did in the study itself, by breaking them into manageable parts. Accordingly, I first examine the state-level causes of GRD then the minority-specific causes. Second, I discuss the nature and causes of societal religious discrimination (SRD). Finally, I discuss some policy implications.

WHERE ARE WE MORE LIKELY TO FIND GRD?

In Chapter 2, I discussed the potential state-level causes of GRD *in theory*. These include religious ideology, religious monopolies, antireligious ideologies, the majority religion, regime, regime stability, and world region. In this section, I cover much of the same territory, but I emphasize how these theories play out *in practice*. All these factors play a role in practice. As these factors combine to create a complex economy of cross-cutting causes of GRD, when I discuss any single cause, it is with the caveat of all other things being equal.

Religious Ideologies and Religious Monopolies

The roles of religious ideology, religious monopolies, and antireligious ideologies all play out in practice in the context of government religion policies. That is, governments use policy to put their ideological and other preferences into action. Three aspects of government religion policy can predict levels of GRD. Each of them is complex in practice. It is also important to keep in mind that each of these influences competes with other influences, and there are outright exceptions to all these principles. Usually these exceptions are due to other influences on GRD, but not in all cases.

First, the stronger a country's connection to religion, the more it engages in GRD. As the most likely reasons a country would be strongly connected to a religion are religious ideology and the desire to protect a religious monopoly, the link between these causes of GRD in theory and government religion policy in practice is clear. Specifically, those countries that are influenced by a religious ideology and wish to maintain a religious monopoly will be more strongly connected to religion as measured by the RAS variables. In addition, states that are secular but not hostile to religion are more likely to have neutral religion policies where the government either maintains separation of religion or state or treats all religions equally. These states will tend to have low levels of GRD. I discuss states with antireligious ideologies separately later.

In this study, I measure this connection in two ways, official government policy and support for religion. Each of these directly influence GRD, but this connection manifests differently in different groupings of states. Looking first at official religion policy, there is one common factor across groupings of states. States with neutral religion policies tend to engage in the lowest average levels of GRD within their grouping. This is true of every grouping of states that includes states with neutral policies, but not all groupings contain such states, including Communist and Buddhist-majority states.

Ethiopia and Ukraine, the two Orthodox-majority states that have otherwise neutral policies toward religion, are the two exceptions to this general finding. Nine of the ten minorities in these states experience GRD. In all other groupings, a large majority of minorities in neutral states experience no GRD. As I discussed in detail in Chapter 6, this exception is due in great part to the influence of Orthodox institutions and clergy on policy, especially at the local level. Nevertheless, the level of GRD in these two countries is still lower than the average for Orthodox-majority states whose official religion policies give more exclusivity to the Orthodox Church. The RAS measures quantify mostly government actions that influence religion, which is appropriate for measures of government religion policy. The link between policy and GRD assumes that government support for religion is related to the influence of religion on government, but other factors can influence government religion policy. Also, it is possible that, as is the case with Ethiopia and Ukraine, this influence of religious ideology manifests primarily as GRD but not in other aspects of government religion policy.

If one looks at the RASM3 dataset as a whole, as official policy more strongly supports a single religion, GRD increases. That is, states that prefer multiple religions engage in more GRD than neutral states, states that prefer a single religion (but have no official religion) engage in more GRD than states that prefer multiple religions, and states that have official religions engage in more GRD that states that prefer a single religion. However, as shown in Table 8.7 in the previous chapter, there are some exceptions when looking at specific groupings of states.

While some of these exceptions are likely due to a small number of states in some of the categories, this is not true of all of them. For example, levels of GRD in European and Western non-Orthodox-majority democratic (EWNOCMD) states are roughly the same in the multiple religions preferred, one religion preferred, and official religion categories. This is likely because in these countries there are multiple crosscutting influences on GRD, including clashes between religious and secular political actors, anticult policies, the securitization of Islam, and the desire to protect national culture from religions seen as nonindigenous. Thus, in these countries, states that maintain neutral policies are more successful at avoiding the influence of religious ideologies as well as most other influences, other than the securitization of Islam – Muslims in four of five neutral EWNOCMD states experience GRD. However, once countries in this grouping begin supporting religion unequally, even if they support multiple religions, these other factors come into play.

The second variable I use in this study of a country's connection to religion is the actual level of support given to religion as measured by the

RAS3 religious support variable. Even when controlling for official religion policy, support for religion is a consistently significant predictor of GRD except when looking only at EWNOCMD states, where it was significant only when excluding official religion policy from the analysis. This is likely due to the same crosscutting influences on GRD in EWNOCMD states that I discussed earlier.

Hostility to Religion

The second aspect of government religion policy can predict levels of GRD is hostility to religion. All fifteen states that overtly exhibit this hostility currently espouse secular antireligious ideologies or have a history of such ideologies in the past. Three democracies had antireligious ideologies in 2014. France's *laicite* ideology advocates that public space and behavior be secular. Religion is allowed but it should be kept in the private sphere. Mexico's anticlerical approach to religion dates back to the 1830s. Mexico's 1917 constitution essentially outlawed the Catholic Church and appropriated all religious property. This occurred at least in part in response to a church-supported counterrevolution in 1913 to the Mexican Revolution (1910–1920). This remained in force until Mexico softened but did not eliminate its anticlerical policy when it amended its constitution in 1992 (Gill, 2008: 146–165).

Uruguay's anticlericalism is milder than in France and Mexico but is still significant. For example, it designates December 25 as "Family Day" and Easter week as "Tourism Week." In contrast, Uruguayans tend to be less religious than Mexicans. Most Uruguayans are nominally Catholic, but religious practice is low. Perhaps this milder antireligious ideology is why Uruguay is the only state with an antireligious official policy to engage in no GRD.

The five Communist states, China, Cuba, Laos, North Korea, and Vietnam, engage in high levels of GRD. As I discussed in more detail in Chapter 6, in theory GRD should be low in these states because their ideology should inspire hostility to all religions equally. However, in addition to significant levels of restrictions on all religion including the majority religion, in practice they single out some religious minorities for extra repression for a variety of reasons. These include attempts at rebellion, other forms of security threats, oppositional activity, other political threats, perceived nonindigenousness, a greater willingness to tolerate the majority religion as compared to minority religions, and as part of a government program to bring all religious organizations under its control.

Likely antireligious elements of their national ideologies magnify the impact of these factors on GRD.

The five Muslim-majority states that are hostile to religion – Azerbaijan, Kyrgyzstan, Tajikistan, Turkmenistan, and Uzbekistan – are all former-Soviet republics. In this respect they have not strayed far from their antireligious Communist histories. They all have similar policies of maintaining state-controlled religious organizations for the purpose of controlling and limiting religion. All minorities in these countries experience GRD, most of them at high levels. However, the highest levels of GRD are reserved for minorities that are considered nonindigenous.

The final two countries hostile to religion are Eritrea and Rwanda. Eritrea engages in a milder form of control than found in the former-Soviet republics. The government recognizes only four religious organizations, the Eritrean Orthodox Church, the Evangelical (Lutheran) Church of Eritrea, Islam, and the Roman Catholic Church. It appoints the country's Muslim mufti and the head of the Orthodox Church. While the Pope appoints Eritrea's highest-ranking Catholic official, the government pressures the church to conform its activities to government policies. In addition the law prohibits religious groups from becoming involved in politics and discourages the religious media from commenting on politics. It also limits contributions to religious organizations to contributions from the government, local followers, and government-approved foreign sources. Most GRD in Eritrea is against unrecognized religious groups.

Rwanda is similarly considered hostile to religion due to high levels of regulation of religion in general in the country. These regulations include a general hostility to religion in politics. The country's constitution bans religious political parties. It also restricts holding religious services outside designated places of worship and bans the use of private homes for this purpose. Until 2003, the government banned nighttime religious meetings. Since then it allows nighttime meetings only with advance notice from the religious group. Most of this is motivated by the fear of religion being used to organize political opposition.

Overall, setting aside the influence of religious ideologies, the motivations for GRD in these states that are hostile to religion mirror those in other categories of states. Also, as I already noted, antireligious ideologies should result in limiting all religions, including the majority religion. This is not GRD as this study defines GRD as restrictions placed on the religious institutions or practice of religious minorities that are not placed on the majority religion. Given this, we must ask why would similar motivations for GRD cause such high levels of GRD in states with antireligious ideologies? I posit that once motivated to engage in GRD by one of these other motivations, the antireligious sentiment likely acts as a multiplier. That is, an antireligious ideology is unlikely to by itself motivate GRD, though it will likely motivate restricting religion in general, but a separate motivation for GRD provides an avenue for these antireligious sentiments to come to the fore, and this intensifies the levels of GRD.

Regulating Religion

The third aspect of government religion policy that can predict levels of GRD is the regulation of the majority religion. This factor, though related to and correlated with the first two, predicts GRD in most of the multivariate tests when controlling for these other factors. It did not predict GRD in the tests looking at EWNOCMD states exclusively, but it did when EWNOCMD states were included in a larger set of states including all Christian-majority democracies. Like GRD, the relationship between a government's attitude toward religion and regulating the majority religion is U-shaped, highest in states that most strongly support religion and those that are the most antireligious. Governments that support religion tend to also regulate it, likely in order to maintain doctrinal purity and to prevent the state religion from challenging the government for power.

Overall, in practice, government religion policy is a strong predictor of GRD. The exact mix of elements within government religion policy that influence GRD differs across states and groupings of states as well as how this influence manifests. Nevertheless, government religion policy is likely the most important predictor of GRD. Yet, even this factor on its own is not fully determinative.

Regime: Autocracy and Democracy

Classic theory on repression and discrimination in general has it that autocracies discriminate more than democracies. Classic theory on liberal democracies specifically expects that liberal democracies will be the most religiously tolerant states, as freedom of religion is an integral element of liberal democratic ideals. This study calls both of these assumptions into question. Western liberal democracies are not the most religiously tolerant countries in the world. Also, not all categories of autocracy are intolerant of religious minorities compared to other countries.

Four related findings show this to be the case. First, the "southern" democracies – those that are not European, Western, Buddhist-majority, or Muslim-majority – engage in less GRD than the "northern" EWNOCMD states. Second, the "southern" nondemocracies, those that are not European, Buddhist-majority, Muslim-majority, Orthodox-majority, or Communist also engage in less GRD than the "northern" EWNOCMD states and, in fact, engage in levels similar to their "southern" democratic neighbors. Third, among Christian-majority states, "southern" non-Orthodox Christian-majority states engage in less GRD than the "northern" EWNOCMD states.

Fourth, the states that engage in more GRD than EWNOCMD states are Orthodox-majority, Buddhist-majority, Muslim-majority, and Communist states, regardless of whether or not they are democracies. Thus, the combination of world region and majority religion arguably provide a better prediction of which states will engage in GRD than regime.

Yet regime clearly plays a role. Overall, democracies engage in less GRD than do nondemocracies. Among Orthodox-majority, Muslim-majority, and Buddhist-majority states average levels of GRD are lower in democracies, though democracies are less common among these states compared to Christian-majority states. Also, in the multivariate analyses that take other factors into account, democracy, as measured by the Polity score, does reduce levels of GRD.

These findings have some interesting and interrelated implications as well as raise some important questions. First, given these findings, it is fair to say that democracy does influence GRD, but its influence is limited and is often overridden by other factors. That is, all other things being equal, there is a correlation between democracy and lower GRD, but not all things are equal. That a major category of nondemocracies engages in less GRD than the liberal democracies of the EWNOCMD states demonstrates this. I discuss the specific factors that can override democracy in the context of the larger discussion of the causes of GRD. That is, any of the potential causes of GRD I discuss in this chapter could potentially counteract the influence of democracy on GRD.

In addition, democracy is itself a complicated concept. Recent studies show that different elements of democracy such as free elections and an independent judiciary have independent influences on discrimination (Finke, Martin, & Fox, 2017).

That being said, I argue that the fact that other factors regularly override the influence of democracy is an important result. That is, while a list of factors can explain why particular democracies engage in GRD, that this GRD is present at all much less at the high levels found in many Western democracies means that liberal democratic ideology's ability to promote equality and tolerance is weaker than the influence of these factors. Put differently, this is not a correlation that is only important in theory. Real people are having their lives and religious freedom disrupted, and this occurs more often in Western democracies than it does in many other categories of states, including a major category of nondemocratic states. This is in and of itself important. That we can identify the factors that override the liberal democratic impetus to religious freedom is also important, but it should not be taken to mitigate this basic finding. All of this has significant implications for our understanding of the role of religion in liberal democracies as well as for what types of policies are likely to increase religious freedom.

Second, perhaps it is the "liberal" aspect of liberal democracies that results in higher GRD. The fifteen states with ideologies hostile to religion, I posit, engage in more GRD precisely because these antireligious ideologies compound other causes of GRD. Perhaps this is also the case with Western liberal ideologies. Liberal ideology, as interpreted by many in Western democracies, tends to support secularism as well as religious freedom. Yet there may be some tension between these two principles. Theorists such as Bader (1999: 601) argue that to pursue the secular goals of liberal democracies in effect restricts religion by giving preference to secularism. Perez et al. (2017: 432) argue similarly that the principle of equality may be undermined when the proponents of secularism are unwilling to be tolerant of those who do not share their ideals. That is, secularists may not see those who are religious as their equals and, more important, may feel that religious ideals and practices that are not compatible with secular liberal ideals must give way to those ideals. Thus, there is an inherent tension between the principles of secularism and religious freedom. Religious freedom is guaranteed but only if the use of this freedom does not contradict secular liberal ideals.

In Fox (2015) I argue that much of religious politics is a clash between secular and religious political actors. This is certainly true in Western democracies in practice. In fact, at least some interpretations of Western liberal secular ideology demand that religious believers cease any religious practices that are in conflict with secular liberal ideals. There are currently at least three policy areas where either Western countries restrict religious practices considered central to Islam and Judaism or where advocates in these countries are actively seeking to impose such restrictions.

First, several countries restrict the right of Muslim women to cover their hair and in some cases restrict their right to dress modestly in public spaces. Many argue that these practices undermine secular public space and are a form of oppression of women. Interestingly, many Orthodox Jewish woman follow similar head-covering practices once they are married, but there has been little resistance to this practice. Perhaps this is because many of the forms of head coverings favored by Orthodox Jewish women such as wigs and hats are less obvious than the Muslim hijab, for example. It is also possible that because many of these restrictions are specifically in schools, the fact that Jewish Orthodox women do not begin the practice of covering their hair until after they are married and tend to attend private Jewish schools reduces the potential clashes between this practice and secular ideology.

Second, several countries restrict Kosher and Halal slaughter of animals because they consider it cruel to animals and therefore a violation of the principle of animal rights. Third, many are also questioning the right to male circumcision of children on the grounds that it is a barbaric ceremony that undermines the child's right to bodily integrity. While this right has not been restricted other than some limitations on who can perform this ritual in Sweden, Denmark, and Norway, and a brief ban due to a court ruling in Germany that was overturned by a law, it is present on the political agenda in several countries. I discussed all of these issues in more detail in Chapter 5.

These are very tangible examples of secular-religious competition as well as of secular-liberal intolerance for religious practices that contradict secular-liberal ideology. RASM3 considers restrictions on any of these three types of religious practices to be GRD, as each of these are religious practices central to their respective religions. Structurally, secular-liberal ideologically motivated restrictions on these practices are not different from a majority religion restricting minority religious practices considered abhorrent to that religion. Thus, the "Gods" of secularism are arguably inspiring a form of intolerance similar to the intolerance that is often inspired by religious ideologies. Like many of the "Gods" of various religions, these secular "Gods" will tolerate no other "Gods" before them.

There is strong evidence that this can explain part of the gap between the "northern" EWNOCMD states and the "southern" TRD states. These types of restrictions are common in liberal Western and European democracies. Sweden, Norway, and Denmark regulate circumcisions, and Germany banned them briefly. Kosher and Halal slaughter are banned or restricted in Denmark, Germany, Iceland, Norway, Sweden, Switzerland, and, as of 2019, Belgium. The wearing of religious clothing by Muslims is restricted or banned in parts of Belgium, Croatia, Denmark, France,

Germany, Italy, Malta, Norway, Switzerland, and the UK. In contrast, no TRD state restricts either circumcision or ritual slaughter. Only Kenya and Panama restrict head coverings by Muslim women, and these restrictions are relatively minor. In Kenya, beginning in 2007, public schools occasionally banned head scarves worn by Muslim students. In Panama beginning in 2014 some officials sometimes required Muslim women to remove their hijabs when taking photos for official documents such as identification cards or passports. However, they allowed head coverings.

Overall removing these three factors from the equation would reduce the gap in GRD between TRD and EWNOCMD states by about 26 percent. Thus it accounts for some but not all of the differences. Yet it is likely that secular distaste for religion is motivating other elements of GRD in EWNOCMD states in a less obvious manner. All of this leads to two conclusions. First, secular liberal ideology can, like any other ideology, be a source of intolerance. Second, this liberal impetus to intolerance of religious minorities manifests far more often in the liberal democracies of the "north" than in the democracies of the "south."

There are two potential alternative explanations for this finding. None of the twelve EWNOCMD states that engage in at least one of these types of restrictions have neutral religion policies. France is hostile to religion. Belgium, Germany, Sweden, and Switzerland prefer multiple religions. Croatia and Italy both prefer Catholicism without declaring it the official religion. Denmark, Iceland, Malta, Norway (until 2017), and the UK all declare official religions. Thus, other than France, which is perhaps the clearest case of a secular ideology motivating policy among these states, all these policies may have a religious ideological motivation.

In addition, all of the three types of restrictions target Muslims, though they also have a similar impact on Jews. Those that support these types of restrictions include far-right anti-immigrant groups. For example, "far-right groups in Norway and elsewhere in Scandinavia, ... oppose [infant circumcision] on the grounds that they regard it as a foreign element in Nordic societies, which they say are under threat from immigration from Muslim countries" (JTA, 2014).

Likely, the actual explanation is a combination of secular ideology, religious ideology, and anti-immigrant sentiment. Societies can be divided between advocates of secularism and religion, but these two sides can find common ground along with other political interests such as those who espouse anti-immigrant sentiments. In this case, these forms of GRD may be that common ground.

A third, and related, implication is that ideology, whether it is secular or religious, is a significant cause of GRD, perhaps the most significant cause. Both the findings on government religion policy and the findings on regime, point to this implication. The strength and exact types of GRD caused by ideology may vary across types of ideology, but this basic relationship is clearly robust.

While this has already been stated in the context of the previous three implications, a fourth implication deserves to be highlighted. The true bastions of religious tolerance are not found in the developed Christian democracies of the "north" but in the less-developed states of the "south," many of which are not democracies. It is difficult to fully sort out the reasons why this is the case. It may be due to less adherence to liberal ideology. It may be because GRD is costly in resources and these states have fewer resources to devote to the luxury of GRD. It may be due to a stronger culture of tolerance or perhaps even a political theology of tolerance (Philpott, 2007, 2019). Or, it may be because the issue of religion is simply less important politically in the "south" as demonstrated by the higher proportion of "southern" states with neutral religion policies. Yet, the fact of this finding, in and of itself, regardless of what explains it, falsifies the assumption that the developed liberal democracies of the West and Europe are the most religiously free and tolerant countries in the world.

Other State-Level Causes of GRD

This study examines five additional explanations for GRD that impact all religious minorities in the state mostly equally: the majority religious tradition, world region, the country's population, regime durability, and economic development. All of these factors influence GRD under at least some circumstances.

Majority religious tradition is not a variable I use consistently in this study's quantitative analyses because my methodology has been to break the problem set into smaller groups of states that are largely homogeneous with regard to their majority religion. However, a comparison of these groupings of states shows that the majority religious tradition has a large impact on GRD as well as other aspects of government religion policy. Overall the mean level of GRD is highest in Muslim-majority countries (12.28), followed, respectively, by Orthodox-majority countries (11.11), Buddhist-majority countries (7.36), and non-Orthodox Christian-majority countries (2.13). All other states (2.18) engage in levels similar to non-Orthodox Christian-majority states. This excludes Communist states (17.28), who engage in more GRD than any of these categories of majority religion.

This is not to say that states from any of these religious traditions are homogeneous with regard to GRD. There is considerable variation, which I discussed in more detail for most of these religious traditions elsewhere in this book. Factors like government religion policy can explain much of this variation. Yet, even when taking this into account, Muslim-majority and Buddhist-majority states still engage in more GRD than Christian-majority states. Thus, there is some aspect of GRD's intersection with religion, government, and society that differs across religious traditions as they are understood and lived today. Obviously, the nature of this inter-section varies from country to country within religious traditions, but collectively the evidence shows this to be the case.

World region also matters. In this chapter, as well as Chapters 7 and 8, I discussed the differences between "northern" and "southern" countries, especially among non-Orthodox Christian-majority states. In Chapter 4, I showed that much of the variation in GRD, as well as in government religion policy, across Muslim-majority states is based on how culture and interpretations of Islam differ from world region to world region. While this is likely explained to some extent by similar culture and history, Mataic (2018) shows that cultural variables do not provide a good explanation for geographic clustering of GRD scores and argues that mimicry of bordering states provides a better explanation. Be that as it may, Appleby (2000) argues that most major world religions have complex theologies that can be interpreted very differently. This study provides evidence that these differing interpretations often cluster geographically.

This study addresses the country's population size mostly as a control variable in the multivariate analysis. It is a standard control that is often used but infrequently discussed. Yet, Christian-majority countries as a whole with larger populations engage in more GRD. However, population is not significant when looking only at EWNOCD states. I suggest that this may be because in smaller countries, people, especially group leaders, are more likely to know one another and have more contact across religious traditions. It is more difficult to discriminate against people one knows in person than a minority that one sees more in the abstract. Lijphart (1977) makes this argument when he posits that accommodation between identity groups is easier to accomplish in less-populous countries.

Regime durability is another standard control. In most of the tests it was not significant, but in the tests for Muslim-majority states and Christian-majority democracies it resulted in more GRD. This indicates that when it is a factor, discrimination by governments occurs more often in stable countries as opposed to those whose regime is more in a state of flux. This suggests that GRD is often a deliberate policy choice that occurs after a period of consideration in stable governments

Finally, economic development, as measured by per capita GDP is another standard control. It is also theoretically relevant as I argue that GRD is costly in government resources, and wealthier states have more resources, which allows them to engage in the luxury of GRD. This theory was confirmed in tests for Christian-majority states as a whole and the "southern" states as well as some subsets of these groupings but not for Muslim-majority states and EWNOCMD states. This indicates that while the resources argument likely has the potential to influence GRD, it does not do so in all cases. This suggests that it is a factor that can either overshadow or be overshadowed by other factors depending on the circumstances.

WHY ARE SOME MINORITIES TARGETED FOR MORE GRD?

One of the most basic findings of this study and analyses of previous versions of the RASM dataset (Fox, 2016) is that most countries that discriminate do so unequally. That is, some minorities within a state are subject to more and different types of GRD than others. In Chapter 2 I discussed several potential causes of this differential GRD in theory. In this section, I review this study's findings on how these causes influence GRD in practice.

Ideology and Objectionable Practices

Both religious and secular ideology can play a role in differential GRD. In theory, if a religious ideology considers a religion particularly objectionable, this can motivate more GRD against that minority. In Chapter 4, I find that this is a plausible explanation for the relatively high levels of GRD against Buddhists, Hindus, and Bahais in Muslim-majority states. Theologically, in classical Islam, these religions are considered less acceptable than religions like Christianity and Judaism.

While secular ideologies in theory should have similar levels of hostility to all religions, in practice this is not the case. While much of the GRD in states where secular ideologies are influential can be attributed to other causes, these ideologies can motivate restrictions on minority religious practices that these ideologies consider objectionable. As I discussed in the previous section, in several Western and European countries these ideologies have motivated restrictions on Jewish and Muslim practices, including modest dress, head coverings, circumcision, and ritual slaughter.

Nationalism, Culture, and Cults

Many countries seek to protect their national cultures and identity from outside, nonindigenous influences. For example, a number of European countries have specific laws or policies that recognize those religions they consider indigenous or traditional to the country, give those religions specific benefits not given to others, and often restrict those not included in the list of approved religions. As I discussed in Chapter 6, in 1997 Russia passed such a law that recognizes religions such as Christianity, Islam, Judaism, and Buddhism as part of Russia's cultural heritage and restricts other religions that are not part of this heritage. However, this type of policy does not necessarily lead to more GRD. For example, Belgium by law recognizes six religions as well as a secular organization called *Culte Laïcité,* but there is no substantial GRD against nonrecognized religions. They simply do not get the benefits from the state given to recognized religions that include subsidies for clergy salaries, maintenance and equipment for facilities and places of worship, clergy pensions, support for religious education in schools, tax exemptions, and free access to public broadcasting. Thus, this type of policy tends to lead to unequal treatment but it does not necessarily lead to restrictions on religious practices and institutions.

Formal policies are not a necessary condition for a perceived lack of indigenousness to lead to higher GRD. In this study, I find this type of motivation for GRD particularly in Orthodox-majority states, Buddhist-majority states, the five former-Soviet Muslim-majority states, Communist states, and some TRD states. However, this type of motivation is less common in other groupings. For example, I found little evidence that this motivates GRD in EWNOCMD states. While GRD against Muslims in these states is high, it is not high against immigrant minorities of other religions, which indicates that the motives are unlikely to be purely anti-immigrant. However, with the rising influence of anti-immigration political parties in the West, this may change.

Anticult policies are closely related to the nationalism and culture explanation for GRD. These policies seek to protect citizens from religions that the state considers to be potentially dangerous for other reasons. For example, Germany considers Scientology to be a predatory profit-seeking business masquerading as a religion that takes advantage of vulnerable members of society. In most cases, however, the animus is less specific and targeted at religious groups that are small and new, at least in the context of the country in question. The same religions may be more mainstream elsewhere. Thus, the designation of cult is often intertwined with perceptions of nonindigenousness.

Most groups considered cults are too small to be included in RASM3. However, RASM3 measures whether a minority is declared a "dangerous or extremist sect" (The Religion and State Project, n.d.). As this is included in the GRD index, I removed this component of the index in order to compare levels of GRD for the thirty-two minorities coded as being subject to such government policy to all other minorities. The sects considered dangerous and extremist by governments have a mean (modified) GRD level of 17.81 as compared to 5.55 for all other groups. Thus, when a government goes to the effort to call a religious minority a cult, it is clearly motivated to discriminate against that minority. I posit that even when there is no such official designation, anticult sentiment can still influence GRD.

Perception of Threat and Past Conflict

Much of the discussion of security threats in this study focuses on the securitization of Islam. On a more general level, securitization theory argues that when a minority is perceived as a security threat, this can lift it from normal politics and allow government actions that otherwise might not be legitimate. This theory attempts to explain how democracies justify actions taken against minorities that are not acceptable to liberal democratic ideals in normal circumstances. Thus it is a narrower example of the more general principle that groups perceived as threats may attract more discrimination.

The findings of this study show that the securitization of Islam is likely a motivation for GRD throughout the Christian world. However, most studies that focus on securitization, and particularly those that address the securitization of Islam, focus on Western countries (e.g., Cesari, 2013; Chebel d'Appollonia, 2015; Donnelly, 2007; Gearty, 2007; Razack, 2008). In fact, one of the reasons the theory was developed was specifically to explain why Western liberal democracies sometimes engage in discriminatory practices that run counter to their liberal values.

However, this study finds similar patterns of GRD against Muslims in most groupings of Christian-majority states and not just EWNOCMD states. This pattern is present, though weaker, in TRD and TRND states. I also found this pattern to be present in my analysis, which includes all Christian-majority states, in Chapter 8. This pattern involved particularly high levels of GRD against Muslims, that SRD against Muslims, when present, enhances levels of GRD, and higher GRD against Muslims in states where at least some Muslims are responsible for violent and semi-violent attacks against members of the majority religion. Overall, this set of findings expands the applicability of securitization theory and, more specifically, the securitization of Islam to a larger group of countries.

These findings combined with securitization theory have a larger implication. Securitization theory shows an understanding that liberal values are not always followed in those countries considered liberal Western democracies. As I discuss throughout this book, the findings on SRD, GRD, and government religion policy in general call into question aspects of this assumption of liberal democracy. The aspects called into question in this book and by securitization theory overlap but are not identical. For example, securitization theory also deals with immigrant minorities who are not religiously distinct in the West such as Latin American immigrants in the United States. In this book SRD and GRD are present against many minorities in the West that are not at all addressed by securitization theory such as North American protestant denominations (outside of the United States and Canada) and Jews. In addition, I confirm previous findings that I discussed in more detail in Chapter 5 that the West is not as secular as many assume. Thus, this study is part of a larger body of theory and findings that questions the liberalism of Western democracies.

Interestingly, there is evidence of a reciprocal process of responding to perceived threats by Christians in Muslim-majority states, but this reaction is not GRD, rather it is SRD. This is not to say there is no GRD against Christian minorities in Muslim-majority states. However it is not high relative to other minorities and does not seem to be motivated by perceptions of Christians as a security or political threat. As I discussed in more detail in Chapter 4, a combination of factors including religious ideology and protection of culture likely motivates GRD against Christians in these countries. That Muslim-majority governments discriminate against Christians is not a new finding (e.g., Fox, 2015, 2016; Grim & Finke, 2011; Philpott, 2019), but the level of detail provided in this study is likely the highest of any previous study. The securitization argument is rarely used to explain this discrimination, likely because securitization theory focuses on the behavior of democracies, and most Muslim-majority states are not democracies.

SRD in Muslim-majority countries, in contrast, is by far highest against Christians. I posit that this is at least in part because of perceptions of threat. As I discussed in more detail in Chapter 4, many Muslims perceive that Islam is in a worldwide, centuries-long struggle with Christianity. Those who see the world this way perceive Christian minorities in Muslim-majority countries as part of this existential enemy. Given the evidence, this view is more common or at least more influential in society than in government as it influences SRD far more than GRD.

On a more basic empirical level, RASM3 measures whether religious minorities engaged in violent and semiviolent actions against the majority (VSVA). This is an empirical measure of groups that pose a security threat and of past conflict. Interestingly, in the multivariate analyses, this variable influences SRD in every test but influences GRD only for some groupings of states, particularly EWNOCMD states and TRD states. Examining the impact of VSVA more generally confirms this finding. Fifty-eight RASM3 minorities engaged on VSVA at some point between 1990 and 2014. Levels of GRD in 2014 among these minorities were slightly higher than levels against other minorities (6.96 compared to 6.03), but SRD in 2014 was considerably higher (6.50 compared to 2.21).

This has two interesting implications. First, the impact of an empirically measurable threat has at best a weak influence on GRD. It is likely that much of this impact is indirect. The results of this study show that VSVA influences SRD. SRD, in turn, as I discuss later, influences GRD. This likely explains the weak direct impact of VSVA on GRD.

Second, perceived threats may be a more important influence on GRD than objective threats. While certainly there is a correlation between the two, perceptions of reality and reality itself are rarely identical, especially in politics. Securitization theory focuses specifically on the perception of threat, how this perception is created, and how it influences policy. According to securitization theory, it is not the threat itself that initiates the process of securitization but, rather, speech acts by leaders. Leaders can create a perception of threat that is, at the very least, disproportionate to the actual threat as well as downplay real threats. The findings of this study imply that it is the perceptions created by these political narratives that motivates policy far more than actual threats.

In retrospect, this finding is logical. Leaders engage in the speech acts that securitize a minority. Political leaders, who are among those leaders who drive this process of securitization, also make the policy decisions that lead to GRD. From this perspective, securitization theory, rather than providing an explanation for GRD, shows how leaders justify the policies they choose.

The results indicate that societal actors are more sensitive to actual threats. VSVA consistently predicts levels of SRD. That is, societal actors are more likely to target minorities that have targeted the majority religion than they are to target those minorities their political leaders choose to securitize. Only 39.3 percent of minorities that did not engage in VSVA between 1990 and 2014 experienced SRD in 2014 as opposed to 75.0 percent of minorities that did engage in VSVA.

While RASM3 has no variable for political threat, there is clear anecdotal evidence that minorities perceived as political threats are often subject to higher GRD. China's religion policy, which I discussed in more detail in Chapter 6, targets precisely those minorities the government sees as political threats. This includes groups that have engaged in opposition activities such as Buddhists in Tibet, the Falun Gong, and Uighur Muslims. It also includes small religious groups that refuse to join the state-sponsored "patriotic" religious organizations, which China uses to monitor religious activity to make sure that it does not become political. Another example is the repression of the Church of Jesus Christ in Madagascar because of its association with ousted former President Marc Ravalomanana. Rwanda similarly bans and monitors many types of religious gatherings in order to prevent them from becoming avenues for political organization.

Sarkissian (2015) argues that this type of policy is common in authoritarian governments. In cases like this the repression is

aimed at diminishing religion's potential influence on politics and society . . . [these states] recognize the danger that independent civil society can pose to a regime's stability and understand that repression can backfire and lead to mobilization. Religious resurgence . . . heightens regime fears of religiously based opposition, and repression comes in the form of strict state control over religious practice and outlawing politicized religious groups.

(Sarkissian, 2015: 52)

Minority Size

Kunovich (2006) argues that larger minorities are seen as posing a greater threat to the religious majority and finds that the presence of larger religious minorities makes religion more salient to national identity. This argument that larger minorities pose a greater challenge to majority groups is not uncommon (e.g., Ellingsen, 2000; Manglos et al., 2013). Others focus theoretically on minorities that are more visible, but in practice measure population size (Ben-Nun Bloom et al., 2013). Some make the opposite argument that repression focuses on smaller and weaker minorities that are less able to defend themselves (Olzak, 1998: 211). However, this study finds no significant relationship between the size of a minority and either GRD or SRD.

Anti-Semitism

Anti-Semitism is a bit of the odd man out in this discussion because it is the only potential motivation for GRD that applies only to a single religious minority. Yet, in Christian-majority states the patterns of SRD and GRD against Jews are distinctive. In all groupings of Christian-majority states, or mostly Christian states, as is the case with TRD and TRND states examined in this study, Jews experience the highest levels of SRD. Interestingly, all the Jewish minorities included in RASM3 are either in Christian-majority or Muslim-majority countries, other than the Jews in Singapore, which has no majority religion, and Bosnia, which has a joint Muslim and Christian majority. Thus, the results for Jews in the TRD and TRND countries apply nearly exclusively to Christian-majority countries.

There is also a "north-south" difference in the patterns. In the "northern" EWNOCD and Orthodox-majority states, these high levels of SRD do not translate to disproportionate levels of GRD, but in the "southern" TRD and TRND states, Jews experience the highest levels of both SRD and GRD. As I discussed in Chapters 7 and 8, this result for the TRD states and TRND states is likely due to the small number of Jewish minorities in these groupings being located in countries that engage in higher levels of GRD. It may also be because the legacy of the Holocaust deters GRD, and Western states are more sensitive to this historical event.

As I discussed in Chapter 5, the origins of anti-Semitism mutate over time. Jews are often compared to whatever is considered evil and wrong in society. Thus, if ideology is the most important cause of GRD in a country, advocates of GRD against Jews will likely use that ideology whether it is secular or religious. If the source of GRD is nationalism and protection of culture, anti-Semites will argue that Jews are nonindigenous. One example of this phenomenon in current US politics is that those who consider "whites" the "oppressors" often explicitly consider Jews to be among these "white oppressors." Yet, white supremacists clearly do not consider Jews to be white. However, both groups apparently agree that Jews have too much power in the media and finance, both of which are considered by the Anti-Defamation League to be core indicators of anti-Semitic attitudes.[1] Thus, all of the causes of GRD discussed here can potentially be applied to Jews.

Societal Religious Discrimination

I discuss SRD last because in many ways it is intertwined with all the aforementioned causes of GRD. On a basic level, Grim and Finke (2011) posit based on extensive evidence from a study using state-level variables that societal restrictions on religious minorities leads to government-based restrictions on religious freedom. As I discussed in more detail in Chapter 3, they define and measure both their independent and dependent variables differently than I do in this study. Yet their variables are sufficiently analogous to mine that it is reasonable to expect that this study will produce similar results. This study does produce similar results, up to a point, but the differences require major modifications to Grim and Finke's (2011) theorizing.

When looking at the state-level, as do Grim and Finke (2011), the results are largely the same. That is, even when looking at 771 religious minorities as the unit of analysis rather than at the state, if one uses a global SRD variable – by this I mean that I use the SRD variable in multivariate tests without modification or interaction with other variables – the results show that SRD leads to GRD with one exception. This relationship does not hold in EWNOCD states. This is not a new finding. Barr (2014) finds the same absence of a correlation when examining Western democracies using Grim and Finke's (2011) data. She argues that this is because these countries developed social and legal mechanisms to deal with religious tensions after the violence of the Reformation and the religious violence that came after it.

However, using a global SRD variable masks a more dynamic finding. This study uses minority-specific SRD variables. That is, each minority has its own SRD variable, which I created by setting the variables at 0 for all cases not involving the specific minority, and the SRD score remains as is for those cases that do involve that minority. This allows an assessment of whether the SRD-GRD relationship exists for each minority separately.

---

[1] For more details, see http://global100.adl.org/.

The findings show it does not. That is, the relationship is present for some minorities in some groupings of states but not others.

I argue that the SRD-GRD link only becomes active in the presence of a trigger that catalyzes the relationship. That is, the potential for SRD to cause GRD is present but in and of itself it is neither a necessary nor a sufficient cause of GRD. Rather, the government needs some additional motivation to discriminate. Not just any motivation will do. In most cases the motivation is one that makes the group seem to be a significant threat of some sort and is most likely to be a trigger if this threat is existential. In the presence of such a trigger, SRD becomes both a measure of how deeply the societal actors feel this threat and a form of pressure on the government to address the threat.

This type of trigger successfully catalyzes SRD as a cause of GRD for a small number of minorities, once one excludes correlations that are driven by a small number of outliers. SRD causes GRD for Muslims in all groupings of Christian-majority countries tested. As I discussed in Chapters 5, 7, and 8, I posit that the trigger in this case is the securitization of Islam. The securitization process precisely depicts Muslims as an existential threat. This means they are perceived as a threat that is certainly of sufficient magnitude to activate the SRD-GRD link.

The SRD-GRD link is present for Christian minorities in all groupings of Christian-majority states other than EWNOCMD states. As I discussed in Chapters 7 and 8, the trigger for this is nonindigenousness. That is, GRD is higher against Christian denominations that are considered to be alien to the local culture. Encroachment by these groups, especially if they proselytize, can be perceived as a significant existential threat. The majority sees them as targeting their friends, relatives, and neighbors for conversion. This is threatening both on the individual level and on the macro-level. An individual who leaves one's religion can be seen as leaving one's family, society, and culture. In addition, denomination switching within religions is more common than conversion to a different religion, so inter-Christian proselytizing can seem especially threatening. If this happens on a large scale it can alter politically relevant demographics in a country.

For example, Gill (1998) demonstrates that in Latin American countries where Protestants are making significant inroads into the Catholic population, the Catholic Church is more likely to support opposition movements. This is because many are leaving the church precisely because it is associated with governments that are seen as nonresponsive to the people. Most of those who leave Catholicism join North American

Protestant denominations. While disassociating from the government can result in a loss of an important source of support and funding, the existential threat of losing the Catholic congregation to Protestant denominations outweighs this consideration. This demonstrates that successful conversion campaigns can have significant political implications.

Finally, in Muslim-majority states the SRD-GRD link is present for Christians and Bahai. As I discussed in more detail in Chapter 4, many Muslims see Christians as part of the larger world Christian population with which they are at war. In addition, many Christians proselytize to Muslims. Both of these factors are potentially significant existential threats. The Bahai pose a different form of existential threat. Many Muslims see them as a heretical offshoot of Islam. This makes their very existence ideologically unacceptable to many Muslims. For example Somer and Glupker-Kesebir (2015: 539) demonstrate that "Islamic actors are less open to accommodating non-Muslim minority and Muslim sectarian differences, perceived 'heterodox Muslim' minorities, and perceived 'un-Islamic' minorities such as gays." There are no other "heretical" minorities in Muslim-majority countries with sufficient numbers to examine this proposition further, but this observation likely applies to the Ahmadis who are present in four Muslim-majority countries.

EXPLAINING SOCIETAL RELIGIOUS DISCRIMINATION

While this book does not focus on the issue, in the process of analyzing the causes of GRD, it also addresses the causes of SRD. Perhaps the most relevant finding is that the causes of GRD and SRD do not greatly overlap. As I discussed earlier, VSVA – violent and semiviolent actions taken by minority groups against the majority – influence both SRD and GRD, but VSVA is more strongly and consistently a cause of SRD than GRD. Similarly, the country's population size influences SRD more consistently than it influences GRD.

However, the variables that most strongly predict GRD, have almost no significant influence on SRD. Regime and government religion policy do not predict GRD. As these are government characteristics, it is reasonable that they would have a stronger connection to GRD than SRD. However, one would expect some connection to SRD. Democratic culture teaches ideals of tolerance, so we might expect more societal tolerance in democracies. Government religion policy reflects the influence of religious ideology in a country that ought to have societal implications. Yet this study provides little evidence that these connections and processes exist.

As discussed earlier, anti-Semitism is a far better predictor of SRD than GRD. Anti-Semitism is to a great extent derived from long-lasting societal prejudices with deep historical roots. Also, anecdotally, regional culture, national culture, and nationalism appear to influence levels of SRD. In many cases, SRD interacts with a minority's perceived nonindigenousness.

Taking all of this into account, SRD seems to be more deeply rooted in two factors. The first is violence by the minority. This study has demonstrated a clear link between violence by the minority and SRD, but only a small proportion of minorities engage in violence against the majority, so this explanation has a narrow utility. The second is history and culture. Has there been a history of enmity and prejudice? Is a minority seen as not belonging in a given society and culture? Is the minority seen as being in some way a threat to the local culture and society? Future research needs to develop measures for these factors in order to properly analyze these causes of SRD.

A NOTE ON CAUSALITY AND FUTURE RESEARCH

While there is direct empirical evidence for many of the causes of GRD I discuss in this study, this is not always the case. In many cases, the empirical evidence shows higher GRD for certain group, and I use the causes I list in this chapter to explain the empirical findings. Nevertheless, social science research has a long history of providing plausible explanations for empirical findings, even if it is not currently possible to directly test the causality of these explanations.

Social science research is a process. Asking and answering one set of questions often raises new questions and reveals new phenomena and possible relationships. This study has done both. While I cannot currently test the causality of many of the explanations and phenomena that I discuss in this chapter, these findings and explanations provide a roadmap for future data collection and empirical research.

This study is the result of an evolving RAS and RASM project. Limited only to the GRD, SRD, and VSVM variables for a twenty-five-year period for 771 minorities, this involves 1,291,425 data points. Adding in the control variables including all their components increases this to over 11 million data points. Each of the three rounds of RAS and RASM has allowed a more detailed analysis of a wide range of issues using more detailed data. This study is no exception. As I discussed in Chapter 1, this study makes use of more accurate and detailed information than any previous study of any topic related to GRD or religious freedom. Yet, as has been the case for each of the previous rounds, this analysis both provides new insight into the causes of GRD and sheds light on the data we need to take this understanding a step further. The factors that I theorize influence GRD in this study will, to the extent that it is possible, be those that I add to future data collections.

POLICY IMPLICATIONS

The principal goal of this study is to discover and understand why governments discriminate against religious minorities. Yet the findings from this study have real-world implications. Both the United States and Canada, for example, have passed laws that make promotion of religious freedom an official part of their foreign policies.[2] As is the case in the academic literature, foreign policy makers often assume that democracy and religious freedom go hand in hand. Yet this study shows that the relationship between the two is more complicated. These recommendations focus on some policy guidelines to make as efficient and focused as possible a foreign policy designed to promote religious freedom for religious minorities worldwide.

First, democratization will only substantially improve religious freedom for some countries. Democracy has, at most, a minor impact on levels of GRD in non-Orthodox Christian-majority countries. While this seems to be a very specific designation, it applies to 90 of the 183 countries included in this study. That being said, the promotion of democracy likely has many benefits aside from increased religious freedom. Given this, promoting democracy is a laudable goal, but it is important to have reasonable and accurate expectations if the goal is to increase religious freedom through democratization.

In contrast, the democratization approach is likely to be particularly useful in Muslim-majority, Buddhist-majority, and Communist countries. In the former two groupings, there is evidence that democracies engage in substantially less GRD. In the Communist states, it is difficult to see how democratization would fail to improve matters.

Second, societal prejudices play a role in causing GRD, but general programs promoting tolerance will have a limited impact on GRD. While reducing on SRD is in and of itself a worthwhile endeavor, it is not an

---

[2] For a full discussion of these laws, see Joustra (2018).

efficient means to reduce GRD. SRD leads to GRD only in cases where minorities are seen as existential threats. This requires a policy that looks for signs that minorities are seen as existential threats and especially one that monitors political and religious leaders for signs of promoting such perceptions. The focus of this element of policy should be to prevent, undermine, eradicate, dissipate, and delegitimize efforts to paint a religious minority as an existential threat.

Third, religious freedom in general and GRD specifically are linked to the state's ideology. Whether the ideology is secular or religious, it leads to more GRD. Associating with a single religion makes states more likely to discriminate against other religions, and secular ideologies can motivate discrimination against all religions and exacerbate other causes of GRD. In the case of secular democracies, secularism can promote restrictions on religious practices that are seen as not in accordance with secular ideals. Thus, promoting religious freedom requires encouraging that governments be nonideological but have a positive attitude toward religion.

Put differently, GRD is lowest in states that are neutral on the issue of religion, but there is more than one kind of neutrality. Full separation of religion and state can promote GRD if that separation is itself separated from secular ideologies. A benevolent, and perhaps laissez-faire, neutrality that is based on equal treatment for all minorities and supports all religions equally, assuming it supports them at all, is more likely to protect religious freedom. Put even more bluntly, religious freedom is more likely in a state that considers religion none of its business than in one with an explicit secular ideology.

Fourth, the perception that a minority is not indigenous, that its presence in the country is illegitimate is a common motivation for GRD. It is difficult to change this kind of perception, but any policy seeking to increase religious freedom needs to find a way to change this type of perception.

Fifth, the perception that a minority is a threat is also a potent motivation for SRD. Addressing this issue is likely to require working with both the religious minority and the majority group to change behaviors and perceptions on both sides.

Finally, if the West wants to promote religious freedom, it needs to clean up its own house. This is not true of all Western countries, many of which engage in very low levels of GRD, but only Canada engages in none. It is difficult to promote a foreign policy intended to end GRD when GRD is occurring at home.

SOME FINAL THOUGHTS

The general topic of religious freedom is becoming more prominent in politics and academia. Yet there is relatively little empirical research on the topic. This study is intended to help add to our knowledge of the causes of GRD. The evidence undermines some of our basic assumptions such as the assumptions that the West is the most religiously free region of the world, that secular liberal democracy is the best environment for religious freedom, and that SRD generally leads to GRD.

GRD is a subset of the larger issue of religious freedom. While, as I discussed in Chapter 2, there is no agreement on what the term *religious freedom* means, all conceptions of the term agree that GRD violates religious freedom. In this study I show that while GRD is ubiquitous, there are pockets of states around the world that engage in little to no GRD. However, most of these pockets are not where one would expect. They include Muslim-majority states in West Africa and many of the Christian-majority states of the "south," including several that are not democratic. This stands in stark contrast to the assumption of religious freedom in the West.

The causes of GRD are complex, and there is no one attribute a state can possess that guarantees it will engage in no GRD. However, there are steps a state can take to improve the freedom of its religious minorities such as disassociating from both religious and secular ideologies and taking a benevolent but equal attitude toward all religions. Yet, the devil is in the details. How to motivate a state to adopt this type of policy remains an open question.

Bibliography

Abouharb, M. Rodwan & David L. Cingranelli "The Human Rights Effect of World Bank Structural Adjustment, 1980–2001" *International Studies Quarterly*, 50 (2), 2006, 233–262.

Abramowitz, Michael J. *Freedom in the World 2018: Democracy in Crisis*, Washington, DC: Freedom House, 2018; https://freedomhouse.org/report/freedom-world/freedom-world-2018.

AFP "Myanmar Christians Forced to Convert to Buddhism, Claims Rights Group" *The Express Tribune*, September 5, 2012.

Ahmad, R. "Malaysia Mosque Vandalized amid Allah Row" *Reuters*, January 16, 2010; http://in.reuters.com/article/idINIndia-45443920100116.

Ahmed, Azam *A Christian Convert, on the Run in Afghanistan*, Washington, DC: International Christian Concern, 2014.

Aid to the Church in Need International, *Religious Freedom in the World: Report 2008*, Brooklyn, NY: Author, 2008, 58.

AJC "AJC Urges Bolivia to Ensure Safety of Jewish Community" *U.S. Newswire*, September 18, 2014.

Akbaba, Yasemin & Zeynep Tydas "Does Religious Discrimination Promote Dissent? A Quantitative Analysis" *Ethnopolitics*, 10 (3), 2011, 271–295.

Alexseev, Mikhail A. & Sufian N. Zhemukhov "From Mecca with Tolerance: Religion, Social Recatagorization, and Social Capital" *Religion, State and Society*, 2016, http://dx.doi.org/10.1080/09637494.2015.1127672.

Almond, Gabriel, R. Scott Appleby, & Emmanuel Sivan *Strong Religion: The Rise of Fundamentalism around the World*, Chicago: University of Chicago Press, 2003.

Alon, Ilan, Shaomin Li, & John Wu "An Institutional Perspective on Religious Freedom and Economic Growth" *Politics and Religion*, 2017, doi:10.1017/S1755048317000098.

Anderson, John "The Catholic Contribution to Democratization's Third Wave: Altruism, Hegemony, or Self-Interest?" *Cambridge Review of International Affairs*, 20 (3) 2007, 383–399.

Anti-Defamation League *2011 Audit of Anti-Semitic Incidents*, New York: Author, 2012.

"ADL Condemns Attack on Jews in Sydney," October 27, 2013; www.adl.org/press-center/press-releases/anti-semitism-international/adl-condemns-attack-on-jews-in-sydney.html.

  Global Anti-Semitism in 2014, New York: Author, 2014; www.adl.org/anti-semitism/international/c/global-antisemitism-2014.html#.VLaUytKUeSr.

Appleby, R. Scott *The Ambivalence of the Sacred: Religion, Violence, and Reconciliation*, New York: Rowman and Littlefield, 2000.

Arora, V. "In Myanmar Christian Rebels Are Double Trouble" *World Watch Monitor*, May 18, 2015.

Arutz Sheva 7 "Anti-Semitic Protests Rage in Algeria against Synagogue Plans," July 11, 2014.

Associated Press, "Religion Helps Heal Cyprus' Ethnic Division as Muslim, Christian Leaders Wage Quiet Diplomacy" *Fox News*, April 19, 2014; www.foxnews.com/world/2014/04/19/religion-helps-heal-cyprus-ethnic-division-as-muslim-christian-leaders-wage/.

Bader, Veit "Religious Pluralism: Secularism or Priority for Democracy" *Political Theory*, 27 (5), 1999, 597–633.

Baig, Rachel "Scientology Is Still a Red Flag in Germany" *Deutsch Welle*, February 22, 2013.

Baptist Mid-Missions, *Ethiopia*, n.d.; www.bmm.org/country/ethiopia/.

Barr, Kasey "Measuring the Impact of Social Regulation on the Cycle of Religious Persecution: A Risk Assessment Model" MA Thesis. Interdisciplinary Center, Hertiziliya, Israel, 2014.

Barret, D. B., G. T. Kurian, & T. M. Johnson *World Christian Encyclopedia*, 2nd ed. Oxford, UK: Oxford University Press, 2001.

Basedau, Matthias Georg Strüver, Johannes Vüllers, & Tim Wegenast "Do Religious Factors Impact Armed Conflict? Empirical Evidence from Sub-Saharan Africa" *Terrorism and Political Violence*, 23 (5), 2011, 752–779.

Benge, Michael "Vietnam's Two-Front War on Religion" *American Thinker*, July 22, 2012; www.americanthinker.com/articles/2012/07/vietnams_two-front_war_on_religion.html.

Ben-Nun Bloom, Pazit "State-Level Restriction of Religious Freedom and Women's Rights: A Global Analysis" *Political Studies*, 2015, doi: 10.1111/1467-9248.12212.

Ben-Nun Bloom, Pazit, Gizem Arkian, & Udi Sommer "Globalization, Threat, and Religious Freedom" *Political Studies*, 2013, doi: 10.1111/1467-9248.12060.

Berger, Peter L. "Faith and Development" *Society*, 46 (1), 2009, 69–75.

  "Secularism in Retreat" *The National Interest*, Winter 1996/1997, 3–12.

Bhatta, Nita "Fear Stalks Displaced Muslims after Muzaffarnagar Riots" *BBC*, September 19, 2013; http://in.reuters.com/article/muzaffarnagar-riots-muslims-displaced-fe-idINDEE98I0CA20130919.

Bingham, John "Atheist Afghan Man Granted Asylum in UK to Protect Him from 'Religious' Persecution; An Afghan Asylum Seeker Who Become an Atheist Has Been Granted Leave to Remain in Britain Because He Would Face

'Religious' Persecution for Abandoning Islam" *The Telegraph*, January 13, 2014.

Blaydes, Lisa & Drew A. Linzer "Elite Competition, Religiosity, and Anti-Americanism in the Islamic World" *American Political Science Review*, 106 (2), 2012, 225–243.

Bohman, Andrea & Mikhaek Hjerm "How the Religious Context Affects the Relationship between Religiosity and Attitudes toward Immigration" *Ethnic and Racial Studies*, 2013, doi:10.1080/01419870.2012.748210.

Bond, Anthony "Anger of Israel Fans after Pig-Shaped Balloon with Star of David released at Roger Waters Concert in Belgium" *Daily Mail*, July 25, 2013.

Boomgaarden, Hajo G. & Andre Woost "Religion and Euroscepticism: Direct, Indirect or No Effects?" *Western European Politics*, 32 (6), 2009, 1240–1265.

Boomgaarden, Hajo G. & Andreas M. Woost "Religion and Party Positions towards Turkish EU Accession" *Comparative European Politics*, 10 (2), 2012, 180–197.

Bos, Stefan "Crackdown on Churches Spreading in Southern Laos" *Worthy News*, May 15, 2012; www.worthynews.com/11484-crackdown-on-churches-spreading-in-southern-laos.

"Bosnia and Herzegovina Education" UNICEF; www.unicef.org/bih/education.html.

Bowen, John, R. "Secularism: Conceptual Genealogy or Political Dilemma?" *Comparative Studies in Society and History*, 52 (3), 2010, 680–694.

Brackman, Harold "Europe and the Jews 2012: Dramatic Rise in Anti-Jewish, Anti-Israel Prejudice" *Simon Wiesenthal Center Special Report*, March 22, 2012.

Branas-Garza, Pablo & Angel Solano "Religious Favoritism in Europe: A Political Competition Model" *Rationality and Society*, 22 (3), 2010, 333–352.

Brathwaite, Robert & Andrew Bramsen "Reconceptualizing Church and State: A Theoretical and Empirical Analysis of the Separation of Religion and State on Democracy" *Politics & Religion*, 4 (2), 2011, 229–263.

Brekke, Torkel "Halal Money: Financial Inclusion and Demand for Islamic Banking in Norway" *Research and Politics*, 2018, doi 10.1177/2053168018757624.

Bridge, Adrian "Attack on Jewish Memorial" *The Independent*, November 7, 1991.

Brown, Davis & Patrick James "The Religious Characteristics of States: Classic Themes and New Evidence for International Relations and Comparative Politics" *Journal of Conflict Resolution*, 2017, doi.org/10.1177/0022002717729882.

Bruce, Steve "Secularization and Politics" in Jeffrey Haynes, ed. *Routledge Handbook of Religion and Politics*, New York: Routledge, 2009, 145–158.

God Is Dead: Secularization in the West, Malden, MA: Blackwell, 2002.

Bruguière, P. "Ethiopia's Muslims Protest against Being 'Treated Like Terrorists'" *The Observer*, July 25, 2012; http://observers.france24.com/en/20120725-ethiopia-muslims-protest-labeled-terrorists-addis-ababa-muslim-council-awoliya-mosque-al-ahbash-anawar.

Brummitt, Chris "Vietnam Lets Churches Thrive, but Keeps Control" *Associated Press*, October 10, 2013.

Burling, Stacy "Vandals Hit Synagogue" *The Philadelphia Inquirer*, March 29, 1998.

Buzan, B. & Segal, G. "A Western Theme" *Prospect*, February 1998, pp. 18–23.

Buzan, Berry, Ole Waever, & Jaap de Wilde *Security: A New Framework for Analysis*, Boulder, CO: Lynne Rienner, 1998.

Cairnduff, Julia "Vietnam's Priest Prisoner; He's 65, Part-Paralysed and Has a Brain Tumour. Yet the Vietnamese Authorities Think Father Ly, a Priest and Human Rights Activist, Deserves Prison" *The Times* (London), September 16, 2011.

Calfino, Brian R. & Paul A. Djupe "Religious Clues and Electoral Support" *Political Research Quarterly*, 62 (2), 2009, 329–339.

Calhoun, Craig "Secularism, Citizenship and the Public Sphere" in Craig Calhoun, Mark Juergensmeyer, & Jonathan VanAntwerpen, eds. *Rethinking Secularism*, New York: Oxford University Press, 2012, 86–102.

Campbell, C. "Once Again Racial Tensions in Burma Turn Deadly" *Time*, July 4, 2014.

Candia, Steven "Govt Persecuting Us – Muslims" *New Vision*, April 6, 2013.

Canetti, Daphna, Stevan E. Hobfoll, Ami Pedahzur, & Eran Zaidise "Much Ado about Religion: Religiosity, Resource Loss, and Support for Political Violence, *Journal of Peace Research*, 47 (5), 2010, 1–13.

Cantilero, Monica "Christians in the Middle East Facing Worst Persecution as Population Drops Sharply" *Christian Today*, July 26, 2015.

Carlin, John "Anti-Semitism Added to SA's Racist Brew; John Carlin in Johannesburg Reports on the Return of Swastikas and Pigs' Heads" *The Independent*, April 29, 1990.

Carol, Sarah, Mark Helbling, & Ines Michalowski "A Struggle over Religious Rights? How Muslim Immigrants and Christian Natives View the Accommodation of Religion in Six European Countries," *Social Forces*, 2015, doi: 10.1093/sf/sov054.

Casanova, Jose "The Secular and Secularisms" *Social Research*, 76 (4), 2009, 1049–1066.

Cederman, Lars-Erik & Luc Girardin "Beyond Fractionalization: Mapping Ethnicity onto Nationalist Insurgencies" *American Political Science Review*, 101 (1), 2007, 173–185.

Cederman, Lars-Erik, Andreas Wimmer, & Brian Min "Why Do Ethnic Groups Rebel? A New Data Analysis" *World Politics*, 62 (1), 2010, 87–119.

Cesari, Jocelyne *Why the West Fears Islam: An Exploration of Islam in Liberal Democracies*, New York: Palgrave Macmillan, 2013.

The Awakening of Muslim Democracy: Religion, Democracy, and the State, New York: Cambridge University Press, 2014.

What Is Political Islam? Boulder, CO: Lynne Reinner, 2018.

Cesari, Jocelyne & Jonathan Fox "Institutional Relations Rather than Clashes of Civilizations: When and How Is Religion Compatible with Democracy?" *International Political Sociology*, 2016, doi: 10.1093/ips/olw011.

Chebel d'Appollonia, Ariane *Migrant Mobilization and Securitization in the US and Europe: How Does It Feel to Be a Threat?* New York: Palgrave-Macmillan, 2015.

Chiaramonte, Perry "Mexico's Christians Face Beatings, Forced Conversions at Hands of Hybrid Faiths" *Fox News*, April 18, 2016; www.foxnews.com/world/2016/04/18/mexicos-christians-face-beatings-forced-conversions-at-hands-hybrid-faiths.html.

Chin Human Rights Organization "Prayer to Boycott 'Religious Conversion Law' Draft" *Khonumthung News Group*, June 29, 2014.

"Christian Preachers Closely Monitored by Regime" *Burma News International*, January 27, 2010.

"Christians Arrested on Charges of Proselytizing" *Official Vatican Network*, 2015; www.news.va/en/news/asialaos-christians-arrested-on-charges-of-prosely.

"Church Responsible for Bias in Greece Says Report" *The Hurriyet Daily News*, September 15, 2009.

Ciftci, Sabri & Gunes M. Tezcur "Soft Power, Religion, and Anti-Americanism in the Middle East" *Foreign Policy Analysis*, 12 (3), 2016, 374–394.

Copley, Caroline & Katharina Bart "Right-Wing Firebrand Shakes Up Cozy Swiss Politics" *Reuters*, February 1, 2015; www.reuters.com/article/2015/02/01/us-swiss-politics-blocher-idUSKBN0L515U20150201.

Corley, F. "Georgia: Will Police Protect Muslim Prayers from Mobs?" *Forum 18 News Service*, July 4, 2013.

"Kyrgyzstan: Jail Terms Overturned but Investigation Continues" *Forum 18 News Service*, June 24, 2011.

"Kyrgyzstan: Eight Raids, Two Official Warnings in Three Months" *Forum 18 News Service*, April 8, 2013.

Cosgel, Metin & Thomas J. Miceli "State and Religion" *Journal of Comparative Economics*, 37 (2), 2009, 402–416.

Crouch, Colin "The Quiet Continent: Religion and Politics in Europe" *The Political Quarterly*, 71 (Supplement 1), 2000, 90–103.

Cumming-Bruce, Nick & Steven Erlanger "Swiss Ban Building of Minarets on Mosques" *The New York Times*, November 29, 2009.

"Cyprus Considered the Law on Cremation" *Cyprus Today*, September 6, 2013; http://en.cyplive.com/ru/news/na-kipre-rassmatrivayut-zakon-o-krema cii.html?selcat=1.

Deisher, J. (29 September 2013) "Sweden Children's Rights Official Calls for Ban on Infant Male Circumcision" *Jurist: University of Pittsburgh's School of Law*, September 29, 2013; http://jurist.org/paperchase/2013/09/sweden-chil drens-rights-official-calls-for-ban-on-infant-male-circumcision.php.

Demerath, N. J. III *Crossing the Gods: World Religions and Worldly Politics*, New Brunswick, NJ: Rutgers University Press, 2001.

Demerath, N. J. III & Karen S. Straight, "Religion, Politics, and the State: Cross-Cultural Observations" *Cross Currents*, 47 (1), 1997, 43–58.

Dempsey, Judy "Germany, Jews and Muslims, and Circumcision" *New York Times*, September 17, 2012.

Djupe, Paul A. & Brian R. Calfino "Divine Intervention? The Influence of Religious Value Communication on US Intervention Policy" *Political Behavior*, 35 (4), 2013, 643–663.

Donnelly, Jack *International Human Rights*, Boulder CO: Westview Press, 2007.

Dons, Anne Mette "Vejledning om omskaering af drenge" [Guidance on Circumcising Boys] National Board of Health, April 2, 2014; www.retsinformation.dk/Forms/R0710.aspx?id=162591.

Doorley, Neil "Logan Mosque Bombarded with Anti-Islamic Leaflets in Latest Hate Attack" *The Courier Mail*, September 15, 2014; www.couriermail.com

.au/news/queensland/logan-mosque-bombarded-with-antiislamic-leaflets-in-latest-hate-attack/story-fnihsrf2-1227058301127?nk=7d5611e20762bdbaec9e dec902f7a318.

Driessen, Michael D. P. "Religion, State and Democracy: Analyzing Two Dimensions of Church–State Arrangements" *Politics and Religion*, 3 (1), 2010, 55–80.

Durham, W. Cole Jr. "Perspectives on Religious Liberty: A Comparative Framework" in John D. van der Vyver & John Witte Jr., eds. *Religious Human Rights in Global Perspective: Legal Perspectives*, Boston: Martinus Njhoff, 1996, 1–44.

Eddy, Melissa "Germany Clarifies Its Stance on Circumcision" *International Herald Tribune*, December 13, 2012.

Eisenstein, Marie A. *Religion and the Politics of Tolerance: How Christianity Builds Democracy*, Waco, TX: Baylor University Press, 2008.

Ellingsen, Tanja "Colorful Community or Ethnic Witches' Brew? Multiethnicity and Domestic Conflict during and after the Cold War" *Journal of Conflict Resolution*, 44(2), 2000, 228–249.

Embury-Dennis, Tom "Law Forcing Jews to Obtain Permits for Kosher Meat Proposed by Austrian Politician" *The Independent*, July 18, 2018; www.independent.co.uk/news/world/europe/kosher-meat-ban-permits-register-jews-lower-austria-freedom-party-gottfried-waldhausl-a8453011.html.

Erdbrink, Thomas "An Ayatollah's Daughter Prompts a Debate on Religious Persecution in Iran" *The New York Times*, May 18, 2016; www.nytimes.com/2016/05/19/world/middleeast/iran-bahais-kamalabadi-hashemi-meeting.html.

Esbeck, Carl H. "A Typology of Church–State Relations in American Thought" *Religion and Public Education*, 15 (1), 1988, 43–50.

European Commission against Racism and Intolerance *ICRI Report on the Netherlands*, Strasbourg, France: Author, 2013.

Express News Service "Vadodara Violence Flares Up, Mobile Data Services Off" *The Indian Express*, September 29, 2014; http://indianexpress.com/article/india/india-others/vadodara-violence-flares-mobile-data-services-off/.

Farha, Mark "Global Gradations of Secularism: The Consociational, Communal, and Coercive Paradigms" *Comparative Sociology*, 11 (3), 2012, 354–386.

Farr, Thomas F. "Diplomacy in an Age of Faith: Religious Freedom and National Security." *Foreign Affairs*, 87 (2), 2008, 110–124.

Fetzer, Joel S. & J. Christopher Soper "The Root of Public Attitudes toward State Accommodation of European Muslims' Religious Practices before and after September 11" *Journal for the Scientific Study of Religion*, 42 (2), 2003, 247–258.

Fetzer, Joel S. & J. Christopher Soper. *Muslims and the State in Britain, France, and Germany*. New York: Cambridge University Press, 2005.

Feuerberg, Gary "Religious Persecution in Vietnam: Government Spies, Forced Renunciations of Faith" *Epoch Times*, April 3, 2014; www.theepochtimes.com/n3/598710-religious-persecution-in-vietnam-government-spies-forced-renunciations-of-faith/.

Finke, Roger "Religious Deregulation: Origins and Consequences" *Journal of Church and State*, 32 (3), 1990, 609–626.

"Origins and Consequences of Religious Restrictions: A Global Overview" *Sociology of Religion*, 74 (3), 2013, 297–313.

Finke, Roger & Jamie Harris "Wars and Rumors of Wars" Explaining Religiously Motivated Violence" in Jonathan Fox, ed. *Religion, Politics, Society, and the State*, New York: Oxford University Press, 2012, 53–71.

Finke, Roger & Robert R. Martin "Ensuring Liberties: Understanding State Restrictions on Religious Freedoms" *Journal for the Scientific Study of Religion*, 53 (4), 2014, 687–705.

Finke, Roger, Robert Martin, & Jonathan Fox "Explaining Religious Discrimination against Religious Minorities" *Politics & Religion*, 10 (2), 2017, 389–416. doi:10.1017/S1755048317000037.

Finke, Roger, Dane R. Mataic, & Jonathan Fox "Assessing the Impact of Religious Registration" *Journal for the Scientific Study of Religion*, 56 (4), 2017, 720–736.

Flere, Serge J. "Registration of Religious Communities in European Countries" *Politologie Des Religions*, 4 (1), 2010, 99–117.

Flere, Serge J., Miran Lavric, & Dragoljib B. Djordjevic "Religious References in the Institutions of Post-Communist Countries and Ethno-Symbolism" *Journal of Church and State*, 2016, doi:10.1093/jcs/csw029.

Forum 18 News Service, *Russia: Religious Freedom Survey*, 2012; www.forum18.org/archive.php?article_id=1722.

Fox, Jonathan *Ethnoreligious Conflict in the Late 20th Century: A General Theory*, Lanham, MD: Lexington Books, 2002.

Religion, Civilization and Civil War: 1945 through the New Millennium, Lanham, MD: Lexington Books, 2004.

A World Survey of Religion and the State, New York: Cambridge University Press, 2008.

"Building Composite Measures of Religion and State" *Interdisciplinary Journal of Research on Religion*, 7 (8), 2011, 1–39.

Political Secularism, Religion, and the State: A Time Series Analysis of Worldwide Data, New York: Cambridge University Press, 2015.

The Unfree Exercise of Religion: A World Survey of Religious Discrimination against Religious Minorities, New York: Cambridge University Press, 2016.

An Introduction to Religion and Politics: Theory and Practice, 2nd ed., New York: Routledge, 2018.

"A World Survey of Secular-Religious Competition: State Religion Policy from 1990 to 2014" *Religion, State & Society*, 47 (1), 2019, 10–29.

Fox, Jonathan & Yasemin Akbaba "Restrictions on the Religious Practices of Religious Minorities: A Global Survey" *Political Studies*, 2014, doi: 10.1111/1467-9248.12141.

"Securitization of Islam and Religious Discrimination: Religious Minorities in Western Democracies, 1990 to 2008" *Comparative European Politics*, 13 (2), 2015, 175–197.

Fox, Jonathan, Chris Bader, & Jennifer McClure "Don't Get Mad: The Disconnect between Religious Discrimination and Individual Perceptions of Government" *Conflict Management & Peace Science*, 2017, doi: 10.1177/0738894217723160.

Fox, Jonathan, Roger Finke, & Dane R. Mataic "New Data and Measures on Societal Discrimination and Religious Minorities" *Interdisciplinary Journal of Research on Religion*, 14 (14), 2018.

Friedman, H. "In Mexican Village, Utility Shut-Off Used to Force Protestant Families to Contribute to Local Catholic Festivals" *Religion Clause*, March 2, 2014.

Frieland, Roger "Religious Nationalism and the Problem of Collective Representation" *Annual Review of Sociology*, 27, 2001, 125–152.

Froese, Paul "After Atheism: An Analysis of Religious Monopolies in the Post-Communist World" *Sociology of Religion*, 65 (1), 2004, 57–75.

Gearty, Connor "Terrorism and Human Rights" *Government and Opposition*, 42 (3), 2007, 340–362.

Gill, Anthony *Rendering unto Caesar: The Catholic Church and the State in Latin America*, Chicago: University of Chicago Press, 1998.

"The Political Origins of Religious Liberty: A Theoretical Outline" *Interdisciplinary Journal of Research on Religion*, 1 (1), 2005, 1–35.

The Political Origins of Religious Liberty, New York: Cambridge University Press, 2008.

Gill, Emily R. "Religious Organizations, Charitable Choice, and the Limits of Freedom of Conscience" *Perspectives on Politics*, 2 (4), 2004, 741–755.

Gillet, Kit "Gay Rights Could Be Major Hurdle for Moldova's EU Bid" *The Christian Science Monitor*, November 29, 2013; www.csmonitor.com/World/Europe/2013/1129/Gay-rights-could-be-major-hurdle-for-Moldova-s-EU-bid.

Goldberg, Dan "Rising Anti-Semitism in Australia Leaves Jews Feeling Vulnerable" *Haaretz*, August 28, 2014; www.haaretz.com/jewish-world/jewish-world-news/.premium-1.612430.

Gorski, Phillip S. & Ates Altinordu "After Secularization" *Annual Review of Sociology*, 24, 2008, 55–85.

Grim, Brian J. & Roger Finke "International Religion Indexes: Government Regulation, Government Favoritism, and Social Regulation of Religion" *Interdisciplinary Journal of Research on Religion*, 2 (1), 2006, 1–40.

"Religious Persecution on Cross-National Context: Clashing Civilizations or Regulating Religious Economies" *American Sociological Review*, 72 (4), 2007, 633–658.

The Price of Freedom Denied, New York: Cambridge University Press, 2011.

Griswold, Eliza "Is This the End of Christianity in the Middle East?" *New York Times*, July 22, 2015.

Grotsch, Florian & Anette Schnabel "Integration – What Integration? The Religious Framing of the European Integration Process between 1990 and 2000" *European Societies*, 14 (4), 2012, 586–610.

"The Ambiguous Roles of Religion: The European Integration Project as a Multilevel Case" *Interdisciplinary Journal of Research on Religion*, 9 (7), 2013, 1–32.

Grzymala-Busse, Anna *Nations under God: How Churches Use Moral Authority to Influence Policy*, Princeton, NJ: Princeton University Press, 2015a.

"Thy Will Be Done? Religious Nationalism and Its Effects in East Central Europe" *East European Politics, Societies and Cultures*, 29 (2), 2015b, 338–351.

Gurr, Ted R. *Minorities at Risk*, Washington DC: United States Institute of Peace, 1993.

"War Revolution, and the Growth of the Coercive State" *Comparative Political Studies*, 21 (1), April 1988, 45–65.

Peoples versus States: Minorities at Risk in the New Century, Washington, DC: United States Institute of Peace Press, 2000.

Hagevi, Magnus "Religiosity and Swedish Opinion on the European Union" *Journal for the Scientific Study of Religion*, 41 (4), 2002, 759–769.

Halman, Loek & Veerle Draulans "How Secular Is Europe?" *British Journal of Sociology*, 57 (2), 2006, 263–288.

Haynes, Jeff "Religion, Secularisation, and Politics: A Postmodern Conspectus" *Third World Quarterly*, 18 (4), 1997, 709–728.

Haynes, Jeffrey *Religion in Global Politics*, New York: Longman, 1998.

Haynes, Jeffrey, ed. *Routledge Handbook of Religion and Politics*, New York: Routledge, 2009.

Hazou, Elias "Church Sticks to Its Guns on Cremation" *CyprusMail*, November 1, 2013; www.incyprus.eu/cyprus-news/church-sticks-to-its-guns-on-cremation/.

"Head of Town in Mexico Sends Mob to Beat, Abduct Christians" *Morning Star News*, November 11, 2013; http://morningstarnews.org/2013/11/head-of-town-in-mexico-sends-mob-to-beat-abduct-christians/.

Hefner, Robert H. "Public Islam and the Problem of Democratization" *Sociology of Religion*, 62 (4), 2001, 491–514.

Helberg, Marc "Opposing Muslims and the Muslim Headscarf in Western Europe" *European Sociological Review*, January 13, 2014, doi:10.1093/esr/jcto38.

Helbling, Marc & Richard Traunmuller "How State Support for Religion Shapes Attitudes toward Muslim Immigrants: New Evidence from a Sub-National Comparison" *Comparative Political Studies*, 2015, doi: 10.1177/0010414015612388.

Henne, Peter S. & Jason Klocek "Taming the Gods: How Religious Conflict Shapes State Repression" *Journal of Conflict Resolution*, 2017, doi: 10.1177/0022002717728104.

Hookway, J. "Vandals Strike at Malaysia Mosques with Boar Heads" *Wall Street Journal*, January 28, 2010.

Horowitz, Donald L. *Ethnic Groups in Conflict*, Berkeley: University of California Press, 1985.

"Human Rights Violations Perpetrated against the Chin in Burma March 2011–March 2013" Chin Human Rights Organization, April 8 2013; http://burmacampaign.org.uk/media/HRVs_against_the_Chin.pdf.

Human Rights Watch, *World Report 2015: Cuba, Events of 2014*, New York: Author, 2015; www.hrw.org/world-report/2015/country-chapters/cuba.

Human Rights Watch, *Persecuting "Evil Way" Religion: Abuses against Montagnards in Vietnam*, New York: Author, June 26, 2015.

Huntington, Samuel P. "The Clash of Civilizations?" *Foreign Affairs*, 72 (3), 1993, 22–49.

The Clash of Civilizations and the Remaking of the World Order, New York: Simon and Schuster, 1996.

Hurd, Elizabeth S. "The International Politics of Secularism: US Foreign Policy and the Islamic Republic of Iran" *Alternatives*, 29 (2), 2004a, 115–138.

"The Political Authority of Secularism in International Relations" *European Journal of International Relations*, 10 (2), 2004b, 235–262.

Iceland Review On-Line "Protest against Mosque May Be Defined as Hate Crime," November 29, 2013; http://icelandreview.com/news/2013/11/29/pro test-against-mosque-may-be-defined-hate-crime.

Imboden, William "Religion and International Relations: How Should Policy-makers Think about Religion?" In Michael C. Desch & Daniel Philpott, eds. *Religion and International Relations: A Primer for Research*, Mellon Initiative on Religion across the Disciplines, South Bend, IN: Notre Dame University, 2013, 163–175.

Importing Personal Property into Kuwait, 2010; www.state.gov/j/drl/rls/irf/2009/127351.htm.

International Center for Law and Religious Studies "People's Republic of China: Law and Religion Framework Overview" Provo, UT: Religlaw, 2012; www .religlaw.org.

International Holocaust Remembrance Alliance "Working Definition of Antise-mitism," Berlin: Author, 2018; www.holocaustremembrance.com/working-definition-antisemitism.

Inter-Religious Council in Bosnia-Herzegovina *Monitoring of Attacks on Reli-gious Buildings and Other Sites of Importance for Churches and Religious Communities in Bosnia and Herzegovina – Protection of Holy Sites*, January 2015; www.mrv.ba/images/stories/Monitoring/izvjestaj%202013-2014%20-%20english.pdf.

Iran Press Watch "Mahnoush Shafi'i, A Baha'i, Has Been Expelled from Univer-sity," January 27, 2016; http://iranpresswatch.org/post/13967/.

Ireland, Michael "Christian Presence, Missionary Activity, Not Wanted in Afghanistan," *ANS/International Christian Concern*, January 15, 2008; www.persecution.org/2008/01/17/christian-presence-missionary-activity-not-wanted-in-afghanistan/.

Isani, Mujtaba & Daniel Silverman "Foreign Policy Attitudes towards Islamic Actors: An Experimental Approach" *Political Research Quarterly*, 69 (3) 2016, 571–582.

Islam Today "Negotiations Underway to Open Greek Cyprus's Most Prominent Mosque for Prayers," December 16, 2011; http://en.islamtoday.net/artshow-229-4289.htm.

Jackson, T. "Al-Shabaab Capitalises on Muslim Grievances in Kenya" London: Tony Blair Institute for Global Change, October 3, 2014; http://tonyblairfaith foundation.org/religion-geopolitics/commentaries/opinion/al-shabaab-capital ises-muslim-grievances-kenya.

Jaggers, Keith & Ted R. Gurr "Tracking Democracy's Third Wave with the Polity III Data" *Journal of Peace Research*, 32, (4), 1995, 469–482.

Jain, Bharti "Government Releases Data of Riot Victims Identifying Religion" *Times of India*, September 24, 2014; http://timesofindia.indiatimes.com/india/Government-releases-data-of-riot-victims-identifying-religion/articleshow/22998550.cms.

Jelen, Ted G. & Clyde Wilcox "Denominational Preference and the Dimensions of Political Tolerance" *Sociological Analysis*, 51 (1), 1990, 69–81.

Jenkins, Phillip "Religion, Repression and Rebellion" *Review of Faith and International Affairs*, 5 (1), 2007, 3–11.

Jones, Jeremy *Antisemitism Report, 2009*. Edgecliff, New South Wales: Executive Council of Australian Jewry, 2009; www.worldjewishcongress.org/uploads/documents/781a970bf9cafeaf4de310e62986fa8bc347f5b9.pdf.

Joustra, Robert *The Religious Problem with Religious Freedom: Why Foreign Policy Needs Political Theology*, New York: Routledge 2018.

JTA "Jews Ruined Russia, Says Politician from Putin's Party" *Times of Israel*, February 14, 2014.

"Norway Passes Act Regulating Circumcision" *Times of Israel*, June 28, 2014; www.timesofisrael.com/norway-passes-act-regulating-circumcision/.

"Juche" *New World Encyclopedia*, June 12, 2018; www.newworldencyclopedia.org/p/index.php?title=Juche&oldid=1012244.

Kaplan, Edward H. & Charles A. Small "Anti-Israel Sentiment Predicts Anti-Semitism in Europe" *Journal of Conflict Resolution*, 50 (4), 2006, 548–561.

Karpov, Vycheslav "Religiosity and Tolerance in the United States and Poland" *Journal for the Scientific Study of Religion*, 41 (2), 2002, 267–288.

Kaspersen, Kars B. & Johannes Lindvall "Why No Religious Politics? The Secularization of Poor Relief and Primary Education in Denmark and Sweden" *Archives of European Sociology*, 49 (1), 2008, 119–143.

Keane, John "Secularism?" *The Political Quarterly*, 71 (Supplement 1), 2000, 5–19.

Kellner, Mark A. "The New Law Making It Harder for People in Burma to Switch Religions" *Deseret News*, August 25, 2015.

"Kenya Cleric Sheikh Mohammed Idris Shot Dead in Mombasa" BBC, June 10, 2014; www.bbc.com/news/world-africa-27776743.

Kim, Myunghee "Spiritual Values, Religious Practices, and Democratic Attitudes" *Politics and Religion*, 1 (2), 2008, 216–236.

Koesel, Karrie J. *Region and Authoritarianism: Cooperation, Conflict, and the Consequences*, New York: Cambridge University Press, 2014.

Kortmann, Matthias "Secular-Religious Competition and the Exclusion of Islam from the Public Sphere: Islamic Welfare in Western Europe" *Politics & Religion*, 2018, doi:10.1017/S1755048318000706.

Koziol, Michael & Leila Abdallah "We Are the Ones Being Terrorized, Muslims Say" *The Sydney Morning Herald*, September 21, 2014; www.smh.com.au/federal-politics/political-news/we-are-the-ones-being-terrorised-muslims-say-20140920-10jdkw.html.

Kuhle, Lene "Concluding Remarks on Religion and State in the Nordic Countries" *Nordic Journal of Religion and Society*, 24 (2), 2011, 205–213.

Kulush, Nicholas "German Ruling against Circumcising Boys Draws Criticism" *New York Times*, June 26, 2012.

Kumar, Ruchi "Kalaghoda Axes Play after Hindu Groups Call It 'Anti-National'; Producers Move It to YouTube" *DNA India*, 2014; www.dnaindia.com/mumbai/report-kalaghoda-axes-play-after-hindu-groups-call-it-anti-national-producers-move-it-to-youtube-1959801.

Kunovich, Robert M. "An Exploration of the Salience of Christianity for National Identity in Europe" *Sociological Perspectives*, 49 (4), 2006, 435–460.

Kuru, Ahmet T. *Secularism and State Policies toward Religion, The United States France and Turkey*, New York: Cambridge University Press, 2009.

"Lao Christians Evicted from Village amid Religious Tensions" Radio Free Asia, November 13, 2014; www.rfa.org/english/news/laos/christians-11132014150735.html.

"Laotian Christians Evicted for Refusing to Renounce Faith" Ecumenical News, November 21, 2014; www.ecumenicalnews.com/article/laotian-christians-evicted-from-village-for-refusing-to-renounce-faith-27284.

Larsen, Odd "Almost No Religious Freedom for Migrant Workers" *Forum 18*, June 23, 2009; www.forum18.org/Archive.php?article_id=1316.

Lassner, Jacob & S. Ilan Troen, *Jews and Muslims in the Arab World*, Lanham, MD: Rowman & Littlefield, 2007.

Laustsen, Carsten B. & Ole Waever "In Defense of Religion: Sacred Referent Objects for Securitization" *Millennium*, 29 (3), 2000, 705–739.

Laythe, Brian, Deborah G. Finkel, Robert G. Bringle, & Lee A. Kirkpatrick "Religious Fundamentalism as a Predictor of Prejudice: A Two Component Model" *Journal for the Scientific Study of Religion*, 41 (4), 2002, 623–635.

Laythe, Brian, Deborah Finkel, & Lee A. Kirkpatrick "Predicting Prejudice from Religious Fundamentalism and Right Wing Authoritarianism: A Multiple Regression Approach" *Journal for the Scientific Study of Religion*, 40 (1), 2002, 1–10.

Lee, Morgan "US Wants Answers on Evangelical Persecution – in Mexico" *Christianity Today*, July 17, 2015; www.christianitytoday.com/gleanings/2015/july/mexicos-evangelicals.html.

Lewis, Bernard *The Political Language of Islam*, Chicago: University of Chicago Press, 1988.

Semites and Anti-Semites: An Inquiry into Conflict and Prejudice, New York: W. W. Norton, 1999.

LFNC "Decree on Management and Protection of Religious Activities in the Lao PDR" Lao Front for National Construction (LFNC), 2001; http://lib.ohchr.org/HRBodies/UPR/Documents/Session8/LA/LFNC_UPR_LAO_S08_2010_LaoFrontforNationalConstruction.pdf.

Lijphart, Arend, *Democracy in Plural Societies*, New Haven, CT: Yale University Press, 1977.

Little, David "Religious Militancy" in Chester A. Crocker and Fen O. Hampson, eds. *Managing Global Chaos: Sources of and Responses to International Conflict*, Washington, DC: United States Institute of Peace Press, 1996, 79–91.

Lodge, Carey "Religious Freedom Abuses at Risk of Increasing in Vietnam" *Christian Today*, October 19, 2015; www.christiantoday.com/article/religious.freedom.abuses.at.risk.of.increasing.in.vietnam/68070.htm.

Mabee, Bryan. "Re-imagining the Borders of US Security after 9/11: Securitization, Risk, and the Creation of the Department of Homeland Security." *Globalizations*. 4 (3), 2007, 385–397.

MacEoin, Denis "The Baha'is in Iran" *Gatestone Institute*, June 10, 2014; www.gatestoneinstitute.org/4347/bahais-iran.

Madeley John T. S. & Z. Enyedi (eds.) *Church and State in Contemporary Europe: The Chimera of Neutrality*, London: Frank Cass, 2003.

Manglos, Nicolette D. & Alexander A. Weinrab "Religion and Interest Politics in Sub-Saharan Africa" *Social Forces*, 92 (1), 2013, 195–219.

Mantilla, Luis F. "Church–State Relations and the Decline of Catholic Parties in Latin America," *Journal of Religious and Political Practice*, 2 (2), 2016, 231–248.

Marquand, D & R. L. Nettler "Forward" *The Political Quarterly*, 71 (Supplement 1), 2000, 1–4.

Marshall, A. "Myanmar Gives Official Blessing to Anti-Muslim Monks" *Reuters*, June 27, 2013.

Martin, David A. *A General Theory of Secularization*, Oxford, UK: Blackwell, 1978.

Mataic, Dane R. "Countries Mimicking Neighbors: The Spatial Diffusion of Governmental Restrictions on Religion" *Journal for the Scientific Study of Religion*, 2018, https://doi.org/10.1111/jssr.12518.

Mazie, Steven V. "Rethinking Religious Establishment and Liberal Democracy: Lessons from Israel" *Brandywine Review of Faith and International Affairs*, 2 (2), 2004, 3–12.

Israel's Higher Law: Religion and Liberal Democracy in the Jewish State, New York: Lexington, 2006.

McLaughlin, Bryan & David Wise "Cuing God: Religious Cues and Voter Support" *Politics & Religion*, 7 (2), 2014, 366–394.

Miles, Jack "Religion and American Foreign Policy" *Survival*, 46 (1), 2004, 23–37.

Miller, Ann "U.S. Embassy Warns of Terror Threat against Christians in Uganda" *Mission Network News*, June 2, 2014.

Milligan, Scott, Robert Anderson, & Robert Brym "Assessing Variation in Tolerance in 23 Muslim-Majority and Western Countries" *Canadian Review of Sociology*, 51 (3), 2014, 241–261.

Ministry of Culture Sweden *Changed Relations between the State and the Church of Sweden*, 2000; www.sst.a.se/download/18.4c1b31c91325af4dad38000 15546/1377188428760/Fact+sheet+about+state-church+relations.pdf.

Minkenberg, Michael "Religion and Euroscepticism: Cleavages, Religious Parties and Churches in EU Member States," *West European Politics*, 32 (6), 2009, 1190–1211.

"Between Christian and Multicultural Democracy: Religious Legacies and Minority Politics" *West European Politics*, 2017, doi.org/10.1080/01402382.2017.1343967, 1–27.

"Christian Identity? European Churches and the Issue of Turkey's EU Membership" *Comparative European Politics*, 10 (2), 2012, 149–179.

Morning Star News "Police in India Slow to Investigate Torture, Killing of Christian Boy," November 30, 2013; http://morningstarnews.org/2013/11/police-in-india-slow-to-investigate-torture-killing-of-christian-boy/.

"Hindu Extremists Accused of Killing Pastor in Andhra Pradesh, India," January 30, 2014; http://morningstarnews.org/2014/01/hindu-extremists-accused-of-killing-pastor-in-andhra-pradesh-india/.

Mostafa, Mohamed M. & Mohaned T. Al-Hamdi "Political Islam, Clash of Civilizations, U.S. Dominance and Arab Support of Attacks on America: A Test of a Hierarchical Model" *Studies in Conflict and Terrorism*, 30 (8), 2007, 723–736.

"MP Urges Czechs to Bother Muslims" Prague Post, January 4, 2015.

Murdoch, Lindsay "Cambodia Refuses Asylum to Refugees Fleeing Persecution in Vietnam" *Canberra Times* (Australia), June 4, 2015.

"Muslim Clerics Who Preach Hatred Face Deportation" DutchNews.nl, August 25, 2014; www.dutchnews.nl/news/archives/2014/08/muslim_clerics_who_ preach_hatr.php/.

"Must Provide Burial Site for All" The Norway Post, April 1, 2010.

Mutiga, M. "Al-Shabaab Militants Kill 36 Christian Quarry Workers in Kenya" *The Guardian*, December 2, 2014; www.theguardian.com/world/2014/dec/ 02/kenya-quarry-massacre-leaves-36-dead-says-red-cross.

Myanmar Ministry of Religious Affairs "Department for the Promotion and Propagation of Sasana," 2005; www.mora.gov.mm/mora_sasana1.aspx.

Myers, David G. *Social Psychology*. New York: McGraw-Hill Publishing Company, 1990.

Nair, Rupam Jain, "Police Arrest 140 for Religious Clashes in Vadodara as Modi Tours U.S.," *Reuters*, September 29, 2014; http://in.reuters.com/article/india-religion-violence-idINKCN0HO0NW20140929.

Nebehay, Stephanie "China Rejects Allegations of Detaining Millions of Uighurs in Xinjiang" *Reuters*, August 13, 2018.

Nelsen, Brent F. & James L. Guth *Religion and the Struggle for European Union: Confessional Culture and the Limits of Integration*, Washington, DC: Georgetown University Press, 2015.

Nelsen, Brent F., James L. Guth, & Cleveland R. Fraser "Does Religion Matter? Christianity and Public Support for the European Union *European Union Politics*, 2 (2), 2001, 191–217.

New Brunswick Department of Energy and Resource Development "New Brunswick Hunt & Trap 2014," 2014; www2.gnb.ca/content/dam/gnb/Depart ments/nr-rn/pdf/en/Wildlife/HuntTrap.pdf.

Nguyen, Jennifer "Jennifer Nguyen on Religion in Communist Vietnam" Berkley Center for Religion, Peace and World Affairs, August 18, 2008; http://berkleycen ter.georgetown.edu/letters/jennifer-nguyen-on-religion-in-communist-vietnam.

Nirenberg, David *Anti-Judaism: The Western Tradition*, New York: W. W. Norton, 2013.

Norris, Pippa & Ronald Inglehart "Islamic Culture and Democracy: Testing the 'Clash of Civilizations' Thesis" *Comparative Sociology*, 1 (3–4), 2002, 235–263.

Sacred and Secular: Religion and Politics Worldwide, New York: Cambridge University Press, 2004.

"Norway Bans Niqab in Schools" The Local, June 8, 2018; www.thelocal.no/ 20180606/norway-bans-burqa-and-niqab-in-schools.

Nova Scotia Department of Lands and Forestry "Nova Scotia 2014–2015 Hunting and Trapping Seasons," 2014; www.novascotia.ca/natr/hunt/pdf/ SeasonDates.pdf.

Novnite-Sofia News Agency "Bulgaria Church Organizes Anti-Jehovah's Witnesses March" *World-Wide Religious News*, October 8, 2009.

Olzak, Susan "Ethnic Protest in Core and Periphery States" *Ethnic and Racial Studies*, 21 (2), 1998, 187–217.

Ontario Federation of Anglers and Hunters "Sunday Gun Hunting"; www.ofah .org/hunting/Sunday-Gun-Hunting.

OSCE *Tackling Hate Crimes: An Analysis of Bias-Motivated Incidents in Bosnia and Herzegovina*, Sarajevo: Author, November 25, 2012.

Hate Crimes in the OSCE Region: Incidents and Responses, Annual Report 2012, Sarajevo: Author, November 2013.

Oweis, "Iranian Media Publish List of Bahai Businesses for Boycotting and Closure," May 18, 2016; https://sensday.wordpress.com/2016/05/23/iran ian-media-publish-list-of-bahai-businesses-for-boycotting-and-closure/.

Parmar, Vijaysinh "Evict Muslims from Hindu Areas: Pravin Togadia" *Times of India*, April 20, 2014; http://timesofindia.indiatimes.com/india/Evict-Muslims-from-Hindu-areas-Pravin-Togadia/articleshow/34017292.cms.

"Pastors Released after Arrest for 'Spreading Christian Religion'" *Christian Today*, April 8, 2013; www.christiantoday.com/article/pastors.released .after.arrest.for.spreading.christian.religion/32072.htm.

Perez, Nahshon & Jonathan Fox "Normative Theorizing and Political Data: Toward a Data-Sensitive Understanding of the Separation between Religion and State in Political Theory" *Critical Review of International Social and Political Philosophy*, 2018, doi.org/10.1080/13698230.2018 .1555683.

Perez, Nahshon, Jonathan Fox & Jennifer M. McClure "Unequal State Support of Religion: On Resentment, Equality, and the Separation of Religion and State" *Politics, Religion & Ideology*, 2017, doi: 10.1080/ 21567689.2017.1400429.

"Persecution Continues in Laos as Christians Are Detained for Meeting to Pray" AsiaNews, September 30, 2014; www.asianews.it/news-en/Persecution-con tinues-in-Laos-as-Christians-are-detained-for-meeting-to-pray-32297.html.

Pfaff, Steven & Anthony J. Gill "Muslim Interest Organizations and Political Integration in Europe" *Comparative Political Studies*, 39 (7), 2006, 803–828.

Philpott, Daniel "Explaining the Political Ambivalence of Religion" *American Political Science Review*, 101 (3), 2007, 505–525.

"Has the Study of Global Politics Found Religion?" *Annual Review of Political Science*, 12, 2009, 183–202.

Religious Freedom in Islam: The Fate of a Universal Human Right in the Muslim World Today, Oxford, UK: Oxford University Press, 2019.

Pitman, T. & G. Peack "Myanmar Anti-Muslim Violence Fueled by 969 Radical Buddhist Movement" *Huffington Post*, May 31, 2013.

Posner, Sarah "Kosher Jesus: Messianic Jews in the Holy Land" *The Atlantic*, November 29, 2012; www.theatlantic.com/international/archive/2012/11/ kosher-jesus-messianic-jews-in-the-holy-land/265670/.

"Pro-Government Kenyan Muslim Cleric Shot Dead in Mombasa" Reuters, November 4, 2014; www.reuters.com/article/us-kenya-killings-idUSKBN0IO 2420141104.

Puddington, A. & T. Roylance *Populists and Autocrats: The Dual Threat to Global Democracy*, Washington, DC: Freedom House, 2017; https://freedom house.org/report/freedom-world/freedom-world-2017.

Razack, Sherene H. *Casting Out: The Eviction of Muslims from Western Law and Politics*, Toronto, Canada: University of Toronto Press, 2008.

Rebe, Ryan J. "Re-examining the Wall of Separation: A Cross-National Study of Religious Pluralism in Democracy" *Politics & Religion*, 5 (3), 2012, 655–670.

Reimer, Reg "Vietnams' Religion Law" *World Watch Monitor*, May 8, 2015; www.worldwatchmonitor.org/2015/05/3844615.

Religlaw International Centre for Law and Religion Studies "Mongolia," Provo, UT: Author, 2013; www.religlaw.org/common/document.view.php?docId= 6142.

Research Directorate, Immigration and Refugee Board of Canada *Russia: Information on the Law "On Freedom of Conscience and Religious Associations" and Its Impact on Religious Minorities*, Ottawa: Immigration and Refugee Board of Canada, 1997; www.refworld.org/docid/3ae6ab968.html.

"Ritual Circumcision Ban Recommended in Sweden and Denmark by Medical Associations" Huffington Post, January 27, 2014.

Ryland, J. "Committee Support Use of Hijab in the Police" *The Norway Post*, January 17, 2012.

   "Hijab Will Not Be Permitted in the Police Force" *The Norway Post*, January 8, 2013a.

   "Muslims in Norway under Illegal Surveillance" *The Norway Post*, April 25, 2013b.

Sabel, Robbie "A Role for International Law in Combating Antisemitism?" *Israel Journal of Foreign Affairs*, 10 (3), 2016, 451–456.

Sacks, Jonathan "The Mutating Virus: Understanding Antisemitism," London: The Office of Rabbi Sacks, September 27, 2016; http://rabbisacks.org/mutat ing-virus-understanding-antisemitism/.

Saiya, Nilay "The Religious Freedom Peace" *The International Journal of Human Rights*, 19 (3), 2015, 369–382.

   Weapon of Peace: How Religious Liberty Combats Terrorism, New York: Cambridge University Press, 2018.

Sandal, Nukhet & Jonathan Fox *Religion in International Relations Theory: Interactions and Possibilities*, New York: Routledge, 2013.

Sarkissian, Ani *The Varieties of Religious Repression: Why Governments Restrict Religion*, New York: Oxford University Press 2015.

Saskatchewan Human Rights Commission "Annual Report 2010" http://saskatch ewanhumanrights.ca/+pub/documents/publications/SHRC_AR_09-10.pdf.

Schatz, J. "In Myanmar Attacking the Rohingya Is Good Politics" *Al-Jazeera*, May 29, 2015.

Schnabel, Annette & Mikael Hjerm "How the Religious Cleavages of Civil Society Shape National Identity" *Sage Open*, 2014, 1–14, doi: 10.1177/ 2158244014525417.

Schreuer, Milan "Belgium Bans Ritual Slaughter" *New York Times*, January 6, 2019.

Seiwert, Hubert "The German Enquete Commission on Sects" in James T. Richardson, ed. *Regulating Religion: Case Studies from around the Globe*, New York: Springer, 2004, 85–101.

"Seven Christians Arrested for Prayer Gathering, Released in Laos" Ecumenical News, October 17, 2014; www.ecumenicalnews.com/article/seven-christians-arrested-for-prayer-gathering-released-in-laos-26903.

Shaheed, Ahmed *Report of the Special Rapporteur on the Situation of Human Rights in the Islamic Republic of Iran*, Geneva: UNHCR, 2015; http://shaheedoniran.org/wp-content/uploads/2015/03/HRC-2015.pdf.

Shia News Association "Ugandan Muslims Criticize Government's Discriminatory Acts" *Press TV*, April 1, 2015.

Shibani, M. "Have Papers, Still Can't Travel: Pilot Program in Myanmar Gives Citizenship to Some Rohingya Muslims, but Fears of Violence Keep Them Trapped in Camps" *Wall Street Journal*, December 31, 2014.

Silberman, Israella "Religion as a Meaning System: Implications for the New Millennium" *Journal of Social Issues*, 61 (4), 2005, 641–663.

Sito-Sucic, D. "Catholic Schools Form Rare Oasis amid Bosnia's Ethnic Strife" *Reuters*, November 25, 2009.

"Six Dead in Gun Attack Near Mombasa" Christian Solidarity Worldwide, March 24, 2014; www.csw.org.uk/2014/03/24/news/2196/article.htm.

Smith, Anthony D. "Ethnic Election and National Destiny: Some Religious Origins of Nationalist Ideals" *Nations and Nationalism*, 5 (3), 1999, 331–355.

"The Sacred Dimension of Nationalism" *Millennium*, 29 (3), 2000, 791–814.

Sokol, Sam "Venezuelan Government Accused of Doing Little to Curb Anti-Semitism" *The Jerusalem Post*, January 5, 2015; www.jpost.com/Diaspora/Venezuelan-government-accused-of-doing-little-to-curb-anti-Semitism-386731.

Solholm, R. "Believers in the Norse Gods Get Their Own Graveyard" *The Norway Post*, May 14, 2009.

Somer, Murat and Gitta Glupker-Kesebir "Is Islam the Solution? Comparing Turkish Islamic and Secular Thinking toward Ethnic and Religious Minorities" *Journal of Church and State*, 5 (3), 2015, 529–555.

Somerville Sustainable Conservation "Africa – News and Analysis, Kenya – ICG Says Al Shabab Exploiting Local Grievances" *Africa Sustainable Conservation News*, September 27, 2014; https://africajournalismtheworld.com/2014/09/27/kenya-icg-says-al-shabab-exploiting-local-grievances/.

Stark, Rodney, *For the Glory of God*, Princeton, NJ: Princeton University Press, 2003.

One True God, Historical Consequences of Monotheism, Princeton, NJ: Princeton University Press, 2001.

Stark, Rodney and William Bainbridge, *The Future of Religion: Secularization, Revival and Cult Formation*, Berkeley: University of California Press, 1985.

Stark, Rodney & Roger Finke *Acts of Faith: Explaining the Human Side of Religion*, Berkeley: University of California Press, 2000.

Stark, Rodney & Lawrence R. Iannaccone "A Supply Side Reinterpretation of the 'Secularization' of Europe" *Journal for the Scientific Study of Religion*, 33 (3), 1994, 230–252.

Stepan, Alfred "Religion, Democracy, and the 'Twin Tolerations'" *Journal of Democracy*, 11 (4), 2000, 37–56.

"The Multiple Secularisms of Modern Democratic and Non-Democratic Regimes" in Craig Calhoun, Mark Juergensmeyer, & Jonathan VanAntwerpen, eds. *Rethinking Secularism*, New York: Oxford University Press, 2012, 125–155.

Strathern, A. "Why Are Buddhist Monks Attacking Muslims?" *BBC News*, May 2, 2013.

Straziuso, J. & T. Odula "Four Dead in Kenya Riots after Muslim Cleric Killed" *Times of Israel*, May 10, 2013; www.timesofisrael.com/four-dead-in-kenya-riots-after-muslim-cleric-killed/.

Supreme Court of Canada "Saskatchewan Human Rights Commission v. Whatcott 2013 SCC 11" https://scc-csc.lexum.com/scc-csc/scc-csc/en/item/12876/index.do.

"Sweden Restricts Circumcisions" *BBC News*, October 1, 2001.

Tausch, Arno "The New Global Antisemitism: Implications for the Recent ADL-100 Data" *Middle East Review of International Affairs*, 18 (3), 2014, 46–72.

Taylor, Charles *A Secular Age*, Cambridge, MA: Harvard University Press, 2007.

Ten Veen, R. *Myanmar's Muslims: The Oppressed of the Oppressed*, London: Islamic Human Rights Commission, 2005.

Tezcur, Gunes M., Taghi Azdarmaki, & Mehri Bahar "Religious Participation among Muslims: Iranian Exceptionalism" *Critique: Critical Middle Eastern Studies*, 15 (3), 2006, 217–232.

The Institute on Religion and Public Policy "Religious Freedom in the Kingdom of Bhutan," n.d.; www.justice.gov/sites/default/files/pages/attachments/2015/10/30/bhutan_immigration_report.pdf.

The Polity Project *About Polity*, Vienna, VA: Center for Systemic Peace, 2018; www.systemicpeace.org/polityproject.html.

The Religion and State Project "RAS3 Codebook"; www.religionandstate.org.

Thomas, George M. "Religions in Global Civil Society" *Sociology of Religion*, 62 (4), 2001, 515–533.

Thomas, Jeff "Exile" *World Watch Monitor*, April 18, 2014; www.worldwatchmonitor.org/2014/04/article_3105563.html/.

Thomas, Scott M. "Religions and Global Security" *ISPI: Quaderni di Relazioni Internazionali*, 12, 2010, 4–21.

Tibi, Bassam "Post-Bipolar Disorder in Crisis: The Challenge of Politicized Islam" *Millennium*, 29 (4), 2000, 843–859.

Ticudean, Mircea "Gloves Come Off in Moldova's Church–State Battle" *Radio Free Europe, Radio Liberty*, July 3, 2013; www.rferl.org/content/moldova-orthodox-church-eu/25035131.html.

TNH Staff "Athens Will Build, Manage, Greece's First Crematorium" *The National Herald*, December 11, 2017; www.thenationalherald.com/178806/athens-will-build-manage-greeces-first-crematorium/.

Toft, Monica D., Daniel Philpott, & Timothy S. Shah *God's Century: Resurgent Religion and Global Politics*, New York: W. W. Norton & Company, 2011.

Toft, Monica Duffy "Getting Religion? The Puzzling Case of Islam and Civil War" *International Security*, 31 (4), 2007, 97–131.

Tolerance and Diversity Institute *Assessment of the Needs of Religious Organizations in Georgia,* Tbilisi, Georgia: Author, 2014.

"Top Court Upholds Key Part of Sask. Anti-Hate Law" CBC News, February 27, 2013; www.cbc.ca/news/politics/top-court-upholds-key-part-of-sask-anti-hate-law-1.1068276.

UCANews "Curfew Imposed after Hindu Muslims Clash," August 21, 2013; www.ucanews.com/news/curfew-imposed-after-hindu-muslim-clash/69070.

UN Human Rights Council "Report of the Commission of Inquiry on Human Rights in the Democratic People's Republic of Korea" 2014; www.ohchr.org/EN/HRBo dies/HRC/CoIDPRK/Pages/ReportoftheCommissionofInquiryDPRK.aspx p. 7.

UNHCR, The UN Refugee Agency, Refworld, *USCIRF Annual Report 2015 – Tier 2: Russia,* May 1, 2015; www.refworld.org/docid/554b355815.html.

United Kingdom Home Office *Country of Origin Information Report – Iran,* London: Author, 2013; www.refworld.org/docid/5385a43d4.html.

United Nations Association of Georgia *Joint Submission on Minority Rights in Georgia for the United Nations Universal Periodic Review,* November 2015.

United Nations Human Rights Office of the High Commissioner *Report of the Commission of Inquiry on Human Rights in the Democratic People's Republic of Korea,* Geneva: United Nations, 2014; www.ohchr.org/EN/HRBodies/ HRC/CoIDPRK/Pages/CommissionInquiryonHRinDPRK.aspx.

"Un maiale-day contro la moschea" CorriereDella Sera, September 7, 2007.

US Department of State "Australia," October 26, 2009; www.state.gov/j/drl/rls/ irf/2009/127264.htm.

Religious Freedom Report Netherlands 2009, Washington, DC: Author, 2009.

Human Rights Report Sweden 2013.

"International Religious Freedom Report 2014" Washington, DC: Author, 2014; www.state.gov/j/drl/rls/irf/religiousfreedom/index.htm?year=2014& dlid=238316.

International Religious Freedom Report, 2011; www.state.gov/j/drl/rls/irf/ 2011religiousfreedom/index.htm#wrapper.

"Defining Antisemitism," Washington, DC: Author, May 26, 2016; www.state .gov/s/rga/resources/267538.htm.

US Department of State, Bureau of Democracy, Human Rights, and Labor "Country Reports on International Religious Freedom 2004, 2005, 2006, 2007, 2008: Bhutan," Washington, DC: Author; www.state.gov/g/drl/rls/irf/ index.htm.

US State Department "Report on Religious Freedom 2014, India," 2014; www .state.gov/j/drl/rls/irf/religiousfreedom/index.htm#wrapper.

USCIRF "Press Briefing: Iran's Imprisoned Baha'í Leaders and Educators" USCIFR, February 13, 2012; www.uscirf.gov/news-room/press-releases/ uscirf-press-briefing-irans-imprisoned-baha-leaders-and-educators.

van der Brug, Wouter, Sara B. Hobolt, & Claes H. de Vreese, "Religion and Party Choice in Europe" *West European Politics,* 32 (6), 2009, 1266–1283.

Vandenbrink, Rachel "New Law Limits Religious Freedom" *Radio Free Asia,* November 29, 2012; www.rfa.org/english/news/vietnam/religion-112920121 91108.html.

Vennard, M. "Kyrgyzstan Keeps a Tight Grip on Religion" *BBC News*, January 19, 2010.

Verkutyten, Maykel, Mieke Malieparrd, Borja Martinovic, & Yassine Khoudja "Political Tolerance among Muslim Minorities in Western Europe: The Role of Denomination and Religious and Host National Identification" *Politics & Religion*, 7 (2), 2014, 265–286.

Vlas, Natalia & Sergiu Gherghina "Where Does Religion Meet Democracy? A Comparative Analysis of Attitudes in Europe" *International Political Science Review*, 33 (3), 2012, 336–351.

Voicu, Malina "Religion and Gender across Europe" *Social Compass*, 56 (2), 2009, 144–162.

Wæver, Ole. "Securitization and Desecuritization" in Ronnie Lipschutz, ed. *On Security*. New York: Columbia University Press, 1995.

"Politics, Security, Theory" Security Dialogue, 42 (4–5), 2011 465–480.

Wald, Kenneth D. *Religion and Politics in the United States*, New York: St. Martins, 1987.

Wald, Kenneth D. & Allison Calhoun-Brown *Religion and Politics in the United States*, 6th ed., Lanham, MD: Rowman & Littlefield, 2011.

Wald, Kenneth D., Adam L. Silverman, & Kevin S. Friday "Making Sense of Religion in Political Life" *Annual Review of Political Science*, 8, 2005, 121–143.

Warner, Carolyn M. *Confessions of an Interest Group: The Catholic Church and Political Parties in Europe*, Princeton, NJ: Princeton University Press, 2000.

WAToday.Com.Au "Rise in Attacks against Aussie Muslims," September 24, 2014; www.watoday.com.au/wa-news/rise-in-attacks-against-aussie-muslims-20140924-10lhl9.html.

"Why Is There Communal Violence in Myanmar?" *BBC News*, July 3, 2014.

Woodbury, Robert D. "The Missionary Roots of Liberal Democracy" *American Political Science Review*, 106 (2), 2012, 244–274.

"Yemen Curbs Extremism in Religious Teaching" *United Press International*, July 15, 2004.

"Yemeni Constitution" (as amended 1994); www.religlaw.org/common/docu ment.view.php?docId=898.

Zaimov, Stoyan "Iran Religious Persecution Increasing Despite Nuclear Deal, USCIRF Reports" *Christian Post*, May 4, 2016; www.christianpost.com/news/iran-christian-persecution-increasing-nuclear-deal-uscirf-report-163403/.

Zitum, Yoav "Haredim Protest 'Missionary Activity' in Holon" *Ynet News*, May 1, 2010; www.ynetnews.com/articles/0,7340,L-3883204,00.html.

Index